The Curious Antipodean

The Journal of an Australian family sidetracked for 365 days halfway between the Pacific Ocean and the Canadian Rockies. The highs and lows, adventures and realisations of living in a flipped hemisphere. 94 degrees of separation from home and an 18-hour time difference.

Stuart. L. Scott

Copyright © 2019 Stuart. L. Scott.

All rights reserved. Except as permitted under the Australian Copyright Act 1968 (for example, a fair dealing for the purposes of study, research, criticism or review), no part of this book may be reproduced, stored in a retrieval system, communicated or transmitted in any form or by any means without prior written permission.

First Published in 2019 by Stuart Lyon Scott Publishing

Author Disclaimer: This is a recollection of events and how I felt during a period of my life. I have written to the best of my knowledge and acknowledge that others may have perceived situations differently. No effort has been made to purposefully deceive. The names of people we met on our journey have been changed as well as identifying details to protect their identity. In some cases, I may have changed details such as physical properties, occupations and places of residence.

Book Layout ©2017 BookDesignTemplates.com

The Curious Antipodean/ Stuart. L. Scott. -- 1st ed.
Paperback - ISBN 978-0-6485976-0-5
Ebook   - ISBN 978-0-6485976-1-2
Hardcover - ISBN 978-0-6485976-2-9

 A catalogue record for this book is available from the National Library of Australia

For Dad.
You would have loved being part of our adventures and we would have loved to have you along for the ride.

Definition of ANTIPODE
plural an·tip·o·des
1: the parts of the earth diametrically opposite —often used of Australia and New Zealand as contrasted to the western hemisphere
2: the exact opposite or contrary
3: Standing sole to sole
.

"antipode." Merriam-Webster.com. 2019.
https://www.merriam-webster.com
(5th October 2019) N.B descriptions 1 & 2 only

Contents

Prologue 1

Winter 9

Spring 119

Summer 205

Autumn 287

Conclusion 319

PART ONE

Prologue

Essentially, we engaged in a sociology experiment wrapped in an adventure. Simultaneously the participant and observer. Therefore, it was important for me to be honest, to document our perception. Our reality. No rose coloured glasses and certainly not holding back. I had grappled with the format of this book, its focus and who the target audience would be. In the end, the decision was obvious. This is a snapshot in time, a special and out of the ordinary experience to add to our family history. Chronicled for my little family and hopefully cherished by future generations. I know if I had the opportunity to read the adventures of my Grandparents and Great Grandparents it would have intrigued and added to my sense of being. Anyway, this decision freed up the process and took away the worry of whether it would be interesting to others, politically correct or commercial. By publishing I offer it out to the general populace who may wish to gain an insight into this rather radical sidestep in our lives and just maybe throw caution to the wind and try it for themselves. Que sera sera.

Far from pondering the existential meaning of life, although a bit of that happened by default, the goal was simply to observe and respond to what was in front of me. Looking at some of the history, traditions and quirks of another nation and occasionally, well maybe often, comparing it to other places I have travelled and with my own country. Australians are a very proud race but are also well known for our irreverence and having the ability to laugh at ourselves. Therefore, I hope my writing does not offend, but inform or at least describe a point of view. The everyday, in another land, may still seem prosaic or mundane to some. However, those who have ripped themselves away from their comfort zone, scratched a little deeper than a sanitised group bus tour and ventured down the narrow laneways of this earth just to explore, will know that physically, emotionally and aesthetically, the everyday is an adventure. This is an insight into the joys, frustrations and realisations of life on the other side of our planet and the human condition. A snapshot of life lead by curiosity.

Travel. It's contagious, out of control. Dinner in Brisbane, breakfast in LA. It's fast as a mad tuk tuk in the back alleys of Bangkok or as slow as a pirogue plying the doldrums in Baie dÚpi. It can be challenging or pampered, confronting or beautiful, or all that and more rolled into one. It smashes down preconceived ideas, leaving no room for counter argument. It flips you from being comfortably part of the cultural, linguistic and ethnic majority to a minority, reduced to hand gestures and hopeful smiles, jumping headlong into opportunity. Travel smells, it gets stuck to your shoes and under your fingernails. It startles, surprises, it takes wrong turns that become the highlight of the day. It is noisy hotel rooms with sagging beds, musty pillows, paper thin walls and that unexpected view from a tiny window that transports you back in time, takes your breath away and makes it all worthwhile. Travellers contemplate their place in the world, their lot in life. They get the chance to be who they really are. The mundane becomes an unforgettable experience. Childhood exuberance reigns supreme. It is climbing a hill just because it's there and the likelihood of something amazing just over the ridge.

Finally, I would like to share a quote, which I stumbled across and find to be very true, from Mark Twain's novel, The Innocents Abroad, published in 1869. It described his adventures through Europe, the Middle East and American West. "Travel is fatal to prejudice, bigotry, and narrow-mindedness, and many of our people need it sorely on these accounts. Broad, wholesome, charitable views of men and things cannot be acquired by vegetating in one little corner of the earth all one's lifetime."

Oh, and please have a laugh.

Wind hustled through the She Oaks, the waves lapping the shore; I awoke from my daydream by seeds dropping around me, dislodged by the raucous black cockatoos out for a feed. It is summertime in North Queensland, Australia. People say we only have two seasons, the Wet and the Dry. If you live in a place long enough, there is much more to it than that. If you take the time to go outside and stand still, even the small changes jostle for the spotlight of your existence, if only fleeting. The frangipani trees are in full bloom and fill the entire garden with the unmistakable smell of summer. The elusive Torres Strait Pigeon hurriedly leaves his feast of palm seeds and glides away to play his own version of hide and seek. His crisp white and black garb, a contrast to the deep greens of the tropics. An early morning walk disturbs the wallabies eating mangrove leaves on the beach. A spoonbill and egret chat away while foraging for breakfast in the shallows of the lagoon. Are they talking about the weather? Noisy Rainbow Lorikeets hyped up on sugar, fight over nectar. I love where I live and where I was born. Like many people, I am deeply rooted to the little things and the collective of North Queensland. Unexpectedly the last twelve months away have led to an even deeper realisation of how thoroughly I am ingrained in the elements that are my part of the world. When you truly love a place, it's hard to imagine you can love it even more. But now I do. Unequivocally! We have just returned from a migration of sorts, like our humpback whales. A full rotation of the seasons has passed. My family are glad to be home, but constantly recalling, both verbally and quietly in our thoughts, the great adventure we have just returned from. The challenges and triumphs, the changes in perspective. The greater understanding and, very importantly, a pride of who we are and where we come from. It will take some time to fully process, but we have done it.

It is not often in one's life, in fact, comparatively only the fortunate few, have the opportunity to live in another country for a year, swapping house and job. Importantly, with the wonderful guarantee that both will be there on our return. My family and I have been on a journey that has not only taken us to the other side of the world, another hemisphere, from the tropics to a place of snow and ice. New friends, acquaintances, school and all that goes with it. Different clothes, different food, people noticing our accent and at times, finding it hard to be understood. We have been afforded the view of another country from within. A vantage point infrequently scaled by foreigners.

Why? Well for all intent and purpose, the time seemed right. Previously there had always been reasons why we should wait, establish our careers, pay off our house, have a baby, wait until the children are at school. Tick, tick, tick we were ready. Several colleagues had waited for years to get a suitable teacher exchange family, so when we filled out the paperwork, we fully expected it to take a while. It only took three months, but we were proactive and kept in contact with the powers to be on both sides of the Pacific. Our daughter would spend part of her childhood abroad and we saw it as a gift to her. She has become more adaptable and it has shaped her into a tolerant and more worldly little lady. Achievements like that are priceless.

It tugged at our heart strings to leave our beloved old Beagle billeted out for the year. I knew she would miss us dearly. The pet fish stayed in their outdoor terracotta pot ponds oblivious. As long there were mosquito larva and a bit of rain to keep it topped up, they would be ok. The guinea pigs had passed away a few months earlier via a stray dog attack which left us all in shock. So, things were all sorted one way or another on the pet front. We hoped our automatic irrigation system would sustain our large tropical garden but didn't like to think about what may happen to twenty-five years of establishing our little oasis on a sand dune.

Some context is necessary. We found that many people we met only imagined Australia as a desert with a large red monolith in the centre and a city called Sydney with kangaroos hopping down George Street. Some think we are a tiny island nation, when in fact we are the world's largest island, sixth largest country and thirty-two times bigger than the United Kingdom. Australia has roughly the same land mass as the lower 48 states of the USA, which excludes Alaska and Hawaii. The most northern tip of Australia is 10 degrees south of the equator through to the southern tip at 48 degrees south. As a result, there is a range of climatic zones from snowy alps, dry sandy deserts, tropical rainforest and just about everything in between. My family are born and bred North Queenslanders, which is on the north east coast. Latitude 19 in the southern hemisphere also runs through the middle of Madagascar, Zimbabwe, Fiji and Tonga. It is Tropical. Our home city of Townsville is geographically closer to New Guinea than to the State Capital of Brisbane. Population 190 000. Our architecture, natural wonders, industries, ethnic diversity, food and climate are in many ways significantly different to our southern cousins. We are situated alongside the Great Barrier Reef and the Wet Tropics rainforest is just to our north. West, just over the Great Dividing Range, lies vast outback cattle country, remnants of gold rush towns and big blue sky. The tablelands to our northwest, have a microclimate which supports dairy and vegetable production. Sugar cane, mining, cattle and tourism are our major industries. Our destination, Blind Bay latitude 50 degrees north. Population 1800, in mid-summer. It gets very cold. It is overcast a lot of the time, snows about five months of the year with an average snowfall in the month of December of 600mm.

Our adventure happened like this...................

With a sigh of relief, we boarded the airplane off to Hawaii for an Aloha stopover, on course to Vancouver. With all the planning and anticipation behind us we had finally started our journey and were now officially expats. I've always liked the word and connected it with intrepid travellers or global citizens. This may be a bit grandiose, but it is the picture that I have painted in my mind. Maybe living in the wilds of Africa or a foreign correspondent in South East Asia. It simply means "out of the fatherland" and that we were. Living in a lake house, at the foothills of the Canadian Rockies, fits the bill just fine and for me, it was suitably exotic. The landscape was the ostensible attraction of our adventure, but the people and weather would prove to be the vital ingredients. Making connections and sense of an unfamiliar environment is all any true traveller desires. We did not wish to upset the apple cart, just be allowed to help push it along for a year.

PART TWO

Winter

A Bing Crosby Christmas standard oozed from the taxi radio on route from the airport, toward our hotel. The streets were adorned with cheerful Christmas shoppers. Chubby children in layers of gaudy winter clothing and wind burnt, cherry checks. The previous night's snow clung steadfastly to any foothold it could find. Hold it! Rewind, this is not a holiday fiction.

The sight of Customs officers in flak jackets and weapons at their hip, was a bit confronting. Their aversion to smile didn't help our fragile, sleep deprived, state of mind. Coming from Hawaii, where it is all "aloha", hibiscus shirts and wide smiles, the disparity was glaring. Not quite as confronting as arriving late on New Year's Eve at an Indonesian airport, where machine gun toting troops lined the hallway to customs. But I digress. We looked for the train sign after spending three hours in immigration with the other flotsam in our discombobulated state trying to sort out a visa issue. It appeared no one wanted to be there including the understaffed, overworked officers. Frustration reined and patience strained. We tried to explain we had a six-year-old who was hungry, thirsty and tired, to no avail. Why do they bother building ten counters then only put two staff on who are not replaced when they take their scheduled breaks? We did witness some interesting people using all sorts of strategies to advance their cause. This was our first experience with visa problems, and I suppose better in Canada than some non-English speaking, third world country. Once outside the cold air slapped us around the face and out of our malaise as we exited Vancouver International. Frustration peaked while negotiating the automatic ticketing. We went up and down the lift a few times, missing the correct floor and got my suitcase bitten and spat out by the train door. Not to mention the last-minute grasp of a handrail to avert an unassisted cartwheel down the aisle as the train took off without warning. The urban landscape was grey and bland. Monochromatic apart from the steadfast soul hitting the pavement in a red trench coat and beret. The predominant deciduous trees stood naked and forlorn. Their cast leaves swirling in eddies, hemmed in by concrete and stone. Our train rattled toward the compact conglomeration of stretched geometric skyscrapers that form the inner city, jutting out on a narrow peninsular into the natural harbour. Framed by a contrasting organic backdrop, the city's playground, a range of mountains covered in a blanket of picket fence white. Although a very foreign scene, it is undeniably beautiful in its own way. The First Nations people, followed by the Spanish and British, sure knew how to pick out the best piece of real estate. More than half of all British Columbians live in the greater Vancouver area, which hugs the beautiful coastline before it is severed by a series of fiords. Tentacles reaching back towards the mountains. We had a very late flight out of Honolulu, a redeye as the Americans say, and an early morning stopover in Seattle. By the time we got settled into our apartment, we had not had any horizontal or sustained sleep for almost thirty-six hours. After a quick bowl of soup from the nearby coffee shop, we crashed into sixteen hours of blissful sleep.

Everything felt and looked better in the morning. We had been researching, making lists, taking advice and making decisions for the last ten months, it was action time. I didn't, however, factor in the extra complexities of being a foreigner doing business. People wanted to see passports and work visas, driving and insurance history, the list went on. We managed to get new sims for our phones and a bank account. From then on it made the other dealings a bit easier. Buying a used vehicle, in good condition, was a priority for our ten-day stopover in Vancouver. We knew that we didn't want our choice of car to hinder our adventure, so decided on a 4WD SUV, not too old, roof racks and a good heater. This meant dealing with used car salesmen in a new country. Or did it? After some searching and emailing various dealers, car brokers and the like, I came across a company based in BC which specialised in buying cars for expats, servicemen or anyone time poor or unwilling to deal with salesmen. All I can say is, what a fantastic service.

The next morning, we caught a train followed by a ferry and then a long walk took us to a huge outdoor apparel warehouse where we stocked up on clothes and footwear to get us through the Canadian four seasons. By this time, we were already two hours late for our car dealership appointment, so we caught a forty-dollar taxi ride to the suburb of Richmond, located on the exotically named Lulu Island. Sure, we crossed a couple of causeways, but I didn't have any idea we were on an island until I looked on a map. Thank goodness the fleet manager and accounts lady were extremely friendly, because we had missed lunch, were very tired and our six-year-old was showing signs that enough was enough. Bribed with chocolate she settled down. The Chevrolet Equinox had one previous owner and low kilometers. We took it for a test drive along the banks of the vast Fraser River. Past fields of, what looked like, cranberry bushes and rows of cabbage left to rot due to poor market price. The pungent stench in the air, like sweaty socks, was now accounted for. I couldn't help wondering why someone didn't take the initiative to donate the crop to welfare groups. Surely big business could partner up with the farmer to make it happen. To our delight, large fluffy rabbits darted in and out of the verge foliage. Apparently, the nearby woodlands are a well-known disposal site for naughty pet rabbits who like nothing more than indiscriminately eating home furniture and fixtures. As the story goes, these domesticated desperados bred like, well, rabbits and before long were impacting the smaller native rabbit community. Of course, the farmers crops were also impacted. So much so that they needed a regular cull. The salesman, who chaperoned our test drive, was very relaxed and shared stories about his family's travels around the world and his upcoming cruise to Norway. Not somewhere I have ever considered, but interesting. We signed the paperwork on our return and added new snow tyres. The costs added up but would prove priceless in the coming months. They even gave us a ride back to the train station. Much appreciated.

So, by the end of a very long day two, we had found a vehicle which ticked all the boxes.

It was the first sunny day in Vancouver for a while and looking at the forecast it would be the last for at least a week. Shards of sunlight cut through an early morning cloud cover. The view from our apartment looked out across the city to the Pacific. Conveniently a few blocks from our hotel was a ferry dock where we caught the tub across to Granville Island Markets. As we approached, I noticed a group of people all leaning on the railing looking into the water. We quickly joined the astonished crowd, expecting to see some unfamiliar wildlife and that we did. From the depths of the briny a man dressed only in his underwear, exploded to the surface and rapidly sucked in some air. He quickly exclaimed "Got the %#@", which turned out to be a wayward credit card. Most of the onlookers were speechless as he climbed up the jetty to be met by his friend holding a handful of clothes. He turned his back to the audience, dropped his dacks and pulled on the rest of his dry clothing before making a rapid departure. No doubt heading for a hot drink and maybe some brandy? He was lucky the water was crystal clear, but the air temperature was only 4 degrees and hyperthermia would be chasing him. I reckon a phone call to the bank to disable the card might have been a better option but much less entertaining. As we disembarked at the market it was mid-morning, but ice still clung to the gangplank. Only becoming evident when we did a bit of a moonwalk on the invisible obstruction. Inside the main pavilion, the contrasting warmth was well received. Buskers churned out a mix of folk standards and originals, providing the soundtrack for vendors spruiking their wares. Lining either side of the many aisles were angled display boxes filled with fruit, vegetables, small goods and baked items, all meticulously laid out and colour coordinated into eye catching patterns. Almost too perfect to disturb. Huge wheels of cheese, wine, display cabinets chocked full of hams, pates and prosciuttos. One particular stall that caught my eye was a sausage company famous in these parts, a Vancouver Christmas tradition. A black truffle and duck salami headed up a list of adventurous concoctions. The lineup was ten deep, but after conquering Tokyo's subway earlier in the year, I reckon we could handle a Christmas Market crowd. After all they were all in the festive spirit.

Amongst the goings on, sat a fellow quietly working away carving intricate jewellery in a white bone like material. I never would have guessed it to be Mammoth tusk, how cool is that and he liked a chat! It turned out that he was a Californian expat who preferred the distinct change of weather and landscape of Canada to his home state. Each to their own. I love California. He seemed to have established himself in Vancouver and made a living from his art. I enquired about the tusks and if he found them himself. "No, while they occasionally are discovered by accident in creek beds and eroded banks, I buy from the gold miners who seem to have a constant supply". Like a good boy, I remembered it was our wedding anniversary a couple of days after Christmas and discreetly bought a three-dimensional heart shaped pendant. I usually would not buy ivory, but I can confidently say that this mammoth's demise was not from poachers. Another lady made casts from found objects, like sea urchin shells, and fashioned them into silver rings. Unique! I could have settled in all day watching the comings and goings on the river as the afternoon breeze pushed up the fiord, the birdlife, the people, but we dragged ourselves away to see what we could see. Another ferry dropped us at the Village part of the old athlete's accommodation built for the 2010 Winter Olympics. The walk back through the city allowed us a peek into the neighbourhoods. Some gritty and historic with curious milliners, cobblers and haberdashery stores just around the corner from bright and shiny chain store boutiques.

The 12 days of Christmas- 2015

Day 1, or in this case it was more like several glorious days at the beach in Hawaii. Warm clear water and sun shining, all masquerading as winter. Yes, we saw Santa in Honolulu, our daughter Imogen hand a photo taken with him doing the universal "surfie shaka" hand symbol, you know the one with the thumb and pinkie pointing outwards and the middle three fingers curled. Not to be mistaken for the heavy metal devils' horns. He wore board shorts, no doubt elasticised, with an extra-large Hawaiian shirt draped over his puddin' belly. Obviously enjoying the good life with a few too many Coconut Mojitos and spam sandwiches. Between obligatory "Ho Ho Ho's" he tossed out a few one liners like "My pet bear likes playing on the beach, so now I just call him Sandy Claws." It made us all smile and surely that is what Christmas is all about.

Day 2 - Stanley Park, Vancouver, Christmas Lights. It was 4 degrees and dropping. The sky was a painting of greys and blues left out in the rain. Colours bleeding into one another. It had drizzled all day, but we had pre-booked tickets for 5.30 that evening. It was either turn up or miss out. We stoically donned our new rain gear and every other piece of warm clothing we had, then trekked over the misty Lost Lagoon causeway to Stanley Park resembling a contingent of explorers heading off on a polar expedition. The evening commute was in earnest, a constant stream slowly emptied the city, all dreaming of their warm homes beyond and wishing someone had invented teleportation, after all it is the 21st century. Shrouded from the wind, the Rowing Club's lights created freeform squiggles across the still inlet, perforated by the droplets of rain. BC Place's large canvas sails, backlit in soft pastels, glowed invitingly in the distance. Sliced into smaller shapes by the mass of silhouetted spinnakers in the foreground. We forged on despite the dark and unsigned path, knowing that eventually we would see or hear some Christmas cheer or bump into a reveler who could show us the way. Sure, enough we turned the corner of a tall garden hedge to be charmed toward a magical, mystical scene emerging from the mist. Over three million twinkling lights. A cacophony of familiar Christmas carols blending into a strangely pleasant pandemonium, not unlike a show circuit sideshow alley in Aus. Presiding over events were larger than life nutcracker soldiers, with their disconcerting facial expressions. Why do they look so scary and in need of a dentist? A thoroughfare of Christmas themed displays funneled us through the park. Papier Mache pop culture characters, in suitably festive poses, sat comfortably beside bales of hay and nativity scenes. Kids of all ages darted around doting grandparents and parents trying to keep their flock together. The smell of roasting chestnuts, gingernut coffee and hot chocolate blended into a heady mix, as people crowded around fire drums, the licking flames illuminating their appreciative faces. Little ones were gleefully lifted up to join in the hypnotic spectacle. To our surprise, and despite the poor weather, there was quite a crowd. We had not yet worked out that in this country, if you waited for good weather you wouldn't do anything. The miniature train ride was fantastic, the park dressed in its season best. Imogen's eyes lit up with each new scene. People sang along with the carols. More marching nutcracker soldiers, this time on stilts, weaved their way along the train track. There was even a backlit silhouette of Elvis. Aliens looking down on this scene would find it hard to understand, but surely note that this form of tribalism gave the earthlings high spirits and a warm glow.

Day 3 - Capilano Suspension Bridge - Christmas Lights - The courtesy bus rattled through Stanley Park, once home to elk, cougar and black bear. Ahead stood another two imposing, regal members of the animal kingdom, but from another continent. Appropriately flanking the entrance to the Lions Gate bridge where two concrete grey kings of the jungle in sphinx pose, guarding large art deco pillars. An interesting mix of Pharaoh and jazz inspired architecture. It shares many similarities with its higher, longer, more well-known and one-year older cousin, the Golden Gate Bridge in San Francisco. I must admit when I first saw the Golden Gate I was in awe. But Vancouver's grand suspension bridge, built in 1938, is impressive. It connects Burrard Inlet to the northern suburbs. The weathered verdigris blue, rust stained span of steel, is a city icon. A part of Vancouver's fabric. So much so that in the 1990's, when faced with the option to replace it with a tunnel, and thus return Stanley Park to its original highway free state, the Government chose to restore. As much as I love the bridge, the thought of removing the traffic from the park would have been too much of a drawcard. Why not build the tunnel and leave the bridge and linked road for bicycles and pedestrians? A win for all. Over the bridge in North Vancouver, the previously mentioned wildlife remain, obviously in less numbers than the early years of the settlement. The bus driver told us that three young male cougars had to be put down earlier that year because they were hanging around a childcare centre creating a real threat. A much larger male was sighted at the back fence of a property in 2014 and would not move despite the locals attempts at scaring it with noise and projectiles. Sadly, he was also destroyed. The driver also recounted the story of a black bear cub who climbing onto the back of a garbage truck, only to be taken for a ride around the streets by the oblivious driver. Now there is an opportunity for a children's picture book if I've ever heard one.

The original hemp rope and cedar plank Capilano bridge, circa 1889, was built by a Scotchman with a dream and a civil engineering degree, which no doubt proved helpful. He purchased some land on the outskirts of a young Vancouver city and proceeded to build a cabin on the very edge of the canyon wall. The name Capilano evolved from the First Nations Squamish Chief Kia'palano who ruled the area during the 1800's. The bridge and river it spans, took his name. We arrived just on dusk as the fairy lights began to take hold of the impending darkness and herald the evenings enchantment. The semicircular cliff walk, jutting out from a sheer granite escarpment, allowed views of the river below, spot lit in several points with revolving colour. As we crossed the bridge, I was surprised that there seemed to be no quota. It was packed from one end to the other. I can only assume that its load capacity must be well in excess of the conservative estimate of one hundred revelers. My girls didn't like its languid sway, but for me, it added to the experience. I mean who wants to cross a rope bridge that doesn't move a little? Certainly, no boy who grew up watching the adventures of Indiana Jones. Once across we climbed a series of elevated boardwalks into the treetops, where a Swiss Family Robinson style of connected pods clung to the ancient cedars, dripping with damp aromatic scent. Surely this would be the perfect antidote to couch bound kids hypnotised by electronic screens.

Day 4 - Very cold and raining. The bleak weather was offset by the frenetic Christmas shoppers on parade in Alberni Street, dressed to impress in their stylish winter apparel. High boots, winter hats and umbrellas. Tinsel, Christmas carols, shop front displays with mechanical Santa workshops, buskers, beggars and me. The traffic horns and crossing beeps, mellowed only by the patter of rain. I left the apartment to do a bit of Christmas shopping of my own, leaving my girls some time together wrapping presents. No matter where you are in the world, it would be hard not to like the lead up to Christmas, you can feel the anticipation in the air. The extra challenge was to buy something that would fit in our suitcase on the way home. A challenge that would be ever present for the following year but sometimes ignored.

That evening after dinner in the apartment, I suggested a movie but ended up going by myself, excited by the prospect of the new installment of Star Wars. I arrived half an hour early thinking I had heaps of time only to find there were no less than six screenings between 6.30 and 10.30. To confuse the issue further, the following options flashed on the digital screen above. *D-Box 3D AVX ATMOS, ULTRA AVX 3D ATMOS, ULTRA AVX 3D, Regular 3D* and *Regular.* Now I understand the 3D part, but the rest? My quandary was soon over as I discovered all screenings were sold out. I have never seen such a crowd at a cinema, but I suppose it's warm and dry entertainment. I happily settled for the new James Bond movie, "Spectre" in *Regular.* It didn't disappoint. The sound and picture were great, and I pondered how much better it could get seeing it in the other formats. There seems to be a lot of highflyers walking the streets of Vancouver at night. As I wandered back to the apartment it was hard not to notice that earthy smell floating on the cool air. The media are heavily covering the push by lobby groups for the Federal Government to legalise Marijuana. Prohibition is clearly not working.

Day 5 - We rugged up and walked the length of Alberni Street, then out to the Lost Lake in between the city and Stanley Park. Photo plaques on the edge showed people dressed in old fashion attire playing ice hockey on the lake, but these days it hardly ever freezes. Oddly, the trees on the bank were covered around their base with chicken mesh. There were remnants of less fortunate trees, reduced to stumps with pointed tops, like an oversize pencil sharpener had been at work. Closer inspection showed small divots left by diligent beaver teeth following their primal instinct. We didn't see one but the fact that wildlife lived in the centre of the city was exciting. Up a bit further we spotted a family of Raccoon, who it appeared, are not at all shy. This outrageously cute cat like mammal, with its black superhero mask, had caught my daughter's attention in the lead up to our adventure. She even did a talk about Raccoons in first grade. This sighting was a real treat and very unexpected. Canadian Geese wobbled and honked around the foreshore park like old women with expansive derrieres and bad hips. Very comfortable they were with the attention from curious humans, casually stepping aside when they felt like it and not before. Further along, near the English Bay headland, we stopped to take in the 360-degree views. Vancouver Island in the distance out to the west, across False Creek to the marinas and museums and behind us to a large sculpture installment. Fourteen three-metre-tall, bronze men, all the same character but faces contorted in the many shades of happy. It was called "A-maze-ing Laughter" and in-scribed with "May this sculpture inspire laughter, playfulness and joy". In my opinion, at least, the artist Yue Minjun achieved his goal. Interestingly it was originally on temporary loan but priced at five million if someone really had to have it. In the end a benefactor negotiated a price of 1.5 million to leave them in place. A great outcome. Earlier in the morning we had spotted Cardero's restaurant on the waterfront just off Hastings Street, with its enviable views of Vancouver harbour and across to Stanley Park, so decided to escape the cold drizzle and head there for lunch. This was my type of place. Great architecture, location, food and wine. We sat watching the poor ducks huddle in the one-degree conditions glad the fire was roaring in the corner and that we indeed were not ducks. There were old fashion kayaks suspended from the ceiling together with all types of vintage maritime paraphernalia. Very cool! A long lunch, something we never get the time to do.

Day 6 - We picked up the Car, I suppose it was a Christmas present, but it felt more like a very expensive, but necessary, outlay. I was not looking forward to the potential hassle of selling it at the end but tried not to think about that. On the bright side, we would be much safer on the interior roads and could confidently go off road to discover hidden gems. We had off loaded our old bomb that I used to commute to work but kept our SUV sitting in the garage at home. I actually got a good price for the seventeen-year-old sedan. A kid bought it for $2000 as their first car and both parties were happy. We tested out our navigational skills with the help of a map's app on our phone. Great free service complete with voice prompts which did a very good job of getting us safely around a town which is notorious for its congested traffic. My wife Anna and I have a long and fractious history when it comes to driving and navigating. During one of these altercations my dear wife tore up the map and threw it out the window as we emerged from the easy drive through the Mojave Desert into Las Vegas where the 11, 564 and 215 freeways intersect in a spaghetti tangle. The petrol gauge was showing empty and we needed to catch a flight. But that is a story probably best left alone. We did catch our flight, without incurring a littering fine, and the road trip through the desert was memorable for all the right reasons. Joshua trees, tumbleweed, red rock and sand complimented by the quirky towns along Route 66.

Day 7 - 20th December- KOOZA - We were very fortunate that a Cirque Du Soleil show was in town and we were able to score some decent seats. Imogen had never seen a Cirque show and I was very excited about experiencing it with her. Hopefully allowing me to see it through the eyes of a 6-year-old. I loved the circus as a kid, but the colour, sound, humour and athleticism of these productions, just blows my mind. Hard to believe the evolution from a small troupe of performers roaming the streets of Quebec City in the early 1980's to the internationally renowned organisation of today with several troupes performing around the globe at any point of time. What better place to see a performance than in its home country? Seeing it in a tent as opposed to the massive venues in Vegas was a pared back delight at close range.

Day 8 - Before our stay, we researched things to do during Christmas in Vancouver. The one that least interested me was the *Omnimax* Christmas Fly Over movie. How wrong this turned out to be. Canada Place is an impressive waterfront convention centre, cruise ship terminal and hotel jutting out into the harbour. Its imposing roof, incorporating several sails, is a prominent landmark. It really does look like it could be uncoupled from its morning and sail off into the deep blue. From the boardwalk we watched seaplanes take off, land and refuel at the floating service station in the bay, a unique experience. Many of the remote communities like the Gulf Islands and beyond rely on the planes for their mail run and urgent supplies. Most use a seaplane like we use a family car. The remoteness and vast distances are very similar to Australia where we have the Flying Doctors and Outback Flying Mail Service.

To Imogen's delight, further along the boardwalk was a tent set up with Christmas craft activities. She made a reindeer antler headband, a cotton wool Santa beard and wrote a lovely letter to Santa, which she posted in the North Pole mailbox conveniently positioned close by. I had a chance to talk with one of the coordinators who had a teacher daughter who married an Aussie. Small world. She told me she loved Sorrento and attended the Bluegrass Festival there each year. It was one degree but she remarked "This isn't winter. It won't be long before you know what I mean. They get loads of snow and subzero temps in the interior." A sobering thought. It was time for the *Omnimax* show. Strapped into our seats, the lights dimmed and the curved screen in front came to life as our mechanical chairs glided out into the space. The action was all around and we quickly forgot that it was a projection. I looked across at Anna and her face was sheer delight. The movie flew over the many and varied landscapes of Canada trying to locate Santa's cheeky elves who had gone AWOL at the busiest time of the year. Imogen loved it and we all agree to come back later in the year to watch the regular show.

On the way back we took a stroll through the historic, and now trendy, Gastown. The original city centre had a lovely old world feel. According to various accounts a British sailor with only six pound in his pocket, paddled ashore in a dugout canoe in 1867. Along with his Indian wife, her cousin Big William and several barrels of whisky. This man obviously had his priorities right. They landed on the shores of what is today, Vancouver Harbour. Although his previous home of New Westminster was only seventeen kilometres away as the crow flies, it would have been dense forest. His vessels path down the Fraser River was over forty kilometres and would have taken several days, hence the need for the cousin. Conveniently he landed right beside Stamp's Sawmill, chose a piece of land to squat on and bribed the workers with alcohol to build him a makeshift "Saloon" in a day. It must have been rough, but I suppose the more whisky they drank as the candles burnt low, the more comfortable it became. No, he didn't get his nickname from the side effects of a cabbage and onion diet, rather Gassy had an ability to spin wild yarns of his adventures around the world, with one account mentioning a desperate escape from the Sydney Docks in Australia. The business and the legend of "Gassy" Jack Deighton grew. Whether or not all the details of the story are totally accurate, does not really matter. This explorer and entrepreneur contributed to the young colony and his story makes people smile 150 years on. Now that is some achievement.

Day 9 - Grouse mountain, wow what a day. We drove our new car through Stanley Park, passed the stone-faced Lions, across the bridge and up the mountain. Beautiful homes and gardens lined the streets of the, what appeared to be affluent, North Vancouver suburbs. Our reliable navigator diverted us around roadworks, through to the base of the mountain and the Gondola parking bay. We have fond memories of Grouse Mountain on a Summer visit some years before baby joined our family, but winter would be a totally different experience. It was a true winter wonderland up on the mountain with Santa's workshop to visit, real reindeer to feed and sleigh rides. Imogen made it very clear that ice skating was where she wanted to be, so we hired the skates and joined the other parents purposefully scanning the flock of skaters like eagles ready to swoop on a rare, but invaluable, support frame. These simple devices could make the difference between a happy child and major dental surgery. After only a short wait I managed to snavel the prize without making any children cry but earning the wrath of envious parents. Skating was a success and Imogen even progressed from using the support to holding my hand as I raced around the edge of the ring in my snow boots of course, not skates. I'm not that silly. As soon as her boots were laced back on, she grabbed my hand and dragged me off to the "Magic Carpet Ride" otherwise known as the sliding hill. We were given two flimsy sheets of plastic mat, because ice is just not slippery enough right? Lots of fun, but the snow was heavily compacted, and the mats were thin, so unless you had some pre-Christmas padding on your derriere, it was a bone jarring dash. I liked the design of the run. It sloped up at the end bringing partakers to a gentle-ish stop. Our first exposure to sledding occurred while spending Christmas in Colorado a few years back. Acting on local advice we ventured out to a slope just on the outskirts of the small village of Minturn. It sat beside a well-used snowshoeing trail and some young families were already into the swing. It looked pretty tame, but what would I know, I come from the tropics. We had a few short runs with

Anna positioned down the slope to catch Imogen. She was having lots of fun and of course wanted to go faster so I gave her a push and ran along behind. She steered it well and the sled zoomed off so fast that in the end I had to do a Hail Mary dive, full stretch, just to stop the red terror. The giggling four-year-old thought it was great and wanted to do it again, but Mother was not as impressed and I decided to be a little less adventurous with our darling girl, at least until she turned five.

As the day progressed, the crowd grew. The snow began to fall heavily, wind lifted the powder, swirling it around any obstacle it could find. We wanted a white Christmas and it sure fit the bill. After a late lunch inside the main Chalet, we escaped the pushing and shoving around the fireplace, which resembled a mosh pit at a rock concert, to venture out along the Christmas lights walk in rapidly decreasing afternoon light. Again, the scenery was breathtaking. Snow covered pines, drooping under the weight, took on cartoon like forms which I never imagined could be real. We climbed up around the ski lifts to a cabin beating out Christmas classics. Then down along a frozen creek bed to a well-lit bridge. With cherry cheeks and lifetime memories. We called it a day.

Day 10 - The girls headed off for some ice skating at the Robson Square rink, just up the road from our lodgings. I am not an ice skate or roller skater for that matter, so let wisdom prevail and avoided spending the morning bruising my backside while trying to maintain a white knuckled grip on the handrail as my six-year-old zipped past me giggling. The alternate route let me visit the famous Bill Reid Gallery in downtown Vancouver. As galleries go, this one was quite intimate, and I had it all to myself. Over his long career Bill and his artwork became National icons appearing on currency, public art installations, galleries and private collections all over the world. Along with his incredible talent, Bill had a real connection to the native Haida people of the Haida Gwaii archipelago of islands. His mother was part Haida and although he grew up in a modern environment on Vancouver Island, his connection with his heritage continued to grow. Haida society was broken up into two groups, the Ravens and the Eagles. Bill was a Raven and this icon features in some of his most famous work. For example, the remarkable two cubic meter, yellow cedar sculpture "the Raven and the First Men" a native version of the birth of mankind. His creativity shone at an early age. On display was a teapot and two cups carved from a stick of board chalk and painted with his mother's nail polish. Apart from the obvious craftsmanship, what caught my eye was the scale of the work, the raw cedar carving and, in particular, the beautiful washed out, earthy colours. The translucent blacks, ochres and sea blue greens, gave the work a real presence. Some of the newer totem poles had solid, vibrant acrylics applied and this I felt detracted from the authenticity of the work. I asked the nice lady at the reception about what the Haida originally used for stains. She seemed thrilled that someone was interested and quickly consulted her database. I was expecting the use of clays but in fact a charcoal mix was used for black and all the other colours were derived from various minerals ground to a powder. Interestingly when the Europeans came onto the scene, they used the bluish-green verdigris from oxidising copper and brass to create those wonderful green shades.

Day 11 - A little Christmas spirit came our way. Due to a late change in our schedule we had to move apartments. We rolled up to our new accommodation three hours prior to check in, hoping only to use their underground car park until later in the day. It just so happened that our room was ready, and we were ushered to the 12th floor with a view of the Harbour and Stanley Park. We quickly unloaded and the girls set to work on a make-shift Christmas tree made of a string of tinsel and sticky tape. They adhered it to one of the large sheet glass window panels and dressed it up with some miniature, flashing, fairy lights. Snowflake window stickers completed their festive artwork. Very effective. It just goes to show a little bit of effort can make such a difference. I bet that tree will be spoken about for many years to come. We called our family back home in Australia, who were already in the middle of Christmas Day due to the time difference. They were staying on the glorious Magnetic Island and had gone to the beach for the morning, spotted Koalas in the backyard and opened all the presents. It was great to hear from them. While people in the Tropics sometimes dream of a white Christmas, having now experienced a couple of cool yules, I must say I prefer our sunny summer version and all the quirky traditions that go with it. Eggnog is replaced by very cold beer and wine. Prawns instead of turkey, a few salads and maybe a Pavlova instead of Christmas Pudding. This type of fair has only recently come to favour. When I was a kid we were still firmly entrenched in the British idea of Christmas, even though it may have been 2 degrees in London and 32 degrees, in the shade, in North Queensland. Traditions are hard to let go because it is not necessarily what they are, but the memories they provoke of people past. I can vividly remember my parents slaving over the oven all morning only to sit down for lunch, stressed out and sweat dripping off the end of their nose.

Day 12 - 25th - Christmas Day. For some reason Imogen woke up at three in the morning and proceeded to drag us out of bed to see if Santa had come. By five am we were all a little weary but once again had the privilege of watching our daughter open her gifts in sheer joy. Somehow Anna got us back to bed and surprisingly we slept until 10. When I was a kid my sister was a shocker for waking us all up very early Christmas day, but never before six. Before lunch I got a bit of fresh, chilly air as I headed out to explore Stanley Park. Just over the causeway a fluffy, black squirrel wagged its tail to greet me before clambering up a tree. Already I was glad I had come. Shafts of light flashed through majestic redwoods holding court in clusters, never ceasing to amaze and hold my attention. If only they could speak, the stories they would tell. I headed east, along the bay, admiring the many and varied yachts and cruisers. The water was so crystal clear I could gaze into the depths, half daydreaming, but also scanning for sea life. May be a mermaid? A congregation of totem poles beckoned ahead, flanked by buses of tourists which reminded me that Christmas Day is not celebrated by many cultures and for them it is just another day to explore. Everything was open for business including the aquarium. At the entrance to a water park, I spotted an air blower, drying station in a short tunnel. Now that's something I have never seen before. I assume if you play in the water park at this latitude you would need to dry off as quick as possible. A women tentatively glided past on her new hoverboard. Very apt, considering 2015 was the year Marty McFly cruised around on a hoverboard in Back to the Future 2. I couldn't help but smile and assume that some of the nostalgia and intrigue was lost on those younger than myself. I read somewhere that Nike is working on a pair of those self-lacing boots from the movie. As I curved around and headed back West, the shipping port laid out in front of me. I heard a passer by telling his friends that wheat was being loaded. Large piles, of what looked like wood chip, sat on the opposite shore, sadly watched by the cypress forest above. The path divided around the Brockton Point Lighthouse and I chose the lower route, near the water's edge. There were not many people walking this section and I was rewarded with some quiet time to reflect on the year ahead.

On a trip to Los Angeles in 2013, I started taking photos of interesting street art and graffiti. Inspired by the range and quality around Santa Monica and Venice Beach. So was delighted to find a life size artwork on the wall beneath the lighthouse. It was a depiction of a homeless man wrapped in a blanket, cup out for charity and a sign that read "Sharing is Caring". Painted beside him was a tourist taking a snapshot of him. A poignant message indeed. Have some places in the world become so used to poverty on the streets that they are desensitised? I have been shocked by the amount of homeless lining the major arteries in Vancouver.

Again, the sun broke through the grey, heavily clouded sky. Suddenly the quiet grounds filled with hordes of people wanting a bit of UV and relative warmth on their face. It would be hard not to notice that very few conversations were in English. Some were Caucasian, but there were many shades of skin and ethnic dress. Everyone was happy, with what appeared to be a live and let live attitude. The Statue of Lord Stanley in the park proclaimed "to be used for the enjoyment of people of all colours, creeds and customs for all time" and it would appear that in that moment, on that small spot on earth, there was peace and harmony despite all of our similarities or differences. Imagine that! Surely Stanley must rival Central Park in NY for position, diversity and wildlife. I was glad to have seen it in such a tranquil, winter state, a pared back version of its greener, boisterous self.

On the 27th of December we pointed the car toward the Rocky Mountains and Blind Bay, our base for the next year. The large sign suspended over the road declared "Trans-Canada Highway" and I couldn't help but sing the chorus of Gene Pitney's hit song of the same name. Now that's showing my age. I tried to get the girls out of the apartment and on the road at a reasonable hour, but scorned I was and successful I was not. By 9.30 we had just left the Vancouver CBD. Wet, raining, cold. Within half an hour the rain turned to sleet and by the time we got to Chilliwack, heavy snow was falling. The road conditions deteriorated, and I felt a bit uneasy on the four-lane highway with people flying past seemingly disregarding the conditions. The landscape was postcard perfect with pine trees dipped in white frosting, pinned to sharp escarpments at all points of the compass. The drive was slow, for us anyway. Cars, buses, semi-trailers all passed us with ease. We came across several cars rolled on their roof and lying in a ditch, justifying my cautious approach. At times the visibility was very poor and my eyes tired from straining to see taillights through the thick fog and snow. Somewhere near the top of the range, between Hope and Merritt, I seemed to lose traction on a steep incline. The accelerator pressed to the floor made no apparent gain. The whole feel of the car on the frozen asphalt was foreign, unnerving. The talcum powder like snow, swirled eerily, like dry ice pouring across a stage. The sheer drop offs were a white out and that was probably a good thing. My girls seemed to be blissfully unaware of the proceedings while I quietly focused on keeping calm and getting us there safely.

Our exchange volunteer welcoming party, Richard and Petra, met us at the house just on dusk. Thankfully the people from across the road kindly used their snow blower to clear a path on the driveway, allowing access to the carport. A very thoughtful welcome. While they were waiting for our arrival, Richard had mentioned to the neighbours that we had struck the worst possible weather to drive up from Vancouver. So much so that the locals would not even consider it. The neighbours response was "well it's probably a good thing they didn't know what they were getting themselves into." Our previous winter driving experience was from Santa Fe, New Mexico up through the Rockies to Minturn, outside Vail, Colorado. This was a couple of winter's ago and although we encountered snow, country roads and higher altitude, it did not prepare me for the Coquihalla Highway. We would find out later that there is a cable TV show called "Highway Thru Hell" documenting the feats of a recovery towing company working this infamous stretch of highway. I am glad we had not seen it.

Within fifteen minutes our greeters had gone. We stood there in that huge house, tired, hungry and quietly hoping it would all be alright. We missed the familiar comfort of our home of twenty-five years, but an adventure beckoned. Thus far we had been travellers in Hawaii and Vancouver, but now the reality had hit. This was it for a whole year. The highs, lows and everything in between. We all slept together in the king size bed downstairs, very aware that our little one would be feeling fragile as well.

Blind Bay, Sorrento and Salmon Arm were as picturesque as expected, pines draped in snow, the lake with Copper Island standing sentinel. Salmon Arm is a small town about twenty-five minutes' drive west on the Trans-Canada Highway and Sorrento is ten minutes in the opposite direction, with a population of 1250 in peak season. There will certainly be no rats to race in this part of the woods. Blind Bay was originally marketed as an exclusive retirement subdivision for people escaping life on the prairies, they now let in folks of any age, but it has a large percentage of retirees. Some are permanent while most keep a holiday home and visit a few weeks each year. Grey is the new blonde in these parts. An aversion to hair dye? Although Anna and I, spent the first twenty years of our lives in a small country town, we have lived in a provincial city for many years now. Small town life will take a bit of getting used to. You don't think you will miss things until they are gone.

We ventured into town on day two to get some groceries. The Salmon Arm welcome sign was partially coated in snow and its logo of a bright sun looking through the mountains proved to be a very optimistic weather outlook indeed. We all craved some of our own home cooked food. Even though Canada implemented the metric measurement system in 1970, four years earlier than Australia, the predominant cost per weight is given in pounds. Kilograms are sometimes in small print. It takes some getting used to, luckily there is 2.2 pounds in a kilo so the maths is easy. I was very surprised there is any reference to the imperial system at all in this day and age and can only suggest that having the US over the border has made the transition very slow. Also having French and English labeling on every product can be frustrating. Just little things that make you appreciate home even more. Having no land borders to other countries and one language is a blessing. There are a few surprises like an open freezer full of haggis and to its left, a rather macabre pile of goose carcasses. They sure are a huge bird but I reckon they would be tough. Like my Dad use to say referring to scrub turkey "Throw a stone with them in the pot and when the stone is tender the bird is ready to eat". Regular black tea is hard to find. There seems to be a strong preference to Orange Pekoe. They have a whole array of brands but all the same variety. I like a strong tea and my ignorance led me to believe that Orange Pekoe actually had little bits of dried orange peel in it, which was simply wrong. I later found out that its name does not refer to the flavour but the size of the tea leaf. In this instance, a fine grade. The Orange part of the name was cast upon it by the historical importer, the Dutch East India Company, who, for marketing purposes, associated the tea with the House of Orange, a respected aristocratic family in the Dutch republic. So, there you go. I tried some and it was weak as water, no matter how many bags I used or how long I drowned it for. I needed to find some-thing hot to drink.

On a whim I picked up a couple of items we had not seen before. Baked beans "Maple Style" espousing the use of "Pure Quebec Maple Syrup". At first glance I thought this would not be a good combination but knowing baked beans at home have added sugar I decided it was worth a go. At only two dollars a can, I could feed it to the Raccoons if I didn't like it. The other item was Black Russian Rye bread. It was the real deal and actually tasted like bread as opposed to that processed white cake like stuff that lines the shelves. Even better was the two combined. Hot beans whacked on top of toast, black pepper and a sprig of parsley. Talk about the simple pleasures in life.

That night I decided it would be best to cook our steak outside and avoid smoking up the closed house. The last thing I wanted was to be dealing with smoke alarms attached to 8-metre-high ceilings. So, a subzero BBQ took place just outside the double-glazed lounge room windows. Although the girls refused to provide me with company, I seemed to provide them with endless entertainment. They sat and watched through the windows; I should have charged an entrance fee. Note to self, let the grill heat up for a lot longer than at home to compensate for the air temperature. Obvious I suppose, but we are conditioned to doing things a certain way. The steak eventually cooked, if not as per the textbook method. No one complained about its toughness and I eventually thawed out once back indoors.

One of Anna's new colleagues dropped over in the afternoon with some soup and took the girls for a tour of their new school at Sorrento. Her name was Tori and she would be a friendly face for them to identify with on day one. What a lovely gesture during her holiday break. The Principal also met us there on Saturday. He also seemed friendly and easy going. I mean anyone who takes the entire school to see the new Star Wars movie on the last day of term, is OK in my books. Even though Imogen would be starting halfway through the Canadian school year, we chose to start her into grade two, but not so sure about putting her in Mum's class. The Principal convinced us it would be best to keep her on track for her return to Australia.

Our greeters Petra and Richard, had us over to their house for dinner the next evening. They had a nice place, only a short drive away, with views of the lake. Both retired, very interesting and easy to talk to. They seemed to be very creative and active within their chosen fields. Petra is an artist with some impressive works on the wall and Richard, who struck me as a Dick Van Dyke type of character, was passionate about music and playwriting. His new Baby Grand piano took pride of place in the living room and we were fortunate enough to hear him play a little, as we arrived.

They were travelling to Australia in March to visit friends. Driving up the East Coast from Sydney in a camper van and keen for some travel advice. I think the key to retirement is to stay active and they sure seemed to be doing that.

New Year's Eve. We woke to minus 8 but it was expected to fall to minus 12 during the afternoon. I scored some Ice Hockey tickets for the Salmon Arm Silverbacks versus the Surrey Eagles. The game started at 5pm and when we arrived in the car park it was already cold beyond belief. We were not sure what to expect inside so wore all our warm gear but were pleasantly surprised that it was at least a bit warmer. The venue was modern, and our seats were right on halfway, just below the press box. After some pre-game entertainment the match began and the home team quickly gained ascendancy, scoring a nice goal. Games are broken up into twenty-minute thirds, with time out for all breaks in play. It takes quite a while to get through. Very fast paced and physical sport with opposition players never letting a chance go by to crunch someone against the glass barrier. This seemed to be acceptable and I noticed opposing numbers getting pay back throughout the match. If you are willing to hand it out, you must be willing to cop it in return. In the final session a big brawl broke out with plenty of punches and verbals thrown. It took the referees about ten minutes to break up and sort out the penalties. Imogen liked counting the players as they were sent to the naughty corner, which was crowded at times. It was a Junior A competition and by the looks of the players they must have been under 21's. What more do young bucks like to do on a Saturday night than play sport and have a brawl. Something to talk about in the pub afterwards. It was hard not to notice the Asian ethnic influence in Vancouver, but if the surnames on the jerseys were anything to go by, it is replaced by French and Russian heritage in these teams. Players are bought from all over North America and are billeted by local families but spend most of their time on the road. When we got back to the car it was that cold outside that we all struggled to function. My muscles seemed to contract and seize up as I fumbled for the keys and tried to safely get out of the parking lot. It took quite a while for the car heater to make any worthwhile impact. From then on, we agreed that -12 is too cold to be outside for the Scott family of tropical North Queensland and should be avoided at all cost. Of course, it was to get much colder before our year was up.

On our first Saturday night in the Interior we ventured out to a concert I found advertised in the local paper. It was at the Sunnybrae Community Hall, about ten minutes' drive up the road. We found the turnoff in the dark and cautiously proceeded down a narrow unlit road. There were signs alerting us to be aware of deer crossing, but we didn't get to see any. I assume they saw us. The young musician hailed from the Appalachian Mountains area of West Virginia and grew up listening to this interesting mixture of music which originated during early colonisation as a blend between European and African styles. The immigrants and slaves brought their music and instruments to the area and it subsequently morphed into a style of its own. This talented, young man had a Degree in Folklore from the University of Kentucky, not sure how that helps with employment, but it sounded interesting. He played banjo, guitar, fiddle, autoharp and dulcimer. I must admit prior to the show I had not heard of the style or some of the instruments. Many of his original songs had a common thread of respecting people's differences and living a happy life. Doesn't the world need more of that! I am not a fan of country music and when the artist strode on stage, well over six foot of him, with a shiny red, pearl buttoned, cowboy shirt, big embroidered boots and a strong southern twang, I thought it may be a long evening. How wrong I was. He was accompanied by a tiny woman who could sing and certainly play a mean fiddle. At times during the show they put down their instruments and per-formed a bit of a jig. Now I hadn't seen that before either, but they certainly got into it. To the onlooker this folk dance appeared to be an enthusiastic combination of tap dancing and line dancing performed with clickety clacking, hard soled shoes, thigh slapping and broad smiles. Depending on which part of the South you come from it is called clogging, jigging, foot stomping and buck dancing. They differ due to the combination of regional rhythms and variants developed over time, but all include toe-tapping, flat-footing, heal and toe steps which are performed with emphasis on the down beat. A whole intriguing new world! The hall was small with only some fifty people in the crowd, but I was glad we ventured out on another very cold night, privileged to hear and view a subculture accomplishing what all performances should, putting a smile on people's faces.

The night was organised by a group who hold regular, what they call, Coffee House evenings throughout the year. We call them open mic or blackboard musician's nights back home. You basically roll up, put your name on the board and have your time on stage. I rang the number in the paper to arrange for some tickets and the lady on the other end instantly recognised my accent. She was a Kiwi and had lived in this neck of the woods for a long time. I did not have the heart to tell her she no longer sounded like our Trans-Tasman cousins. Anyway, she was very friendly and introduced herself on the night along with a friend of hers. I had a good chat to him about what we were doing and his own history. A born and bred Vancouver boy he had spent much of his working life in the very cold northern Alberta oil fields. As I complained about the cold of the previous night, he said that he had moved to the Shuswap partially for the milder winters, which put it in perspective, I guess. They both were part of a band and joined the Appalachians on stage for a few numbers with their double bass and guitar respectively. Towards the end of the evening, someone announced that a blue Chevy had its lights still on in the carpark. It was ours. I quickly grabbed my coat and turned them off, the ice had slicked up outside and I had to do some quick footwork, combined with luck, to avoid hitting the tarmac. While this was going on Anna mingling with the locals over hot drinks and baked slice. Somebody had to do the socialising! One fellow recognised her accent and coincidently he and his wife were from Geelong in Australia. His wife came over on a teacher exchange with him in tow many years ago. They liked it so much that when they retired, they moved to Salmon Arm full time. At the end of the performance we said our good-byes, but the car battery had drained too low and would not turn over the starter motor. With two rather cold girls waiting in the back seat, I went back in for some help. The oil worker rallied a few mates, who happily came to our aide. One was a young fellow with dreadlocks, who only wore a tee-shirt. When he went around to the boot to grab some jumper leads, I asked the others how could he cope without a coat on. One replied "he doesn't know any better, he's from Scotland" which brought a chuckle. When we popped the bonnet, most of us hadn't seen anything like it. Luckily one bloke was a mechanic and pointed out the battery was covered from view, as were the terminals. On top of the box were a bunch of wires and fuses. It took our mechanic friend a few minutes to find an appropriate point to hook up the leads, it then started first kick. Very appreciative and relieved we headed back to the house, pleased with our evening experience.

I figured that I would get a bit more time to play guitar while abroad so packed my tuner, capo and picks. I expected it would be easy enough to pick up a 2nd hand guitar at a flea market, but when we first entered the house, I noticed a guitar leaning up against the fireplace, not the best place for a stringed instrument to live. On closer inspection it was missing a few strings and looked like it had been quiet for some time. After a quick dust down, new strings and a tune up, she sounded just fine. I used to play a lot before Imogen was born, but every time I got out my music when she was younger, she would crawl over and proceed to rip out the pages and giggle cutely. Anyway, I encouraged her to come over and sing along but she was playing on the mat close by and showed little interest. Not disheartened I downloaded a few tunes that she liked on the radio. Stuff I would never play. Sure, enough it got her attention immediately. She came over straight away and started singing. We didn't sound too flash but that's not the point. The things a Dad will do to get some attention. There is also a piano in the lounge just waiting to be heard. I haven't played in forty years but if we get stuck inside too often, I might give it a go.

Day one at school, the alarm clock woke us up at 6 am for the first time in a month. Outside it was minus 8 and snowing. Maybe our bodies were secretly craving routine? We arrived early to find a relatively empty car park, pickup and drop off times at schools' back home are very hectic with traffic everywhere, but not at

Sorrento. The Principal told us that ninety percent of students take the bus, which is great. The classroom was large with a separate wet room where students came in, took off their snow pants, jackets and boots, then put on their inside shoes. All food is eaten inside to avoid litter in the grounds which attracts furry critters small and large. Sorrento Elementary is a P - 5 school located in an enviable position on the banks of Shuswap Lake with views of the water and mountains from Anna's classroom window. It was very utilitarian in design. Much like a 1940's war time airport hangar with a library upstairs, gym in the centre and classrooms fanning out from the central office. It seemed to fit a lot into, what appears from the entrance, a small footprint. I wished the girls luck and took off with my list of errands. I was immensely proud of them both for their courage, adaptability and sense of adventure. I know Anna will be fulfilled by the experience and am sure her class will be engaged in learning and have lots of fun doing it. A year they will never forget.

Dumping rubbish was a bit of a worry. It had been building up for the past week. We are used to a weekly bin pickup at home but the instructions with house were the concise "dump your own." Everyone we asked complained about how complicated the recycling system was, with the majority saying they just dumped it all together at the tip to avoid the problems. There are six categories on top of general waste. Directions to the closest local landfill were obscure and during the first month I couldn't find it online or on a map. When I asked the locals, they said it was a bit complicated to get to in the snow. To get rid of some of it I tried the recycling station and was berated by a fellow dumpee, a rude woman who took umbrage when I failed to separate the lid and the connected milk bottle into separate bins. I know what you are thinking, I'm a rebel even when I am trying to follow the rules. She was one of those types who found it hard to live and let live and obviously enjoyed the confrontation enough to dawdle around a bunch of rubbish in subzero temperatures. I found out later that this sort of thing happens often. It is amazing how people are only willing to divulge this type of information after the fact. I think an altercation must have been a rite of passage to live in the neighbourhood. I temporarily gave up on finding the closest dump and drove all the way into Salmon Arm. After a few wrong turns, I stopped for directions at a produce supply shed in the industrial estate. I walked up to the counter like a cowboy entering a bar, all conversations stopped, the piano player froze, and eyes focused on me. Well maybe not exactly like that but I sure felt foreign. Luckily the barmaid, oops, lady at the counter was pleasant and offered useful directions. I found the dump right next to the airport. Nothing is easy in a foreign land. Strangely enough I managed to take one of the coolest landscape photos I have ever snapped. As I arrived the sun was still low in the East. A ridge above the dump was lined with a thick battalion of aspen, leafless, white, standing to attention. The rest of the landscape, a pure luxuriant white. The fog was thick and refracted the sun's rays into a rich, feather edged glow. The Aspen cast cascading fingers of shadow into the foreground. It was a quick click and run, partly because I was freezing and partly because I could feel my fellow dumpees giving me a look reserved for crazy people. Not sure why I really cared, but that is human nature. When I checked it back at the house that evening, I could hardly believe my luck. I called it "Dawn over the Dump - Nature doesn't Discriminate"

Getting up for school got a little easier each day. But the routine, as soon as I woke, was to check the driveway. Some mornings there was six inches of fluffy snow which had to be removed before we could back out. What a workout, twenty minutes of shoveling with my six-year-old companion. Cherry cheeks and wet track pants. Anna received a text some mornings to say go slow, as the roads were not in great shape. We soon learnt that this meant everyone got to work late. No kids, no teachers, no problem. Copper Island rises out of the lake adjacent to Blind Bay, pretty much in the centre and provides a picturesque distraction from the highway. Pity I have to concentrate on staying in the snow ruts of the car I am following. The township of Sorrento was originally called Trapper's Landing until a resident observed a resemblance to this island and the Isle of Capri, off the coast of Sorrento, Italy. These pioneers petitioned for the change and so it was to be. Now sure Capri is steep, made of rock and has some green foliage but I think a combination of moonshine and homesick Europeans may have fueled the comparison.

Soon enough, due to necessity, I started to observe some snow clearing etiquette. If you get it wrong, the snowplow driver lets you know about it. The first time I cleared the driveway using the push shovel, which I might add is much easier on the back than a regular shovel, I pushed some of the excess snow on to the road, hoping it would be removed by the snow plough. Now I am only talking about the snow on the last half meter of the driveway. I mean they are paid to remove snow, right. Apparently, there is an unwritten demarcation that if the snow falls on the road it is their problem and if it falls on the driveway it is mine. When I got back from the school run, they had pushed the mound of snow I left on the road, plus interest, back into the mouth of the drive, forming an unwanted speed barrier. A welcome to the neighbourhood of sorts. I needed a new plan for the excess. Some Aussie remodeling was required. Over the course of a few days I sculpted the snow into ramps either side of the driveway, which allowed me to slide the full shovel a couple of meters from the edge and deposit it into the gullies. It proved to be a winner and I didn't see anyone standing out front scratching their head at my antics, not that there was anyone around to see. Plenty of people have motorised snow blowers which scrape up the white stuff and throw it onto a pile, where's the fun in that. It is all over too fast and no workout.

Roads are cleared on a priority basis. The highway is of course the first and then major roads. It could be well into the afternoon before they got to our court. This meant on the way to work the snow could be deep. Thank goodness we purchased a 4wd and top-quality snow tyres. After the plough goes through, a truck follows with a salt, crusher dust mix. The slush sure makes a mess of everything. You can hardly tell what colour any of the cars are. After school one day, we made a detour to the car wash. The grime was getting us down. No one bothers to wash their car in Winter and now I know why. By the time we got back to the main road it was as dirty as it was before we started. The car wash was a novelty though and worth the admission. As you drive inside the roller doors close on each end. I briefly thought wow, I am imprisoned, and they may not let me out until someone is satisfied, I have done a good job. No straws were drawn, both my girls just gave me a look which said, "You are the man of the house, get out and do it". I attached myself to the high-pressure sprayer. Within a minute there was so much steam inside that I just had to point in the general direction and hope the gunge was being blown away. By the time I had gone through the multiple stages, I was damp. Although it was warm water it would not stay warm for long. I knew this was not the climate to get around in wet cloths and we still had to refuel at the servo up the road. When we arrived, I drew the short straw again? I jumped out and flipped the fuel hatch open only to find icicles already formed within the last five minutes. I had to crack them off to access the fuel cap, now that was different and yes, I froze while waiting for the tank to fill.

Driving in the snow, on the opposite side of the road than at home, is challenging. The lack of visible centre line markings or roadside reflective guideposts is hard to fathom. When there is paint, it is not fluro and therefore night driving was worse. Being continually covered in snow and muck infinitely compounded the problem. It seems that you just estimate, follow the wheel tracks and keep your outer tyres away from the ridge of snow. I have clipped this ridge a couple of times and it quickly removes your steering control. Not good. The signage is also covered in snow and muck at this time of the year, which makes it hard for newcomers. Maybe a council truck, with a hot water spray could give them a blast every now and again. It sure would be handy, but I appreciate the logistics of this are easier said than done. In town the traffic light rules are also different from home. In some instances, you can go on a red light, which is against all instinct and previous knowledge. You can turn right on a red light if no one else is coming. You can also go "when it is safe" when a flashing red light is suspended over the road. As Salmon Arm is a smallish centre, four way stop signs are everywhere in town, no doubt reducing the need for traffic lights. I would certainly prefer roundabouts, but I suppose it is what you a use to. The official government driving website stated that the vehicle that comes to a complete stop first, has right of way over the other cars to proceed. This can get a bit messy as you are assuming that the other drivers are seeing it the same as each other. If two cars arrive at the same time it is a bit a chicken run or a standoff. Clear as the muck on the road. I asked the locals and they seem to be of the same opinion. At some intersections there were additional lights in the centre median strip. So sometimes when you get a green and begin to accelerate a red light flashes on in the middle island. If you cannot picture it just take my word that is very disconcerting. Apparently, this signals that you cannot turn. Have they not heard of turning arrows lights?

After school one day, our next door neighbour, Samantha, came over with her daughter, Hannah, to introduce themselves. It was great to meet someone and have a chat about the area, school, things for kids etc. Imogen's eyes lit up when she spotted a potential playmate and some four hours later, they had rolled in the snow and played every game in the house. I asked about wildlife and Samantha said she hasn't seen the black bears, but they poo in her yard often overnight. The people across the road had a moose eating away at their lawn last summer. A bobcat and a cougar were spotted on separate occasions last year and she doesn't let her kids go out unless they are in a group or with an adult. Sounds like a good plan. We obviously wanted to see the animals but feel safe while doing it. We cope just fine at home with the snakes, marine stingers and crocs, so will just continue with what we know. On that note, I received a message from home that our exchange family had arrived in Townsville at 10pm. My Mum picked them up and drove them out to our house, even though it was late, they had a tour and when she ushered them outside to show them our extra outdoor shower, a snake slithered across in front of them. We haven't seen a poisonous snake in our yard for a while but at least they now know to have a torch at night and watch where they put their feet. Something for them to post home about the wilds of North Queensland. We do get visits by large carpet pythons which are non-venomous, the most recent was three meters long and Imogen wanted to pick it up. They have beautiful markings, but I have no need to cuddle them. Sand Goannas (Lace Monitors) pass through occasionally and don't seem to cause too much trouble if our dog is asleep, which is most of the time. I wouldn't want to corner one, they have long claws, sharp teeth and can grow up to two metres long. After all they are a member of the Varanidae monitor family of lizards. The same tribe as the well know Komodo Dragon which lives on some of the Indonesian Island to the north of Australia.

On the long quest for the Holy Grail of Teacher Registration for myself, I ventured into Salmon Arm to visit the Royal Canadian Mounted Police, after receiving a letter request for fingerprinting. In this country anyone working directly with kids, including teachers, doctors and dentists, are now required to submit their paws for background checks. So, I fronted up and the nice female officer directed me to "go back out the front door, down to the icy footpath and along to the first driveway, follow the driveway halfway up until you get to a roller door." I followed the instructions and as I approached the roller door, it lifted, and I tentatively walked inside to find a long, empty hall. A voice over the intercom ushered me further along. I was half expecting to be asked for the secret handshake or password. I thought I was part of a Maxwell Smart episode. The lady appeared shortly after and directed me into a small room where my photo and prints were taken several times by a temperamental machine. "It doesn't like dry winter hands" she said "so put on some moisturiser. It doesn't like hands that are too wet so wipe some off. Don't press too softly or too hard." After some time and a significant amount of patience on both our parts, the results came back. I had jumped through another hoop.

We continued along our steep learning curve. Things popped up daily which were far removed from our normal mindset. Like don't fill the windscreen wiper spray tank with water otherwise it will freeze, and your spray won't work until Spring. Fortunately I did not commit this faux pas, as I learnt my lesson the previous day. I placed a vase of flowers onto the outside table because it was making me sneeze. We found the freeze-dried arrangement in the vase cracked by frozen water and stuck to the glass outdoor tabletop. Luckily the vase was only a fruit jar, but I didn't want to crack the tabletop so cautiously poured warm water on it until it let go. Imogen also learnt not to leave her sled out overnight because when it snowed, we couldn't find it, well not until June anyway. We made the obligatory snowman, who was a work in progress throughout winter. He looked very wide and far too short. Even the flying fox (mini zip line for non-Australians) in the backyard got a workout. Note to self "You are too heavy for the apparatus and pull one's trousers over the top of snow boots otherwise you will get cold wet socks!" Conversely, when moving around town, trousers get tucked into top of snow boots. This is Interior BC fashion tip #1.

So next time in town I purchased some minus 46-degree rated antifreeze windscreen wiper fluid. Should do the trick. On the way out of the mall car park, I stopped to give way to traffic and felt a nudge from behind. In the rear-view mirror, I saw the grill of a Ford F250. It was jacked up so high off the ground that an average height man would need a stepping stool to get into the cabin. I crossed the road and pulled over, half expecting the truck to speed off, but it gently came to a stop behind me and both parties got out to check the damage. Thankfully there was none. The driver shook my hand, with a sigh of relief and a coy smile. Nice to see people can sort things out without getting nasty. I suppose I was lucky, several utes and 4wd's in the carpark had hydraulic snow ploughs attached to their front end. I kid you not, they must live on a side road not serviced by the council and have had to take matters into their own hands.

That weekend was the first time since we arrived that the temperature had risen above zero. We reached 1 degree and what a difference it made. The roads became visible from beneath the icy slush. Thick fog rolled in and stayed most of the day. The kids rejoiced because the damp snow was perfect for snowballs and Imogen informed me that she now spends her lunch breaks making snow forts. Apparently, the school oval is covered with staked out claims and icy architecture. She went on to explain "You just make a little ball in your hand Dad, then put it on the ground and roll it. It picks up heaps of snow to make a huge ball which you stack on your fort wall". Back home in Townsville we get an average 320 days of sunshine and the coldest winter night only gets down to 12 degrees but averaging 16. Apart from the snow, the Okanagan Valley is capped in cloud and have been told it stays like that for six months of the year. In 2015 it stayed cloudy for around eleven months. They had a wet summer. Not something that we found in our prior research. We really miss sunshine and we have only been here a few weeks.

Most mornings the slush had refrozen and was very crunchy under tyre and foot. It sounds like crossing a dry creek bed full of river rock. Anna had settled into a routine with her class. One afternoon when the children had been dismissed, she found a note on her desk from a little girl. It simply read "I like you; you make me smile because you are always happy!" Now that would thaw the most hardened soul and sure made one Aussie teacher very glad. She is finding her class to be all good, honest, country kids, similar to back home. Before we left school one Friday, Tori took us down to the sports room to fit us up with some cross-country skis for the weekend. She invited us to Larch Hills, a groomed course just outside of Salmon Arm. Cross country skiing gear and technique are totally different to downhill we are told. The students from year three upwards, practice on the oval at lunch times for the annual Pirate Loppet. There are various distances and age categories in this all district schools' event. Much like a regular cross-country run, just on ski's and dressed as pirates. 'Loppet' is not a word I had come across before and sounded very Scandinavian, which would make sense seeing it is also called Nordic Skiing. It is a Swedish word, basically meaning cross country race. There are some very famous races around the world ski community and even a Kangaroo Hoppet race in the Australian Alps that has been skied since the mid 70's. In these frigid latitudes one needs to find as many ways as possible to get out of the cabin and into the white stuff, I suppose. I am told schnapps helps with creative thinking.

On a crisp Sunday morning we arrived at the course, happy the strong wind of the previous day had dropped off allowing a thick fog to seep across the snowy flats. The local Nordic Ski club had raised money over the years and built a log cabin decked out with toilets, a shared kitchen, tables and the most important feature, a log fireplace. We took quite a while to put on all the layers of clothing and skis. I had on so many garments, all with their own pockets, that I was finding it hard to keep track of my car keys, wallet, glasses. I knew they were there. A bit like pass the parcel. To my surprise the course was groomed by a machine which actually put channels in the snow for you to place your skis, much like an inverted train track. On these narrow skis only the toe of the shoe is connected at a pivot point, so when you walk your heels move up and down independent of the ski. The poles are very helpful and as we set off up a slight incline, I prematurely thought this would be a fun workout. I have done a bit of snow-shoeing previously and enjoyed that. How hard could it be? Imogen had a bit of a hard time going up the slope and complained of freezing fingers. I had doubts that she would last too long, but Tori got her to grab her poles and towed her up while skiing backwards. Cool trick! Soon we came to our first downhill slope and although it was a very slight gradient, all of the Aussies stacked it. After a short while my girls seemed to pick up the technique and were zooming down with glee. Dad, on the other hand, got very acquainted to the snow or should I say hard ice. I managed to have some good runs, followed by some spectacular falls. I would shoot one way; my skis would abandon me when I needed them most and continue gracefully down to the bottom unsheathed from their L plate driver. Talk about fair weather friends. I must admit I preferred the stroll down hill, through the forest, to collect my skis than actually skiing. I even had a chipmunk come out and give me a smile or maybe he was trying to say, "give up mate, before you break a leg". We were on the course for around two hours and by the time I tentatively stumbled across the finish line with my skis and poles over my shoulder, the rest of my group were already perched beside the fire inside preparing a picnic lunch. My dear daughter didn't forget me though. She walked back up the course to meet and encourage me. Imogen assured me that next time we came, she would help me with my technique, or lack of it. She is a good girl and I am really glad she had some success. A good effort for a six-year-old. I think she will enjoy downhill skiing in a couple of weeks. It was good to get back to the house that afternoon, we played checkers and I put some ice on my jarred lower back. Tori sent through the photos of our day in the snow and they sure looked great, so I emailed them to friends and family back home. This was what we came for, new experiences.

There was still no word from the education department regarding a job. My cabin fever intensified even though I tried to keep active with walks when the weather allowed. Which wasn't often. One day I came across an odd sight. Not wanting to stare, but very curious, I watched as a lady guided a snow sled pulled by three poodles, yes you read correctly. I didn't want to be rude, so I took a photo after she passed. I knew no one would believe me otherwise. Further on I took some nice photos of the lake, still with its thin ice sheet close to shore and the marina dock covered in snow. On my way back to the house I passed the Husky impersonating poodles and their owner coming back from the grocer with a week's supply of food in the sled. Now how about that for Canadian ingenuity and multitasking. I was impressed.

My confinement to domestic duties was going OK. I do like cooking and don't mind the laundry tasks but found myself telling the girls to wipe their feet at the door and rinse their plates, oh no Mr. Mum. These tasks only take up a very small part of the day, so I researched impending adventures. Sometimes you really need to scratch below the surface to find the best places to go and things to see. The house we were living in was to a proportion that I have not witnessed before in a single residence. It could easily house several families or a sorority. In total it had eighteen designated spaces which included a basement media theatre, a gym, a huge playroom and several unfinished rooms that we were not sure of their purpose. Maybe a sweatshop some time down the track? Not to forget the enclosed three bay garage. Far from being critical, it was just another cultural difference to observe. They spend so much time inside that it probably makes some sense. The neighbour's house was also quite large, but there are also many homes to the proportions I am accustomed. In the playroom there was an air hockey table. It only took Imogen a few games to work out the tactics. She sure can hit it hard and straight when she wants to. There was no television on the ground level, it was down in the basement. Elvis's Jungle Room, it was not. With no central heating, it was isolated from the rest of the family spaces which prevented having the TV on while preparing dinner or watching a few favourite shows of an evening. In the beginning it was a blessing, as we were all reading more at night. But sometimes you just want to sit back and be entertained by a show. Imogen improved her reading so quickly and before long was rattling off the tongue twisting Dr Seuss tales with delight.

 We were invited to dinner at Tori's along with our neighbours Luke, Samantha and Hannah. The girls played all night and the adults had a good laugh. Tori recounted the time when her husband, Aiden, had gone out in the car and forgot to lower the garage doors. She was in bed and the neighbour rang to say that there was a bear in her carport, having a feast on the garbage. When she opened the door the beast quickly ran off. Not something we have to worry about back home. Their house had views of the lake and a real log fire, which has its own unique ambiance. That being said, I am glad to have the electronic fireplace where we are staying. I once had a mishap in an adobe house in Santa Fe. I filled the dwelling with smoke and had to open up all the doors and windows in the middle of winter, to clear it out. Obviously, the beautiful historic rental did not have smoke alarms. Tori showed the others some pictures of our house that our exchange family had posted on online. While I was glad, they all liked the look of our humble abode, it did make me feel a bit homesick. We built and have lived in our home for almost twenty-five years, the house and garden give us much joy.

Since the adaptations of the 1950's and 60's, to accommodate the baby boom, the government mandated design of the North American school bus has not changed a great deal. Sure, it would have the latest mechanical and safety incorporations, but that classic design, with the engine mounted out in front like a tractor and the boisterous canary yellow skin, maintain a feeling of yesteryear. The cabin cantilevers about two and a half meters past the back wheel, although it is no doubt sound in an engineering sense, it strikes the eye as unbalanced or out of proportion. Something you might see in a child's drawing. Certainly, in my mind, having watched my share of US period movies, I thought the big yellow kid taxi was a leftover design from the wars, much like the Jeep. I expected that they would only be paraded out as props for movies set in a different era. But no, they are alive and well and grace the highways, roads and dirt tracks across North America, complete with their flip out, red stop signs. I suppose if it ain't broke, don't fix it. It made me smile when I saw them coming along and I hope it makes the kids riding them smile as well. Curiously there are no turnouts or shelters at bus stops. The bus stops in the middle of the road, no one can pass in either direction, as it loads. Talking of kids, although the incidence of teenage smoking is on the decline in both Australia and Canada, I was amazed to hear that chewing tobacco is a real issue in some schools. I didn't even know it was manufactured any more. My only exposure was watching Clint Eastwood spit it out before he shot down another good for nothin' horse thief. It has been illegal to buy, sell or use smokeless tobacco products in Australia for a long time. Just another issue for schools to deal with.

In Australia, all school students wear a uniform. Although I am sure any suggestion of this in North America would result in riots on the streets, there is firm research that suggests it is very worthwhile to focus students minds to the business at hand. Namely learning. It makes them feel part of a community, tradition and ethos of a school. It also helps parents trying to get their child to dress respectably and removes some anguish and opportunity for peer pressure about what you should look like. Early on in the year, my daughter was prancing around in the mornings contemplating her wardrobe for the day. I wish she would focus on eating a good breakfast more than her clothes, but that is a work in progress. I am happy that she cares about her appearance and even asks me to help her polish her leather boots. For a bit of fun, I wrote a poem about it all. Although she needs to polish her black leather school shoes back home, in Canada her favourite footwear, when it wasn't snowing, was a pair of high cut leather lace up boots.

MISS MOO'S SHOES

Daddy they are dirty
Daddy they have slime
Daddy they have bits of poo
And every kind of grime

I even saw some chewing gum
Stuck in between the sole
A piece of fruit, a bit of rock
Or maybe it was coal

The leather is all scratched and scuffed
It's faded and it's worn
Oh, please help me polish them
Or other kids will scorn

A brush, some wax, a nice soft rag
We'll whip them into shape
A bit of elbow grease, my dear
They have nowhere to escape

And now Miss Moo your pair of shoes
Glisten brightly in the sun

No goo, no poo, no scuff or scorn
Our work here is now done.

Quite a bit more snow fell the following week. The morning ritual of getting out in the dark to purge it from the driveway, continued. We decided it was time Anna had a go at driving for the first time, but the weather deteriorated along with the roads, so we postponed. Some mornings the highway had not been ploughed, no road markings were visible and the buildup on the edges meant a formerly four lane highway was reduced to a snowy single track in each direction. On one occasion we came around a bend to meet a ute, who decided he was going to pass on a bend. I had to swerve to miss him and expected to lose control, but thankfully the tyres held firm and we were just left shaking our heads. On the same morning, a little further up the road, a small sedan was wrapped around a light pole, which was the only thing that saved it falling over the edge of a hundred-foot drop. I have not seen many road barrier rails and although you don't want to hit one, they give you a bit of confidence if something goes wrong. There seems to be a massive road funding shortage, in this Province at least.

There is no doubt that amongst all the excitement, adventure and meeting new people, there was an emotional burden of choosing to displace your family from everything they know. The challenges of an exchange were ever present, and it took some mental conditioning to stay on top of it. There was an existential angst of having no garden, no family or close friends, no home, no beach to walk on, no city to wander. We were separated from our tribe and our land, but realised it was ok to get down in the dumps at times, just not for too long. We needed to take every opportunity that came our way. Anna and I have always been pretty good at that and try really hard to avoid the "if, but, maybe, would've, could've, should've" excuse mantra, used by those who talk about it, but never do it. This was just a different challenge to be overcome. The premise that you create your own reality is debated. But it is undeniable that when presented with hardship or a problematic situation, one can look at it as a roadblock or an opportunity to learn and grow. Despite our best intentions and efforts in regard to integrating with the locals, many were still very standoffish. Maybe we were expecting too much. Each community is a web of interconnectedness waiting to be discovered. From the bold and loud to the subtle and gentle, each with their own story. Amongst all the natural wonders on offer it is often the people who make an experience. We quickly realised that arriving in the depths of Winter was not an ideal time for meeting people in this neck of the woods. The remnants of the community, left behind to endure winter, are a bit like ant hills. Life is going on, but there were no external signs. There was hope that things would get easier when it started to warm up. Little towns are little towns, no matter where they are. You can flip a coin to whether you will be welcomed straight up or not. Whatever the reason we are Les Marginals, the outsiders. I would have thought curiosity, at the very least, might have fueled some contact early on. We do know how busy families are and had already met some great people. I suppose we just hoped to get to know more. We vowed to say yes to any invites. Thank goodness for Tori and her family who were the enduring shining lights in this regard.

Some eighteen months after our exchange had ended, we met up with a Canadian family while holed up in a dingy little hotel in Siem Reap, Cambodia. They were having breakfast at the neigbouring table and as their children were about the same age as Imogen, we started exchanging stories about our days trekking through the temples of Angkor Wat. They were from Vancouver but had spent time in several towns in the BC Interior. When told we lived in Blind Bay for twelve months, they nearly chocked on their cereal. They couldn't get the "Why? What did you do during Winter?" out of their mouths quick enough. Initially I thought "City slickers, probably don't appreciate nature" but quickly realised that could not be the case. You don't visit Cambodia for a pampered city experience. The wife said "They see the world differently out there! Many like to keep to themselves." Although I am sure this was an over generalisation, we told them it was really difficult to make connections at times, but we figured we just had to try harder. "Oh no, we are not surprised. We found it hard to gain acceptance. But when you do get to know them, they are good people." The father bailed us up the following morning and interrogated us further about our adventure. He was clearly impressed that we lasted the year and after our conversation, we felt justified by our, at times, uneasiness with the social structure that endured during our stay. Our initial thoughts that the psyche of the Interior would be no different to the more populated coastal regions was obviously naive. Secretly I think we were jealous that Imogen was finding it easier to integrate. Anyway, it was nice to meet them, and they gave us a few great ideas for where to explore. They were travelling on a shoestring, just hiring a tuk tuk driver each day and going with the flow. They hadn't decided where they were going to fly to next or how long they were going to stay. Although I like to be quite a bit more organised than that, I was impressed with their obvious travel nous and adaptability.

One day, I spent most of my time on the phone and internet trying to book accommodation for the summer break. I quickly became aware how early popular places book out and was frustrated at the over the top prices in and around the Rockies. After consigning myself to camping, for which we had no gear, or staying in small towns an hour's drive away from where we wanted to be, I came across Hostels International. I rang the reservations centre and a nice lady ensured me that lots of families, and people over twenty, use their facilities. So, we wouldn't be out of place and just as I was thinking I could buy one of those Rastafarian beanies with the dreadlocks attached and use words like "awesome" or "incredibly gnarly dude". Summer hosteling it would be, bunk beds and shared bathrooms for the Scott's. Sounds like an adventure.

Earlier in the week, a quick check of the roads showed that Highway 1 was closed either side of Revelstoke, to our north, due to an avalanche control taking place. The trained crew set off small blasts which drop excess snow from areas that have been identified as a risk, due to their terrain. Then they clear off the road. Our pre booked Saturday night visit and concert looked a bit iffy and the thought of being stuck in Blind Bay for another weekend was depressing. Apart from driving the girls to school and shoveling the driveway, I hadn't been out of the house all week. I tried to take the lake road to Sorrento when time permitted, to avoid the highway and soak up the beauty along the way. Large homes mingled with cute summer cabins to line each side of the road. All had some sort of vessel wrapped up in cling wrap for the winter. I even saw an old Streamliner caravan permanently parked with a roof built over it and surrounded by decks. Like many, it was right on the water's edge, on the thin slice of land between the road and the lake. No one was home. I suspect their owners were lying on a beach in Acapulco waiting for the first glimpse of Spring. A geographically well-planned existence! As mentioned, the elevated highway also offered great views, but I couldn't afford to be distracted, too many crazies driving way too fast. The locals attribute much of the problem to Albertans, or Flatlanders as they call them. A reference to their wide expanses of prairie grasslands, a continuation of the Badlands. They tell me that all of their roads are straight, and they drive fast despite the conditions. I am sure this was just a generalisation, with a bit of inter-provincial rivalry thrown in. They encouraged me to check the next time I witness some poor driving and see if it was a red Alberta plate. I am sure the Albertans say the same thing about British Columbians.

Grocery day was sadly becoming the highlight of my week. I had been told by a colleague back home that exchanged to Alberta in 2014, that the cost of living was similar to back home. She did joke though, that BC stood for Bring Cash. I certainly found goods a lot more expensive. Fruit, vegetables and especially meat and dairy. Fuel was cheap when we arrived but had gone up to around $1.10 a litre by the end of February. Still a bit cheaper than home. While in town I tried to make the most of my visits. I didn't know anybody, but at least there were people around. I found a couple of good spots to pass the time. The Shuswap Pie Company, with its rustic interior, raw timber and flour sack clad walls. Nice hot chocolate and baked goods. A good spot to while away an hour reading the newspaper. One needs to stay abreast of the local comings and goings. Curiously one such occasion I was reading the local rag on Thursday the 14th but it was dated Friday the 15th. How's that for printing efficiency or have I been transported into the future by Doc's DeLorean. If I had the chance to time travel, I certainly wouldn't waste it visiting one day into the future. There's something about the sepia toned

1940's that intrigues me, so maybe that would be my first port of call. The music, well dressed people, politeness, movie stars or maybe because it was a time when my grandparents were young men and women. The way people withstood WW1; a depression followed by WW2. Or maybe a wiser option would be to visit the late 90's and buy shares in a fledgling company with the strange name of Google.

Conveniently our bank was not far from the pie shop on main street, which would be lucky to get five cars pass through an hour outside of the summer holidays. On one visit when I reached the counter, a friendly clerk, having noticed my accent, explained that she was intrigued with Australia and asked, "So is the whole country like what was shown in Crocodile Dundee?" I am a bit taken back by this and enquire what she meant, she said "You know, is it all outback? Do you have industries and large cities?" "Oh, that's right, you have the Great Barrier Reef. So, you must be a skin diver?" she added. Not usually stuck for words, I just smiled and told her it is a great place and she should come and visit sometime. Won't she get a surprise. Anyway, I picked up a family sized Raspberry and Rhubarb Pie on my way back to the car and continued to dream about other points in time I would like to visit whilst driving back to the lake.

That Saturday morning, having checked the BC drive website, we bundled into the Chevy for our first road trip. It snowed heavily from Blind Bay to Salmon Arm, but by the time we reached Sicamous the roads were clear, and the fog had lifted to expose the sheer mountains looking down into the valley. Our destination was Revelstoke. Known for its precipitous skiing slopes and small-town hospitality. We passed frozen lakes and plenty of signage advertising, what sounded like great outdoor activities which were "Closed for the Season." A message we read far too often during the year. Revelstoke is a compact village with a short main street. A cross between the Wild West and a Swiss Alps hamlet. It was cold out, very cold and lunch time. A cozy coffee house provided a refuge and opportunity to check out the locals. The shabby chic decor was warm and friendly. A hard-covered photographic history of Revelstoke Ski culture caught my eye on the table beside the ancient, but comfortable lounge chair I found myself in. The worn cover had a photo of a skier flying off the end of a timber ramp into the crisp thin air. It was a slightly yellowed, black and white photo with handwritten scrawl stating - Nels Nelson, Canadian Ski Champion 1916. I flipped through to see happy punters wearing charming, but not so practical, winter garb of the 1920's, complete with high heel ski boots. The things girls will do in the name of fashion. Some had huge mink coats and Russian Ushanka fur hats, while others appeared to be minimally dressed against the elements. Many photos showed yesteryear ski club patrons posing for portraits in matching club sweaters, beanies or toques as the locals insist. A very European look indeed.

Ski culture rules in this town, snowboards and skis are regular adornments to the shopfronts and fittings. Mixed with the washed-out blues and reds of the buildings draped in icicles, demanding multiple photos. I booked our accommodation online and apart from the reasonable price, the shape and colours of the building caught my imagination. The place was called the Cube, and for obvious reasons. It juxtaposed with the traditional steep pitched roofed architecture of the surrounding buildings and used the designer Mondrian's palette. I learnt that Pieter Mondrian was an early twentieth century painter and contributor to the De Stijl art movement. You know, the one that incorporates rectangular black borders, seemingly random filled with bright red, blue, white and yellow. Imagine the pop of colour against the snow! I have only been exposed to De Stijl design in the last couple of years through my Design classes at school. I prefer an industrial aesthetic but now have developed an appreciation for the it's effective simplistic touch. I applaud the owner and builder for their courage to build such a structure and gauging by the number of guests, it was a case of "build it and they will come".

Acting on a tip from Anna's new Principal, we headed out to the Village Idiot tavern for an early dinner before our concert. The place was bulging at the seams at 5.30 but we managed to prop Imogen up on a stool at the bar while we waited for a table. She didn't seem to mind the loud music and frivolity of the happy crowd. I watched her wide eyes scan the joint with wonder. The walls were covered in various bits of nostalgic bric-a-brac. One sign proclaimed that "Complimentary Air Guitars are available at the Bar". There were no less than six televisions mounted strategically on the walls, all with the gridiron match between the Green Bay Packers and the Arizona Cardinals. Tight match with the Cardinals coming home with the goods. I asked Anna if she thought they would put on the cricket match between Australia and India on at least one screen. She didn't' like my chances and neither did I. The menu used a clever play on words and made us smile with options like "Just for the Halibut" a reference to a Canadian fish species. Good pub food. Afterwards we navigated our way through the dark, heavily snowed, back streets to the impressive Performing Arts complex for our evening entertainment. I certainly didn't expect such a facility in little Revelstoke. A folk band hailing from Vancouver, The Nautical Mile were performing. While lacking some of the harmonies of our favourite bands, the lead singer was very Bob Dylan-esque in the way his songs could easily be removed from the music and read as poetry. He was passionate about his craft and left well timed pauses in his singing to let the music shine through. Both the song list and the instruments were eclectic, with ballads through to up tempo tunes, which the lead rather nicely referred to as "Bombastic Nostalgia", complete with trombone and trumpet. Some songs were very political and focused on issues like the federal government's mass document shredding after losing the election. My favourite of the night was the song "Potted Flowers" which talked about a friend of his that tirelessly worked to leave the world a better place. He also sung "It's exhausting having dreams" which really struck a chord with me. Imogen enjoyed the evening and made a point of telling me what each instrument was. The seldom seen slide guitar impacted the overall feel, shifting from electric guitar to organ like sounds. A great trip away.

Back in Hawaii we afforded ourselves a single piece of kitsch for our anticipated car purchase. We named her Kono and she is a three-inch-tall hula girl complete with little grass skirt and coconut bikini top. We quickly developed a fondness for Kono, she was always smiling, wobbling her hips to the rhythm of the highway and was the only female in my family who always nodded her head in approval to everything I did. Great girl! The following week Kono and I drove into town to pick up our summer tyres from the Greyhound bus. The ones we left behind in Vancouver. It was raining, real rain for the first time, not that half frozen stuff that seems to float, then splat into your windscreen. Strangely it seemed to envelope me in its familiar smell, touch and sound. Very comforting and a feeling of home, something that is tangible in this otherwise uncommon frozen existence. The days continued to be quiet and lonely, as I hoped I would find some kind of work soon.

When we first arrived, the locals seemed to have had enough of winter already, but it was fresh and new for us. However, it was not long until we joined them in the countdown to Spring. There was about six weeks to go before school Spring break and we still had to do some downhill skiing. I hadn't quite given up on ice fishing, but hope was fading. We did see a hearty sole sitting on a frozen lake beside the road to Revelstoke. Even if he didn't catch anything he was rewarded by great scenery.

I had been feeling a bit under the weather, which seemed to intensify the cabin fever and bring on a dose of the doldrums. A number of people had told us to take a daily dose of vitamin D to compensate for the lack of sun exposure on our skin. I assume this is even more important for people who come directly from the sun intense tropics. The radio also regularly gave community advice about Seasonal Affective Disorder or SAD, which is a type of winter depression, not uncommon at this latitude. I suspect the lack of fresh air from hibernating inside didn't help. I did yearn for sunshine and being outdoors, gardening and fresh air. We all did. In what would become a common catch cry from many locals, I am told by a shop assistant "it is not a very nice day, but you wait for the Summer, it is beautiful". I know the intention was encouragement, but Summer was still a long way off, and I don't live for one quarter of the year, nor could I leave for Mexico, Arizona or Florida until it warmed up, like many of the part time local villagers.

I became very determined to find an antidote to the gloomy winter days. First thing I tackled the chores which really didn't take that long, although I got the vibe from Anna that it should take longer than I allocate. I figured I was doing alright when I overheard Imogen telling one of her friends that "Daddy is our Man Maid". Not sure where she picked up that one, but it gave us all a good laugh. The girls have been craving some home cooked goodies so I figured, how hard can it be? Keeping with the Canadian theme, I found a recipe for Nanaimo Bars which are to Canada, what the Lamington is to Australia. Although this sweet is much younger and without the intriguing and sometimes controversial history of the Lamington, it sure packs a punch in the sugar stakes. Named after the city of Nanaimo, a major ferry port on Vancouver Island connecting the mainland. For those adventurous souls with a sweet tooth and a penchant for making a mess in the kitchen, this is my interpretation using what I could find in the pantry.

Nanaimo Bars

The Crust

1/2 cup margarine

1/4 cup sugar

5 tablespoons raw cacao powder

1 egg, beaten

1 3/4 cups crushed corn flakes

1 cup toasted coconut flakes (not desiccated)

1/2 cup almond meal (Imogen won't even notice)

The Gooey Stuff in the middle

2 tbsp custard powder

50ml milk

¼ cup margarine

beat in 2 cups of icing sugar until smooth. Spread over cooled base layer.

Chocolate topping

about ½ to 1 cup of dark chocolate buttons

1 tbsp of thick cream

I gathered all the ingredients on the kitchen bench and after school we made it a group effort. All went really well, including the taste test. Of course, the little one got to lick the chocolate bowl at the end, and she did not share, at all. I must say I like them much more than our Lamingtons. No, it is not treason, I just don't like sponge cake.

So, it was to be that cooking became a regular cabin fever busting fallback activity. The post-Christmas sale turkey we picked up on arrival needed to be consumed. Now I would have much preferred to tell a story of how I tracked this bird through thick snow bound Aspen forest for three hours, dodging bear, moose and cougar, until finally shooting my quarry. But turkey season didn't start until spring, nor had I met any hunters who would let me tag along. At 5.5 kg, it is not huge, but still a lot of protein for my little family. After 48 hours in the fridge supposedly defrosting, it was still solid as a rock. I had considered leaving it out on the front porch for a few days but had visions of a bear walking away with it tucked under his arm. It was much colder outside than in the fridge anyway. Seriously. Now, to brine or not to brine? This was the question. I have had some success with the former, so stuck with that. The process ended up being quite an event, taking as long as a cricket test match (5 days for the uninitiated), but nowhere near as entertaining. After three days to thaw out, a day to brine and three and a half hours in the oven. It came out looking great and smelling better. There was a certain amount of pride when I dumped the beast on the dinner table. What's that saying? "don't wait until the storm has passed, learn to dance in the rain". It certainly kept me occupied for a while.

Hoping for a change in fortune, I went into town to see if any part time work was available. No luck but was told when the snow subsides a few more opportunities may become available. There was still no word from teacher registration. When home alone in the big, yellow house I found myself involuntarily pacing the floor and staring out the front windows at the mounds of snow and leafless skeletal trees. I am sure if I stared long enough, I would begin to see pixies who lived at the bottom of the garden. Then lament that nobody would notice if I did go stark crazy because there was no one around. The warm climate version of having Cabin Fever is to Go Troppo, a condition suffered by some when exposed to the heat and humidity of the tropics. I recall stories of old Diggers using the term to describe men who had gone barking mad during the war in New Guinea, but much of this could be attributed to the stress of battle. There is no doubt that some people cope with the heat of summer better than others. Police statistics in northern Australia reveal that more assaults and alterations occur in summer, but the studies conducted have not referred to it as a seasonal syndrome but rather the fact that some people's bodies do not effectively thermo-regulate causing stress. Sounds like semantics to me. Fortunately, I have never had a problem with the heat of summer, it has always been my favourite time of the year. But I have witnessed the madness slowly creep up and take hold of someone.

A few years back, well more like the turn of the century, Anna, myself and two mates took four days to hike down a remote section of the Herbert gorge from the Kirrama range to Abergowrie. I have recently heard it described as Australia's wildest, least known and most challenging hikes. No tracks or signposts, just following a river full of fish and oversized saltwater crocodiles, which some of my party initially thought were a vivid part of my imagination. They did not believe leftover dinosaurs could live so far inland but soon changed their tune. Swimming was off the itinerary. The going was tough from the steep descent into the gorge through high guinea grass and dodging old tin mine shafts. We passed through some beautiful pockets of rainforest and some heavy undergrowth, following cattle pads where we could. The scenery was untouched. A rugged beauty with an abundance of curious wildlife. We were the only humans around for miles so choosing the best campsite was never an issue. On day two we had crossed a shallow section of the river to find the torso of a calf floating near the water's edge. There was no disputing what had happened, a croc had removed the lower half in one bite, its glazed eyes a forlorn sight. It was getting late in the afternoon, so we set up camp on a high bank close by. Not long after, a helicopter landed on a sandbank and out jumped some keen fishermen. We watched as they flicked lures until one hooked a snag and before we could warn them, one bloke had removed his shirt and jumped in to retrieve it. The four of us sucked in a breath of air in unison and looked away. I had no desire to see someone ripped apart and eaten alive. He made it back to the bank with his lure and his life. Ignorance may be bliss, but it can also be crazy. The next day we ventured overland to cut out a 'W' bend in the river only to find thick rubber vine and lantana to crawl through and steeply eroded ridges to clamber across. At one such ridge, a decent sized boulder became dislodged by one of our party and careered down the slope just missing another. This bloke had already been doing it tough, in fact he was so keen to reduce his pack weight that he had been leaving the previous days set of clothes behind when we broke camp. Personally, I think he could have done without carrying the tetra packs of wine. Anyway, this near-death experience appeared to be the last straw for his poor overheated, mosquito tormented, crocodile neurotic psyche. Without a word he spun on his heels and walked off into the jungle. We had to climb back down and chase after him. It took some convincing, good old chocolate bribery and a bit of rest to get him back on track. He seemed incoherent and later couldn't explain what happened. To Troppo land, that's where he'd gone. That evening myself and another mate crawled under a low-lying branch on the river's edge to fill our water bottles. As we lifted our heads, we startled a monster croc sunning himself on the bank. It dived for the river and we fell back the other way. Now that was an adrenaline burst. What a beautiful part of the world, what an adventure and only one Troppo casualty.

Walking in the clouds! After seemingly endless heavy snow days, the temperature crawled above zero providing the impetus for the fog to roll in. Thick and low lying. Some mornings driving to school, the visibility was reduced to less than sixty metres, more than a bit scary on the highway. On the coast back home, fog visits and evaporates well before most people finish their morning coffee, chased off by a sea breeze and rising ground temperatures, but with the snow covered ground a thermal in-version just hangs around all day. Nothing better to do. At three in the afternoon when I did the school run, it prevailed, with no sign of clearing. Got some great eerie photos of shrouded pines disappearing into the white abyss. The following week came the rain. Before long road gangs were out and about with loaders and trucks, removing volumes of snow. Most people I encountered in town were complaining about the rain and telling me they prefer snow. Not me! The place looked so much different with the sidewalks, signs and carparks clear. I started to get an idea of the lay of the land without snow piled up out front of every establishment.

Every Canadian I met seemed to be fixated with snakes, spiders and "all that other stuff in Australia that can kill you!" It would appear that Australian wildlife crusaders and subsequent documentary shows have had a significant effect on North Americans. Despite our rich geography, culture and traditions, most seem to know little about Australia apart from our reputation as home to some of the deadliest animals on earth. Sure, the majority of Australia's nasties are endemic to our home region of North Queensland, but it is not as if we stare death in the eye on a daily basis, as some would believe. Adding to the hysteria, our exchange family reported back to their friends and family that in early February a 4.7 metre croc was captured off the Strand Beach in Townsville. Now that is a big lizard hanging around a swimming beach. I suppose if you're looking for trouble it is very easy to find. But if you go for a walk alone through the forest in Canada with a pork chop hanging around your neck, chances are you will also gain some unwanted attention. Like anywhere else in the world, Australians who bother to get out of their armchair and into nature, know what to expect with our wildlife and take precautions. The likelihood of a nasty incident is small and road accidents are a far greater threat. However, there is no getting away from the fact that crocodile numbers are on the rise and have been building up since the decision to ban shooting in 1974.

Back in the early 60's my Dad, along with some of his mates, trapped a sizeable croc in the upper reaches of the Herbert river. They used a wild boar's head as bait suspended just above the water level and a submerged snare trap. I wasn't even born then but wondered who would have been more surprised the croc or the young fellows on the bank. Somehow, they extracted the beast from the water, tied it up and lifted it into the back of a flatbed ute where it spent the night. The next day they contacted a zoo a few hours south and drove it down. Dad loved to recount the adventure, in particular the part when they stopped to pick up a hitchhiker. With no room in the cabin, they told him to jump in the back. A tarpaulin was thrown over the croc to keep the sun off. Dad and his mate continued down the highway for a while talking away until Dad glanced back in the rear vision mirror and noticed the bloke gone. He must have been inquisitive and lifted the tarp to see what the lads were transporting. Needless to say, he took his chances and jumped off the moving vehicle. I hope they weren't travelling too fast.

North Queenslanders who want to enjoy our beautiful Coral Sea need to be aware that marine stingers or jellyfish, are a reality which have an equally deadly potential and frustrating impact on our aquatic pursuits. In the summer months these ethereal wisps of translucent blubber, draped in delicate, deadly tentacles cruise the currents. Beautiful to watch through an illuminated fish tank but not to meet in the briny. The main two protagonists are the Box Jelly, which, as the name suggests, is cubic. It can grow to 150 mm square and trails three metre long deadly tentacles behind it. The other, much smaller Irukandji, is equally as deadly and has tentacles up to one metre. Its smaller size makes it difficult to detect when snorkeling. The best precaution is to wear lycra bodysuits, gloves and booties. Alternatively, there are many netted off sections along the northern coast that provide a safe place to enjoy a swim in the ocean and an interesting idiosyncrasy to tourists. Imogen loves snorkeling on the reef and we just have to take precautions. I can't imagine living on the Great Barrier Reef and not getting amongst it.

Yes, we do have snakes in our part of the world, and some are big and ugly. We have been lucky at our home having only spotted two poisonous snakes in the backyard over the years. The first was a young Taipan who reared up at me while I was trying to get the dogs away from it. The other was a Coastal Brown snake. We do get plenty of shy harmless green tree snakes and huge majestic Carpet Pythons who love to live in the roof cavity and take control of the rat population. Unfortunately, they also have a taste for our beautiful green tree frogs. It is common in the evening to hear a poor frog screaming in the jaws of a snake. I am happy to have Pythons live in my garden, but a recent story in the paper caught my attention. It recounted a man who lived near Port Douglas. He told a tale of how his twenty-two-month-old baby son was grabbed on the arm by a 4.2 metre specimen. It quickly wrapped it coils around the boy and started to crush him. The father tried to uncoil and open the jaws to no avail. In the end he had to cut the snakes head off just to get it to release. I also remember my Dad telling us about the story of a bloke that had passed out drunk and placed in a bed at the base hospital to dry out. Now this was the early 70's, there was no air conditioning just wide balconies and doors open to catch any breeze. The story goes that an over ambitious Python saw the comatose drunk as an easy meal. Sometime during the night, it dislocated its jaw and was up to the man's elbow before a distressed nurse walked in.

Spiders, we have many, but I rarely hear of any bites. It is usually a gardener not wearing gloves. Many have minor venom and there are antivenoms for the others. Their webs are magnificent. Some cover massive spans and are true engineering feats. I often find a magnificent St. Andrew's Cross spider has spun a web in my outdoor shower at eye level and not far from the shower head. I get a good look twice a day at its silk cross and check for any prey. She is not venomous to humans but even if she were, I would be at no risk unless I tried to pick her up.

A creature, which is not dangerous to humans at all, but successfully controls the spider population and is cute to boot is the gecko. It may take a while for our exchange family to get used to living with lizards in the house, but it would be hard to find a dwelling in the North that doesn't have a family of these creatures clinging to the walls and ceilings. It is just a natural part of life in Northern Australia. These gregarious, gravity defying reptiles scurry and scamper across the wall, floor and ceilings chasing an insect feed, brawling and playing hide and seek with the human inhabitants. They make a kind of chirping noise that seems far too loud and unsuitable for their sleek body. A sound that means home to me. Their greatest enemy is the sliding window. Geckos have a curious self-defense mechanism. They can drop their tail clean off their body at will if threatened. It is supposed to distract the predator while the gecko absconds. The tail completely regenerates. Unfortunately, this does not help them from the dreaded window squash. I hope our exchange family read our note about wildlife.

By far and away the greatest annoyance for me on a daily basis is not from a member or the world's deadliest but the maligned Green Ant who are graced with super strength, a bad attitude and any notion of self-preservation. I am regularly attacked in my garden by whole armies of these ants complete with foot soldiers, kamikaze paratroopers jumping from overhead foliage and a highly trained special forces, who head straight for the eyes, ears, nostrils and armpits. These are fearsome foe! Admittedly, they do a good job in the garden, killing off a whole range of other pests. But savage! I am generally a peace-loving bloke, happy to gently flick off insects, step around animals on the ground. Live and let live. But a green ant attack would challenge a Buddhist Monk's resolve. Their bite evokes a mad dance involving flicking, slapping and squashing with a finale of ripping off one's shirt and diving into the pool. During the clean up after Cyclone Yasi, the ants were angrier than ever, seemingly wanting to take out their displeasure of Mother Nature's fury on anyone or anything.

Rating second on the annoying natives scale is the reviled Flying Fox. These large fruit eating bats with a wingspan up to one metre, no doubt play an important part in the ecological balance. They live in colonies that smell really bad, they are very noisy and eat fruit crops. Some carry a form of the deadly Rabies virus, but worst of all they delight in spraying their purplish, toxic excrement up the walls of my house, over cars and the clothes drying on the line. The acidic artwork can lift the paint on your car if you don't act quickly and will stain whatever it lands on. I heard an expat Texan woman on the radio suggesting that there is a real opportunity to develop Bat tourism in North Queensland. She believes people will come from across the globe to get a look at our massive bats. Mess and smell aside, they are undeniably magnificent creatures. To witness the evening sky full of thousands moving between roosts and feeding ground is something very special we take for granted. As long as they do not roost in your backyard.

Back to Canada, where you don't have to scratch too deep to find equally interesting stories about the wildlife. Prior to our arrival, I followed the local newspapers online and came across a story that described the events of the previous autumn when a man went for a walk with his Labrador on a forest trail not far from the house, we were living in. He was strolling along and heard a bear crashing through the undergrowth close buy. Following standard procedure, he made lots of noise to deter the beast, but it came into view and walked toward him. At this point his trusty dog ran at the bear and was quickly pinned down and snarled at. Either the bear let the dog go or he wriggled loose, then ran back to hide behind his master. The bear then walked directly toward the man who belted it over the nose with his walking stick. The bear just stared at him and held his ground, so the man hit him again and his stick broke in half. As I am reading, I was thinking, this can't be good! The bear was so close he could smell its salmon breath, the nervous wreck of a dog is hiding, and the weapon is lying on the ground in two pieces. For reasons only known to the bear, it turned around slowly and walked back into the forest. I assume it had a big smile on its face thinking about how his friends are going to laugh when he recounts the story back at the cave. With this encounter in mind and the fact that we wanted to get out into nature as much as possible, I sought local advice. "The best thing is to get a can of bear spray and let them have it in the face" I am told. My first thoughts are how bloody close to this bear do I have to get so that I can spray it in the face? I read the can and found out that you don't need to be a good shot just start spraying in the general direction when the bear is between three to six meters away. I am still not convinced. A bear can cover that distance very rapidly and I reckon few people would have the nerve to wait until it was that close. The active ingredient is capsicum and they recommend walkers should have it on their belt in a quick draw holster. I am yet to see any locals on the trail with their quick draw spray cans, ready to say, "Come on bear, make my day!" But I suppose better safe than sorry.

My little family are self-confessed nature freaks. We are into birds and butterflies, flowers and fruit trees, full moons and everything in between. When we travel at home and abroad, much of the focus is on outdoor activities. On learning of our exchange destination, much of the excitement and discussion was around what we could see, do and eat that was different than home. The prospect of observing new animals in the wild loomed large. The Big 5. Yes, I know we were not living in Africa, but a country with such diverse and iconic wildlife such as Canada should have its own Big 5. These lists are a personal preference and the most obvious may not make everyone's list. The three of us compiled our own and the results are as follows. I included seeing a Bear in the wild (any type would do) and living to tell the tale plus Wolf, Moose, Bison and Orca. Just missing out were Bobcat, Cougar and the agile Bighorn Mountain Sheep. Imogen chose the following and I would not be disappointed to have an up-close moment with any of these cute creatures. Chipmunk, Raccoon, Marmot, Ptarmigan and Puffin. Anna drew from both lists but included the Beaver and Otter. Without giving too much away, by the end of our year abroad we would encounter all but one animal on our list. Incredibly all but one was in the wild and to our delight many, many more animals not on our lists crossed our path.

There are several locals of note, that really should have a higher profile. I knew very little about the Wolverine nor had it piqued my interest until I saw a photo of one. My first thought was that it looked cute and cuddly, but this misconception was quickly overturned when I viewed a video clip of one chasing off a black bear. These feisty balls of muscle are related to weasels and are very rare to encounter. Which is probably a good thing, however they are much more prevalent in the Canadian Rockies and Alaska than the lower 48 states of the US. Another is the wonderfully named, Spirit Bear (Kermode) which are a subspecies of Black Bear. Their beautiful clotted cream coats are a result of a double recessive gene. It is possible for a Black coated mother to give birth to a cream cub. They are not albino and occur in much smaller numbers than the very prevalent black coated variety and hence the mystique of this creature. The first nations people call them Moksgmól and have many legends and stories focused around this special bear.

The banana slug, anecdotally Native Americans used to put the slugs in their mouth to relieve toothache. The slime has a strong analgesic. So what would you prefer, a large needle plunged into your gum or a slug flipped into your mouth to suck on? They are found just up the road in Mount Revelstoke National Park. As far as slugs go, this is one very cool, distinctive dude. Bright yellow, some with black splotches and growing up to 250mm long. Certainly the only Banana that will grow in these latitudes. Apparently, the indigenous people, the early German pioneers and yes even our friend the Raccoon use them as a food source. There even use to be an annual Banana Slug Festival in Russian River, out from the Napa Valley in California. All types of activities took place including a cooking contests, using these creatures as the main ingredient. At least you would not have to worry about spitting out any bones. Forget the beer and prawns; break out a nice Sonoma Pinot Gris and a deep-fried slug canapé, stuffed with feta. Could it get any better than that?

The following weekend we shouted ourselves to a few nights at Silver Star ski resort in the beautiful Monashee Mountains. We arrived at about five in the evening on the Friday, checking into the Vance Creek Lodge, right in the centre of the village. Its Midwest architecture painted in federation yellows, reds and greens, stood out against the pure white of the mountain. Already pitch black the trees took centre stage, spot lit in a multitude of colours and angles. The view from our balcony a pure winter wonderland. Saturday morning, nice and early, we hit the gear rentals shop. We may not be very good skiers but fitted out with boots, skis and poles, at least we looked like we knew what we were doing. Aussie accents regularly punctuated the snowflakes to our delight. The young fellow assigned to fitting us out was from Warrnambool, Australia. He exuded melancholy as he shared his story with us. "It has taken me to travel to the other side of the world to realise that I am a summer person, and much prefer sunny blue skies and warm weather". We gave him an understanding grin and wished him luck hoping that he would gain some solace from the fact that he would be home about nine months before us. I pondered his honest realisation throughout the day and reflected that throughout my own life experience it has taken a shift away from the ordinary to spark an acceptance or instigate a change which needed to occur. I love to travel but every time I return home, I appreciate our country and lifestyle just that bit more and have more understanding and empathy for others. I also think that I make the effort to get out and enjoy the things we have, swim in the creeks, visit the islands, kayak in the river. Some Australians never get to experience those things and it is a shame.

Anna worried that Imogen would get upset when it was time to drop her off at the kids' ski school so I was assigned the drop off duties. She was fine and I was very proud as she toddled off with the nice young instructor, with a Swedish accent, for her two-hour lesson. I raced back to join her Mum and meet our instructor. He was an older gentleman with the perfect amount of humour and patience to guide us through the morning. By the end, we were coming down the beginners' slope with ease and enjoying every minute of it. Imogen emerged from her lesson with the request "when can we do it again". We all went out to practice after lunch and by the evening were very pleased with our newfound skills and ready to relax. Long John's basement bar was the perfect spot to wind down. We followed a worn trail in the snow to a small dimly lit door encrusted in ice. Great meal and music, surrounded by equally happy families discussing their days feats, the jumps and falls getting larger with each retelling.

On Sunday morning we took it easy. We had all struggled through the flu for the previous week so decided to give the tube slides a raincheck. As we headed down the mountain, a warning light started to flash on the dash, which alerted us that the right front tyre was in need of air. There was nowhere to pull over on the narrow mountain road so I crossed my fingers that it wouldn't deflate down to the rims as we limped down to Vernon and into the first servo. It had an air compressor conveniently positioned out the back but to my amazement it was coin operated. As if they don't make enough money selling fuel. As I hooked up the air valve it snapped off with a gush bleeding out the tyre in seconds. Now I have never seen a brass valve collapse like that, they should be able to handle the corrosive salt and freezing temperatures. Anyway, it was cold, very cold, Imogen had skipped breakfast and was now hungry, cranky and in desperate need of a toilet. It never ceases to amaze me that the little one's demeanor regularly transfers to her Mum like osmosis. To add to the morning's revelry, the servo was closed, so I quickly whacked on the spare and found a tyre shop across the road. It was open! Half an hour and one hundred bucks later we were on our way. Vernon seemed like a good sized, small town and the nearby shopping centre provided some welcome warmth and good sushi.

February 2, Groundhog Day. To celebrate the school's Nature Group organised an afternoon hike around Skimikin Lake. About eighteen students and ten brave parents assembled in the school car park as they organised a carpool for the rest of the kids. The drive took around half an hour through some backcountry, past homesteads, various paddocks and livestock quarters. The sun had not graced us with its presence all day, providing no resistance to the enduring gloom and numbing cold. It took another half hour to get everyone fitting out with warm clothing and snowshoes, before a talk about hiking safety and the fragile ecosystem. They described the animals who lived there and that prior to freezing over, the lake evaporates and drains out to at least six meters below peak summer height making the banks very steep. We hiked to the edge of the lake and my little family enjoyed the surreal feeling of walking on a frozen lake even though our first few steps were very tentative. While we played around making snow angels and attempting to polish the ice for a glimpse of its beautiful jewel like, refracted blue green, the other adults had started a fire. Out came the marshmallows and forks and in from the cold came the kids like moths to a flame. Unsurprisingly when the kids were given the option to stay by the fire or hike around the lake, all but five decided to stay. I should say four, because I made Imogen's decision for her. We were not coming halfway around the world to miss an opportunity so ridiculously far removed from our native environment. The walk was gentle and gave the little ones' time to appreciate their surroundings. Duck under fallen trees, scurry up inclines and roll down the snowy lake bank. Once back at the fire, a hot chocolate and gooey marshmallow went down well.

Up until this point in time, I had associated Groundhog Day with the movie from the early 90's and its great soundtrack. But this long-standing tradition throughout North America is even more intriguing (some would say wackier) than the film. Depending on your location, one of a number of so-called mystical groundhogs emerge from their winter slumber to see if the sun casts a shadow from their body. If there is no shadow, it is said that winter will finish early. If the critter casts a shadow, it is proclaimed that winter will last another seven weeks. The holiday started in the 1800's as a Pennsylvanian Dutch tradition of weather prediction. Now there are many hogs throughout the continent with Shubenacadie Sam from Nova Scotia, Queen Charlotte and Sir Walter Wally from North Carolina, Staten Island Chuck from New York, French Creek Freddie from West Virginia, Gus from Georgia and also from the South is General Beauregard Lee. Very prominent on Canada's East Coast is Wiarton Willie, but taking it to a whole new level, are the somewhat clandestine gentlemen who call themselves the Inner Circle. Their Champion meteorologist, the most famous of them all, is Punxsutawney Phil. According to his top hatted, black trench coat wearing posse, Phil has been dispatching predictions since the 1880's and his immortality derives from an elixir, the ingredients are a well keep secret. This organisation, who appear to the onlooker as a cross between a welsh men's choir and a Goth convention, proclaim that Phil speaks a language which only the President of the Inner Circle can understand. Whatever your opinion, it seems like a lot of fun. The event gets national press attention and creates tourism revenue. By the way, in 2016 half of the Groundhogs predicted an early start to Spring and the rest are still in their burrows for another seven weeks.

Family Day long weekend arrived and offered the next opportunity to get out of Blind Bay to scout further afield. Kelowna for two nights fit the bill. Our trip coincided with a Winter festival in Vernon, but we were a little disappointed that the scheduled hot air balloon take off was nowhere to be found. Maybe the wind conditions were not suitable, or the poor pilots couldn't find enough warm clothing to put on. Some of the smaller lakes were frozen, spotted with tiny ice fishing huts like stationary soldier crabs on a sandbar. People strolled the ice with their dogs as if it were a sunny boulevard, all I could think of was their poor frozen paws and hoped they didn't fall through. Although Kelowna is not a large centre, it is a metropolis compared to the tiny places we had encountered thus far. We all enjoyed an afternoon wandering around in the warm shopping mall just to be around people. The city was fringed by snow covered mountains with a glorious lake frontage. We stayed in an older establishment, right in the centre of town. The hallways and lobby walls were adorned with oversize, black and white photos of the town and district in the late 1800's and early 1900's. Paddle steamers, sheep herded up the main street, orchards and crops. Tobacco being tendered by European immigrants. Their swarthy faces telling a story of contentment having escaped the depression and war-torn homelands for fertile soils, space and freedom. The images summoned memories of our North Queensland heritage where thousands of Italian, Maltese, Sicilian and various other groups, came to make a life in the sugarcane fields.

On the Sunday morning we braved the cold and piecing breeze for the Stuart Park outdoor skating rink adjacent the lake. Although it was beautiful, there was absolutely no wind block between us and the icy blizzard. Imogen was very keen to give it a go as long as her Dad ran around the edge holding her hand. Anna had caught a cold and sat as close as humanly possible to the fire at the end of the rink. No mean feat as she had plenty of competition trying to back their bums into the warmth. She looked terrible with a tinge of blue. After an hour we just couldn't handle it anymore. The rest of the day we had planned to visit the museums but surprisingly most were closed for the season. Surely, it was museum visiting weather. Not much else to do. Another example of Canadians bunkering down for a large chunk of the year. I don't think I could ever get used to it and gauging by an article in the paper from a long term local, not many do. Now retired this bloke spends about five months of the year down south in Florida. That year, due to an operation, he had spent the winter at home and was a bit forlorn about the constant overcast skies and cold weather. If he feels like that, what chance have people from the tropics got?

We did find one gallery open. The main exhibit was a collection of Historical British Canadian Women's art spanning from 1792 to 1961. There were some very impressive oils and various ethnic original and inspired weavings. Yet there were two works in particular that caught my eye. The first was a set of framed "Embroidered Samplers" sewn by girls around nine years of age. They had diligently stitched the alphabet and a scene on a piece of cotton cloth. Completed in the early 1800's, no doubt in a school setting with British traditions. It made me think of my mother, who often speaks about the skills developed by creating a sampler with a buttonhole and various other stitching skills. She believes that kids should still do them today and I can't argue. Along with all the technology, kids still need fine motor skills and the ability to look after themselves. Cook a meal, sew on a button. Some would argue that I am clinging to the past but who would have thought the highest selling paperback book of 2015 would be an adult colouring in pad. The wheels constantly turn in both directions. But I digress. The other artwork which amazed me was a photographic manipulation using glass negatives. The Artist, a lady called Hannah Maynard, in 1893 created a series of clever portraits. The most appealing being one where she appeared three times. One seated pouring a cup of tea for the guest, which was herself, again seated looking at the lens. The third image was of the artist appearing to lean out of the picture frame above and pour some more tea onto the guest's head. Skill and humour not always brought to light regarding late 18th century's well-heeled women, with high buttoned collars and dresses scraping the floor. The weather had improved by the time we emerged. I mean it had reached four degrees and the wind had slowed. It's all relative. I took a walk along the lake boardwalk back to the hotel and tried to imagine what it would look like in the summer.

 Back at the hotel the receptionist pointed us in the direction of RauDZ restaurant for dinner. Their mission was to use local produce in extraordinary ways. They didn't accept reservations, so it was suggested that we arrive early or miss out. Housed in a red brick building gracefully showing its age with art deco stone dressings to the doorway and upper windows. Once inside it emitted a rustic, relaxed feel, ambient lighting, background music and a well-appointed bar completed the scene. We choose a white wine Sangria and a quince Martini to start proceedings. Both fantastically unusual but it didn't stop there. The menu revealed a wide range of interesting dishes. We shared a Venison Carpaccio with apple, walnuts and a mustard dressing. It was something new for us, a great combination of flavours that tasted like a holiday. In the end we were all happy with our choices which included pan fried, pressed Bison shoulder with cherry relish, potato bread and roasted onion dip and wild boar with applewood smoked cheddar sauce and grilled portobello mushrooms. Anna was so impressed she wrote her first online food review and a few days later received a congratulatory email saying that 215 people had already read it. If she keeps this up, I might be able to source her out as a critic. In my opinion, this is an example of good social media as opposed to the one-upmanship and hurtful gossip proliferated by some others which has become the communication tool of choice for the extravert, self-perpetuating a look at me society. You know what I am talking about.

Giving nontraditional protein a go is something we are not shy about. Like most things the right cut and best suited cooking method makes a hell of a lot of difference. Kangaroo is a really lean meat and the prime cuts are best cooked on high heat and served medium rare. Much of the animal is best slow cooked like lamb shanks to create a luscious moist meat perfect with red wine. Crocodile is another lean meat and should not be over-cooked. Treat it like lean pork fillet and you won't go wrong. It's a taste most people describe as a mix between fish and chicken. When my Dad was a kid, he and his mates caught a big old sand goanna up on the Herbert River and grilled him on a spit. He reckoned it tasted the same as croc. During the 2nd World War my Grandad was posted up in the Torres Strait. In between watching Japs fly over on their raids of the mainland he was lucky enough to join the islander troops in a feast of sea turtles. He said it was really good tucker, a bit like veal but didn't go for the offal soup they made alongside.

Images and sculptures referencing the infamous Ogopogo are hard to miss in Kelowna. Not only were we living in Sasquatch country but the legend of the Ogopogo Lake Monster lives strong as well. I even found a website which, in Hollywood-esk style, asked the question "Which monster would win in a fight?" Sasquatch Vs Ogopogo. I can just picture it on a Cinema billboard and imagine these poor creatures skulking away saying "I'm not a Monster. I'm just misunderstood." Unlike the Loch Ness Monster and other mythical beasties who are deemed to be friendly or even playful, Ogopogo is a much more fearsome proposition. Centuries of local Indian folklore refer to the water monster as N'ha-a-itk and relate stories of it needing to be appeased with a live sacrifice to allow safe passage. The stories of encounters continued through the early settlers and to this very day. Images and videos can be found on the net offering "proof". Its home is the stunningly beautiful Lake Okanagan. Popular with families and numerous water sports along its 110 klms. I am particularly interested in a bit of kayaking and would like to try Stand Up Paddle boarding. I don't know about live offerings, but I could take a chocolate bar in my pocket, who doesn't like chocolate, right!

Reported sightings of the Sasquatch aka Bigfoot and a whole host of native Indian language versions, have continued for centuries throughout the Pacific Northwest Coast which encompasses British Columbia, Washington State and surrounds. To this day, some strongly believe there are several of these enigmatic missing links roaming around on two legs making bears nervous. Sound recordings, images, videos and written accounts of contact can easily be found. Likewise, in Australia we have numerous sightings and footprints of little apelike men, some are part of indigenous folklore. These Little People of Australia go by many names depending on the area or indigenous tribe. Examples are the Yowie, the Towers Hairy Man, Nimbunj and the Junjuddi. My mate Al reckons he regularly sees forest nymphs in his garden after a few drinks, so who knows. They must like the smell of wine. A common thread to all of these mysteries is that some of the people reporting and researching the unexplained events are otherwise logical, well respected members of the community.

Another friend of mine, who is very sceptical of just about everything, swears he was followed by the famed Min Min lights when driving across the Nullarbor Plain in Australia. But that is a whole other story. There are scientists in Australia who have spent most of their careers looking for tangible evidence. The 2003 discovery in Indonesia of the long extinct race of tiny "Hobbit" people did nothing to quell the intrigue. But if nothing else it is a great topic to bring up at a BBQ to get the crowd talking.

Before long, love was in the air and all the school students were working on Valentine's Day craft. Like many things, dear old Cupid's intentions are interpreted differently in Canada and some would say a bit over the top, but how can a day celebrating love be overdone? Instead of showering a particular sweetheart with gifts, here all the students give their classmates a small gift. It was fun helping Imogen divide an assortment of sweets up into little plastic bags designed just for the occasion. She took delight in writing all her classmates names on the tags and handing them out at school. I am an unabashed romantic and do something every year. I bought a locally made slumped glass heart for Anna to hang in our frangipani tree back home, along with all its other adornments. When I got it back to the house and took Imogen aside to show her what I had for Mummy for Valentine's Day she enquired in her most angelic tone "have you got something special for me too?" Predictably, my heart melted. I went into town the next day and picked up another glass heart for her. Well why not!

While I was browsing the shops in Salmon Arm, for the gift, I somehow got into a conversation with a South African expat. He was quite chatty and recognised my accent. We had a talk about the weather, dull skies and cold, while reminiscing about the warmth and light intensity of our southern hemisphere homelands down under. I spoke of floating over coral reefs on one of those clear calm summer's days or spotting Boab trees in Broome where the horizon is split with the red earth and the turquoise ocean. Is there another place on earth with such an outrageously beautiful contrast of colour, shape and form? This fellow had lived in Alberta for some time before coming to British Columbia and told me that the winters were much colder there, but the sun was always shining, which made it manageable. A story I would hear many times. There was another younger woman in the store, dark skinned and easily recognisable as African. My acquaintance was having simultaneous conversations with her and I, so it was very easy to hear her story. She was a Somali, maybe in her late 20's who had fled the conflict of her country. She said "I feel heavy here, a weight on my shoulders, it is hard to explain. When I am in Africa, I feel light and alive, the sounds, smell, colours and lights are all intense, and I love them." It was as if I was hearing my own thoughts come out of another person's mouth. It somehow normalised the feelings that I was trying so hard to ignore so I could fully embrace the experience. She had spent time in the USA before moving further north and said that many Americans told her "you must be so glad to be in our beautiful country" to which she confessed to thinking that it is beautiful if you have never been anywhere else. I think that was a tough call seeing that they had offered her refuge. Although collectively Americans may not be as worldly or as well traveled as some nations, only 30% have passports compared to 70% of Australians, they often get a bad rap and in my experience are good honest people who always make me feel welcome in their country, as beautiful and diverse as it is. The Somali went on to say that she had been surrounded by conflict most of her life and could only see a bright future from now on. One of the lucky ones I thought.

Valentine's Day arrived and I gave out the gifts, Imogen was delighted and didn't really expect anything, which made it even more special. Later in the morning we took a drive across the bridge to the north shore of Shuswap Lake to check out the small communities of Scotch Creek and Celista. We were surprised by the number of houses, many beautiful log cabins right on the water's edge. There was a quaint pub and a few shops spotted around, but much was closed "for the season". This community is fairly remote, and I wonder what kind of employment opportunities there would be for the residents. Maybe they are mostly retired, like Blind Bay. It was great to explore and get out of the house for a bit.

I had given the girls an invitation, earlier in the week, for a Valentine's dinner. They were most excited and dressed up for the occasion, which was really nice. In the novel I was reading at the time, the characters ate at a high-end restaurant and were served a baked camembert wrapped in prosciutto with a raspberry sauce, baked pork loin and greens. During the week I gathered up the ingredients and had a go. Our candle lit dinner for three was lots of fun. We had a bit of a tough start to our year but were trying hard not let that distract us from living life to the fullest. If you're going to go down the road least traveled, you have to learn how to enjoy the special little things and this was one.

I had the opportunity to attend Imogen's school as a parent helper to celebrate the milestone of completing 100 days of the school year. There is just a procession of acknowledged "Special Days" in the school year and this is a big event in Canada! There are even story books written about it. Anna organised some great activities focused around the number 100. The kids enjoyed it and so did I. She has been teaching little ones for many years. I knew she was good but this was the first opportunity I had to sit back and watch her in full flight. She really does an amazing job. It takes special people to guide them through their formative years. No wonder all her kids over the years simply adore her. Teenagers can be challenging in much different ways and I suppose it is all about knowing your clientele and having your heart in the right place.

In the topsy turvy world we found ourselves in, for one day at least over the weekend we saw sustained sunshine for only the second time since arriving in late December. Despite Imogen and I feeling under the weather with the flu we all drove into town, visited a nice French inspired coffee shop near the lake and walked out to the end of the jetty. Although the small pond at the entrance and the shallow sections of the lake were still frozen, the majority of snow had now melted revealing a beautiful park complete with bandstand rotunda and garden beds. Flower shoots burst from the soil in anticipation of warmer weather and a resilient clump of bulb lilies, which resembled Crocus, stood proud with the beginnings of purple buds forming at the tip. We had missed our garden very much, so any little bit of life emerging was good for our souls. The wharf was curved and quite a spectacle forging out into the lake. I closed my eyes and pictured paddle steamers plying the waters, unloading furs and produce in yesteryear. I am not sure why the timber wharf was constructed with a curve. It would have been significantly more difficult to build that way but adds real character to the entire town. Not usually dawdlers, we found ourselves just standing still almost involuntarily catching the sun's warmth. Steps lead down to mooring platforms, still firmly encased in ice. A stain on the rock breakwater, circling the marina, revealed the summer water level about a meter and a half above the current height. We passed a constant stream of walkers on the way back in, conditioned to drop all other plans and make the most of a visit by the elusive glowing orb in the sky. They hop-scotched opportunistic sheets of ice gathered in the shadows cast by the handrails like miscreants in the night. Teenagers lazed on the grass, partially wrapped in blankets, giggling and generally enjoying the early season warmth. The resident otter family were apparently in hiding from the paparazzi since recently making the front page of the local paper. Preceding the gold rush, Otters, or should I say their magnificent fur, was the main reason British Columbia was colonised. As a result, the otter population was decimated. Slowly but surely numbers are on the rise again.

One of the major players in the fur trade were the Hudson Bay Company, which has an extraordinary history and is now best known for its department stores, spread across the nation known affectionately as "The Bay". Originally started by two Frenchmen who saw the wealth potential of furs. The company lacked backers until it was taken over by the British Government in 1670 who developed its scope and employed many trappers as well as traded pelts for merchandise with the natives. This was a time prior to the formation of the United States of America or Canada. As the Company owned 15% of North America it acted as the de facto Government on behalf of the British King. The only other example of this peculiar arrangement that I am aware of is when the East India Company controlled large tracts of the Indian Subcontinent. The Hudson Bay Company continued along this path for around one hundred and fifty years before merging with its most successful rival in 1821 to control most of the northern part of the continent. By the end of the 19th century, changing fashion tastes brought a downturn to the fur trade which coincided with the Gold Rush. Suddenly there were hordes of cashed up prospectors needing supplies, so the company shifted its focus into retail and transformed many of its trading posts into shop fronts. The rest is history. Is there another part of the world where a company acted as government? Bizarre stuff.

The first student free day was scheduled for the Monday and with it the opportunity to see how other schools ran. Anna went off to a French immersion school in Salmon Arm. Students from grade one onwards are taught almost purely in French. Although there is access to these types of schools throughout the Province, I am led to believe that they are far more common in the East. In Quebec almost all are pure French schools with English only being an option in High School as an elective like we offer Japanese or Italian back home. Very interesting how the Nation has developed in different directions. Although the Government proclaims that officially the country is bilingual, with equal status to both French and English, there are only 22% of the population who speak the former. Although it is very difficult, at least in this area, to extract any strong opinions about social issues, when they let their politically correct guard down it would appear that this creates some considerably angst. It costs the country a significant amount in dual labeling and official documentation. Despite the Feds viewpoint, there is a crazy situation where Provinces counter intuitively can enforce their own linguistic preferences. From the sidelines it appeared to be a push back. A reaction to what Quebec has been able to successfully lobby for over a long period of time. Alberta, Saskatchewan, Nova Scotia and Prince Edward Islands are all officially English, while Quebec is officially French. This French stronghold have gone so far as to try and mandate a whole raft of business and educational Francophile hued laws on their public which has invoked several lengthy legal disputes. I do remember seeing on the news sometime in the 80's that the Province sought independence from the rest of the country. I have even read that religion plays a part in the tension. Now doesn't that sound familiar. All I will say is thank goodness I am an Australian and have not had to deal with such issues.

Imogen and I took the opportunity to bake some brownies and revisit the wharf for a picnic. Even though it only hit seven degrees, it was quite pleasant. Never thought I would ever use those words together to form a sentence. As we looked out across the lake a flock of Swan clumsily came into land. They honked in laughter watching each other touchdown in a much less than elegant fashion. On the way I treated Imogen with a Barbie doll from the toyshop. It came complete with bikinis and windsurfer. We sat in the park and assembled the craft and extracted Barbie from the packaging, which was no mean feat. Imogen had packed several dolls and accessories before leaving home, but we had to remove them when she was sleeping in an attempt to minimise our luggage. When she realised they were not aboard the plane, little miss was not happy.

Forget the Groundhog's prediction, the radio announcer shared that he saw a flock of geese flying in a V formation and it pointed North. Apparently in these parts it means it is about to warm up. I even saw a man in our street pruning the bushes in his front yard, which is a clear indication that we were excited about anything that hinted toward better weather and life out in the neighbourhood, even the most mundane. With eternal hope I decided to get out and wash the car. I found a hose in the shed and figured I should be able to leave it outside without it freezing solid, at least for a few months. The car had been so dirty. It always looked like we had just finished a car rally. We couldn't remember exactly what colour it was. Some sort of bluish green or was that a metallic greenish blue. There seemed to be an aversion to mud guards in this part of the world and our car had also come with none. Might be something to do with the buildup of ice or it might not, I was unable to extract this information. It certainly makes it hard to keep the back windows functional.

Life is too short for bad coffee, so the saying goes. So, with no attempt at sarcasm or arrogance, I say "there is no accounting for bad taste." I was curious to why, oh why do some places accept that brown, burnt, watery substitute when there is a much superior produce out there. Now I know taste is very subjective and don't expect everyone to like the same things I do but surely espresso is where it's at. Over the years during my travels I have noted how bad the coffee is in various parts of the world. Most notably, North America, where it is so bad, I can't drink it. At least in Vietnam their addition of condensed milk transforms the awful brew the French brought with them into something sweet, thick and palatable. With so many Italian immigrants having such widespread cultural influence in America, how did the drink of the contemplative miss out? It must be right up there with the Bermuda Triangle in the mystery stakes. Some suggest it is a philosophy, a mindset which is programed to prefer quantity over quality, but I don't buy it. Literally or figuratively. Coffee was bad long before chain stores churned out super-sized servings to woo their ever-expanding customers. Some acknowledge it is bad but nostalgic. It takes them back to fun times. Well that just sounds like rubbish. I'm sure we had a very nice time the night of my childhood when Nana cooked me tripe in white sauce or when my flat mates made spaghetti Bolognese with three ingredients - a bottle of tomato sauce, a packet of pasta and a can of spam. Both were vile and no reminiscing about the great company has urged me to have either again. Thankfully, later in our journey, we found the winds of change were a blowing. There were espresso huts popping up all over the northern United States. Even in the most remote and unlikely places in Montana, Idaho and Washington. Only a few years back it would have been only a pipe dream, a mirage.

Australians have developed a strong coffee culture around the Italian espresso method and all its variations. Australia has even contributed to gross global happiness by creating our own style, the Flat White, which I am pleased to say has made its way around the world. Even to Canada through a well-known chain. The aforementioned company started an awareness campaign with posters explaining the espresso varieties and various offerings on their menu. It would seem things are changing in Canada too but ever so slowly and I am not convinced it will endure. Espresso coffee is made by passing boiling water through ground coffee under pressure, producing a smoother taste, extracting some of the natural oils and a velvety crema on the top, like the head on a beer. The coffee is in contact with the water much shorter than with the drip method and the outcome is totally different. I read that some jet lagged tourists have been known to get creative when confronted with a blank look from a waitress after ordering their favourite caffeine hit. One compatriot longing for a Flat White asked for a triple shot, no foam, topped up with hot milk, which she reported still did not hit the mark. But full points for effort. Canadians are one of the highest coffee consumers in the world. I would suggest their climate would have something to do with it. They say the national brew is a drip coffee with loads of milk and sugar, eaten with a doughnut. For some preconceived reason I had expected a better offering considering the strong French influence in the country but was disappointed. It turned out my assumption that French coffee would be of the high standard of Italian, was sadly off the mark. The overwhelming belief from anyone using travel social media, who is not French, is that French coffee sucks. Strange in a country with such a fantastic cafe culture and food history. Apparently, the good pastry makes it worth the trip. While the States situation remains a mystery, I have read some fairly lengthy historical reasoning for why Canadian coffee is so bad and they seem quite feasible. The one point they all agree on is that the French did not help the situation. The consensus is that the locals became accustomed to the strong bitter Robusta coffee beans they grew up with. For a very long time France imported coffee predominantly from her colonies around the world. It was duty free, thus cheap, but was mostly the Robusta bean, which is a lot harsher than the Arabica. As mentioned, the French palate grew and even with the deregulation in the 1950's, effectively allowing for more Arabica into the country, there is still 80% Robusta consumption. This combined with the drip or filter methods and you don't have much to work with. To my delight, just after we arrived, we found an espresso machine in an online Boxing Day sale. Buy a quantity of beans and get a free machine. How good is that! It arrived two days later and even on the days when cabin fever took hold, that little red machine positively glowed. It became the fuel for writing this book like the Absinthe green fairy that inspired the art scene in Montmartre. A grand statement indeed but no coffee no writing. All reports are that our little machine continues to work its magic. I left it with the father of Imogen's best friend who hadn't tried espresso and is now a convert. So inadvertently we have contributed to the effectiveness of crime fighting in Canada due to him being a member of RCMP (Royal Canadian Mounted Police). Now that's a quirky little story for the coffee shop.

Maths and English are important but don't have a monopoly on essential skills in life. Pink Shirt Day is celebrated at schools throughout the nation. It is an anti-bullying awareness campaign with a fascinating story. At a school in Nova Scotia in 2007 something happened which should give us faith in the younger generation. The story goes that on the first day of school a year 9 boy wore a pink shirt. Now like bullies anywhere, they roamed in a pack and thought that it would be fun to give this boy a hard time all day. Seeing what was happening, two older male students got together and decided they would send a message to the bullies that it is not OK. After school they went to the local discount store and purchased fifty pink shirts. Then got online and encouraged everyone at school to wear Barbie's favourite shade. The next day they sat in the car park before school and handed out the shirts to those who didn't have one. The message to the bullies was, if you want to pick on that little boy in grade 9, pick on us all. In true bully fashion they were not to be seen. In the nine years since, Pink Shirt Day has been endorsed by the United Nations and is celebrated in several countries around the world, including Australia. We have anti bullying campaigns at our school in Townsville, but the Pink Shirt day has not made it up to north yet, but it should. Nothing inspires kids more than other kids getting out there and making a difference. At Sorrento Elementary, class finished early. They went to the gym to watch a video and discuss why bullying is not OK. Afterwards they had a dance party, well because they could. Imogen said she had a very cool day at school, isn't that what it is all about. She came home with an invitation to a playdate the following Friday evening. It read "bring your togs - we have a hot tub". Ah, one can only dream of having a social life like hers.

 Each day I trudged down to the corner store to check the mailbox in anticipation of my work visa, I even contacted the Immigrant Resource centre in town, but they only told me to be patient. This stretched my patience even more. It required quite a bit of self-control not to scream. We applied for our visa's the previous April and at quite an expense had flown down to Brisbane for our medicals in June because apparently the x-ray machines in Townsville aren't sufficient? I am not sure why things take so long in Canada. You would think it would be a yes or no and that could be decided before you land in the country, which I thought it had. There was an opportunity to apply to teach a Grade Two class for one day a week in the room next to Anna's. I would have enjoyed that immensely and it would have worked out perfectly for transport logistics as well. But no visa, no job. I was hopeful things would fall into place eventually. I had expected to be more involved with the community by that stage.

Saturday brought a discovery trip to Kamloops, only some 87 kilometers up the road. Soon enough, the emerald green of the Shuswap highlands gave way to the arid interior plateau grasslands. Dry eroded hills, barbed wire fences, ramshackled communities and a stretch of asphalt cutting through it all. The town's housing subdivision sprawl, nestled in pockets just off the highway on the eastern access, many looked new, suggesting that the town is a growing concern. The palette of choice consisted of Beige, Mission Brown, Khaki and Military Blue, that blended well with the surroundings to create a landscape desaturated of colour. Few gardens were evident, probably due to the season. It could easily be a snapshot of a Mars colony which had rapidly embraced fast food outlets, neon lights and golf. But I would have expected the migrants from earth to have upscaled their transport to something that hovers. The city sat at the confluence of two tributaries of the Thompson River originally named by the Secwepemc Native Indians as Tk'emlups, describing this natural feature. More of an industry and transportation hub, Kamloops was not touted as a tourist destination, but we found the CBD to be mostly clean with a vibrant cafe scene and quality shopping. Later in the day, on our way out to a suburban shopping centre I inadvertently took a wrong turn and ended up driving the Aussie side of the road in the wrong direction up a four-lane motorway. Thankfully the traffic was light and as this was not my first foray into "minor miscalculations on foreign roads" I stayed calm and avoided eye contact with the oncoming traffic. Their mouthed abuse and waving arms would have only served as a further distraction. I jumped the gutter with two wheels, helpful to have a 4WD for this maneuver, and quickly traveled the last hundred meters or so straddling the gutter. It was all over before the girls could panic. Well that is not entirely true, but they got over it. But seriously no one was hurt and sometimes driving on the opposite side of the car combined with some ineffectual road markings and signage, can disorientate. Back at Blind Bay, the sunny skies had morphed into a clear evening, so we braved the cold and ventured out to gaze at the elusive stars, which we had not seen since leaving Australia. They had become a distant memory and were rapidly descending into a questionable memory zone where one starts to wonder if they are real or a figment of a fairy tale reality. Fortunately, this was averted by a full sky of diamonds strangely devoid of our familiar Southern Cross asterism that watches over the land down under. Imagine going through life without gazing at the stars. I vividly remember standing out front of our house at Forrest Beach one night, I must have been around fifteen. Gazing at the stars and pondering what the future would bring in the year 2000 and my future wife, kids, life. It must have been raining heavy stardust that evening because I struck it lucky on all accounts.

We pondered the possibility of catching a glimpse of the Northern Lights. Although not common, the Aurora Borealis can be seen in the Okanagan if the conditions are right. There are some great photos on the net of its appearance in Kelowna in

2013. The odds improve greatly, the further north you are in the province. I read in the local newspaper, that a man, travelling at 1 a.m. along the Canoe Beach road, was pleasantly surprised by a fleeting glimpse of the dancing green lights coming over the mountains to the north. He managed to take nice photos as well. My Great Grandmother died when I was very young and I do not remember her, but Dad often spoke fondly of her and the tales she told about her homeland in Scotland. He said she reminisced with delight about the wonder of the Northern Lights, the will-o'- the-wisp. I hoped my little family is fortunate enough to have an encounter, but it was not to be on this adventure.

Another opportunity to focus on special members of the community came in the form of Superhero Day at school. We had collected bits and pieces from the craft store and Anna made two felt Cat Woman masks and ears attached to headbands. The girls got dressed in black tights and skivvy tops. They looked fantastic heading off for the day. Superhero Day's goal is to raise money for children's hospitals and bring awareness to the everyday Superheroes in the community. Although many students dress up, they are told that it is not the costume that makes a Superhero but what is inside. What a great initiative! The day was packed full of various activities. A young fireman turned up to tell his story to the eager grade 1's and 2's. A drumming activity coordinated by the school's First Nations Officer followed. Imogen just loves drumming and we often take her along to the Full Moon Drum Circle at home to serenade the rising moon. In the afternoon, a professional National Lacrosse League player visited and ran some skills activities. These kids have all the fun.

Lacrosse, although played in Australia, is a very minor sport which gets virtually no media attention. However, it was interesting to learn we have a national team. The average Aussie would not be able to tell you the rules or much about it at all. I have never seen it played and would have loved to watch a game if the opportunity arose. From what I can figure it's like a cross between field hockey and soccer, with the rubber ball being moved around the field with an oversized ice cream scoop covered in loose mesh. Although you would never guess, Lacrosse is Canada's official Summer sport and was the dominant sport in this country in the early twentieth century. It has a very special history. Today's game is a modified version of the one that was played by the native populations of North America, some accounts referencing it as far back as 1100 AD. Apparently at any given time there could by hundreds of players on each side. Matches could last for days. Certainly, in the 1500's it caught the attention of French missionaries who referred to the game as "La Crosse" the French words for bent stick. It was included in the Olympics in 1904 and 1908. Like many sports these days, it struggles to get younger players interested due to the competition from so many other sports, pastimes and lethargy.

Much to the displeasure of their sport fanatical cousins over the border, a Canadian is credited to have invented the game of Basketball although he was on U.S. soil at the time, so I suppose the bragging rights can be shared. Basketball remains popular in Canada and being an indoor sport makes it perfect for the climate. However, I had my sights on another game. Having experienced the hustle and bustle of the Silverbacks Ice Hockey earlier in our stay, the next goal was to watch a Gridiron match. Before we left Australia; my masseur tried to educate me in the basic rules of Gridiron so that I could at least know the objective. He described the constant stoppages and changes of personnel as a brutally physical game of chess. It is more about explosive power than cardiovascular and mental endurance he explained. The time the ball is in play during a Gridiron match is much, much less than the 80 minutes that many Rugby League players compete each week. The BC Lions play out of Vancouver in the National Football League which has nine teams representing the width of the country. The Canadian and US versions of the game have many differences, but I am told the main difference a novice spectator like myself would notice is the extra passing in the Canadian version due to the need to make more yardage per play.

Speaking of major sports in Canada. Of all the places in the world to witness Curling for the first time, we were sitting in a beach shack, on a French speaking, tiny speck of a tropical Island in the middle of the Pacific. The only channel on television was showing this crazy unknown sport commentated in some unrecognisable European language. Curling intrigued me. Being a Winter Olympic sport only stirred the pot more. From the outside looking in, it seemed to fill the spot taken by sports like Petanque, Bocce and Lawn Bowls in various countries around the world. The National titles had recently cluttered the newspapers with stories about the players, some whom are full time athletes. Where there is television broadcasting there is money and Curling has made it onto the tube. We just had to give it a go before we left.

One morning, after I dropped the girls off, I took a drive west along the lake, crossed the bridge and drove along the shore of Little Shuswap to see what I could see. Intermittently dispersed along the shore were a mish mash of housing from micro cabins to very elaborate homes, complete with timber jetties and various outhouses. Very nice spot indeed. About halfway down the road I came across Quaaout Lodge and Talking Rock Golf Course, run by a First Nations Band. It offers quality accommodation and dining. This small community is even quieter than Blind Bay, but I still passed several vehicles who all gave me, what I call the "three fingered steering salute." You know the one or maybe you don't. I think it is a true indicator of the friendliness and salt of the earth inhabitants. I grew up on a Sugarcane farm outside of a smallish town in North Queensland. Trips to town were continually punctuated by waving to oncoming traffic. I didn't know half of them, but it was just good country manners. Not something I encounter often these days. I didn't notice it anywhere else in my whole year in Canada, so here's to you, the community of Squilax.

In Canada the term Indian Tribe, has been superseded by the term First Nations People, which is a reference to various Aboriginal Canadian groups. Although some groups still refer to themselves as a Tribe, for example the Beaver or Dane-Zaa Tribe from central Alberta, many have broken up into self-governing communities called a Band. These Bands have elected members and are recognised by all levels of government in Canada. The Shuswap region, which includes Blind Bay, is part of the Secwepemc Nation. Having declined from thirty-five subgroups, today there are only seventeen Bands spread out through a region spanning from west of Revelstoke, east of Kamloops and north to Williams Lake. An area of over 30 000 kilometers. Locally the most visible aspects of the Band are administrative offices and the Chief Atahm language immersion school in Chase. The School integrates modern subjects along with Secwepemc reading, writing, speaking and traditional practices. In New Zealand there are similar schools teaching Maori immersion and Aboriginal schools in Australia which also focus on language and tradition. Both foreigners and many Australians probably don't realise that we use to have upwards of 250 dialects in Australia and to this day there are 120 spoken. I called the school to see if I could come and have a look at their program as a visiting educator but the woman who answered the phone was suspicious of my intentions and gave me the impression that it was not a good idea. Well it didn't hurt to ask.

We were learning new words all the time while regularly confronted with very blank looks from the locals, who seem to have no idea what we were saying, they couldn't even get the gist, or join the dots. I mean fair crack of the whip we Aussie blokes use fair dinkum lingo. I can't imagine what the problem was! This enduring "lost in translation" state of play provided some seriously memorable, hilarious and frustrating encounters. I had an amusing conversation at the supermarket deli that went something like this. I enquired, "Hello do you sell tofu?" the deli assistant replies "No sorry. No Thai Food here" I say, "No I am after tofu" assistant "No, sorry no Thai food but we do sell herbs so that you can make it yourself." So, no tofu, but I did get a belly laugh out of it. One lady on the other hand, who watched way too many Australian soap operas, picked my accent in one. She told me her father is a Kiwi, but she had never been to the Southern Hemisphere. I told her that was a shame, not that her father was from NZ but that she hadn't visited either our Great Southern Land or the Land of the Long White Cloud. She worked at the checkout at the corner store and when I walked through the door she would yell out "Crikey Mate that's a big snake" obviously referring to the antics of fellow countryman the late Steve Irwin, who by the way is the only person I have ever heard use the word "Crikey". I didn't have the heart to tell her. I confess that I frequented a certain coffee shop every time I went to town. They were the only ones who knew what a flat white was, so it was my treat for doing the groceries while being misunderstood. Every time I ordered an Oat Slice, the waitress asked me to repeat it and then said "Oh you mean an Oat Slice" in a slightly different intonation? So before entering the store I would practice my pronunciation, not really knowing what to change. Onlookers must have thought I was mad speaking to my imaginary friend. Fortunately, I was concentrating too hard to notice. I tried over sounding the 'O' or "the slice please", even pointing through the glass cabinet didn't work and once I ended up with a cranberry crumble, Yuk! It sounds nothing like oat!

Maybe it is a result of our education, media and foreign films but Aussies seem to know plenty of names for an object used colloquially around the world. Our Canadian friends, not so much. They don't recognise a Chemist, it is called a Drug Store. OK, I can live with that, but one person made the comment that a chemist sounds like someone who cooks up meth. I was polite and said nothing but thought a Drug store evokes images of a bloke selling contraband down a back alley. Toilets are Washrooms, I understand that, but have they never heard of a toilet? I mean toilet paper is called the same, so I don't think it is too much of a stretch to realise that it is used in a toilet? There is no such thing as a bin in Canada, it is simply "garbage". Thankfully, there is a dump, but when I told the toll bridge lady, I had two bags of rubbish she replied "Rubbish, now that sounds very old English to me." Old English, was she for real? I doubt Queen Victoria would have ordered Prince Albert "Don't forget to remind the house maid to put out the rubbish Darling". Maybe some charade type actions would have worked better. Pencils do not get blunt, no they are not magical, they just get dull. If you have a haircut with a fringe, you have bangs, hair clips are called Barrettes, baking paper is parchment and Chinooks are not helicopters but wet, unseasonably warm coastal winds and a rather large salmon. The school cleaner is the Custodian, very regal. Now that sounds Old English! I wonder if the water boy at the Gridiron is called a Hydrologist? Anna's students thought all this confusion quite wonderful and enjoyed being able to correct the teacher and Imogen. I am sure my girls taught them plenty of new words as well. We have had much less trouble being understood in countries where English is a second language.

Although it never ceases to amaze me, when we are abroad, invariably a shopkeeper or taxi driver will say "So that accent, it is British or South African or New Zealand?" which we indignantly respond with "No". Sure, we speak the same language, in the main, but that is where it ends. I find it very cut and dry distinguishing between New Zealanders, South Africans, English and Australians, but I have been told by North Americans that we all sound the same. A while back, I was fortunate to be privy to an explanation by a New Zealand Maori during, a school performance. He explained that Australian and New Zealanders have such different accents because we pronounce our vowels differently. This was a real revelation and helped me become more aware of such things, although we still laugh at them pronouncing "Fish" as "Fush", "Six' as 'Sex" and so on. I became even more intrigued to find out, in an article by a sociolinguist, that Canadians generally pronounce their vowels differently depending what province they inhabit. So yes, it is all about the vowel, meaning "laugh" can sound like "loff" or "red dress" can contort into "rad drass". I was not able to pinpoint exactly how the locals formed their words but have noted that "Nissan" is pronounced "Nesson" and at least the a, e and i sounds are totally different to ours. I tried to explain this to some new friends without much luck. The bottom line is that Australians don't assume we pronounce words the correct way, because there never was a correct way, unless you subscribe to the Poms thinking that they own the English language. I figure if you load up boats of peasants, accuse them of stealing and send them to a prison on the other side of the planet, what they do with the native tongue is their business. I had an amusing experience at a store one day when the cashier asked for the spelling of my name. As I recited, he wrote "Stue", I said "No, a" and again he wrote "e" so I said "A for apple" and then he got it. Isn't the world a wonderful place with so many quirks and differences to keep us entertained. I think my Northern Australian accent is quite broad but nothing like the folk from inland Australia, who we amiably refer to as Ringers or Bushies. To give you some perspective, it is as different as New Yorkers and Texans.

By the end of the month the surrounding mountains had shrugged off most of their crisp white winter apparel, exposing the forest's dark seaweed green, randomly punctuated by bare weathered rock. Some of which, was gilded with that glorious yellow wash, most famously associated with Yellowstone Gorge in Wyoming. It is as if an artist had carefully feathered the brooding greys and blues into the predominant sienna ochres, to create a masterpiece ever changing with the light. Coming from the tropics, I am not unfamiliar with the wonders of nature's palette, but these yellow cliffs always stop me in my tracks. This quirk of quintessential nature appears, to my eye at least, almost unnatural, artistic impressionism. In 2008, I walked to the Lower Falls lookout of Yellowstone Gorge and stood there speechless having never imagined such a vista. Much like when you stare at the markings of a brightly coloured reef fish and ponder how they came to be. In the Shuswap district, one of the best examples of this rock can be seen down Sunnybrae Road. It was one of my favourite parts of the local area.

Having little to do and loads of time to do it in, I took a sortie down Sunnybrae to the Margaret Falls walking track. This short walk up a narrow valley was a bit like stepping back into the time of the dinosaurs. As I entered the main track, cold, wet breeze, created by the gushing waterfall, slapped my face. Hoodie flipped over my head, hands disappeared into my pockets, a rapidly learnt response over the previous few months. The sheer rock walls and valley floor were covered in a close shaven, elfin carpet of moss. The creek was unrelenting, spitting, surging. The snowmelt single mindedly racing to lower ground. So clear, so inviting, so bloody cold. A paradox to the senses. The well-kept path weaved its way from bank to bank on rustic footbridges. Downstream in a quiet backwater, a translucent sheet of ice still covered the surface allowing a view of the pushing and shoving, aerated water below. Mammoth cedars cluttered the gorge. Some stood tall, many toppled sideways, leaning on the sheer rock edge some thirty metres above. All happily continuing to grow while nursing moss, ferns and lichen. Determined seedlings had somehow colonised the rock crevices, creating unusually bent trunks yearning and gasping for the sunlight above. The trill chirp of a chipmunk interjected the wind and water. I could not pinpoint his hiding place.

Despite the weather prediction, the following Saturday was fine and sunny. The perfect combination. It climbed to a positively balmy 16.1 degrees, the warmest March day since records were kept in 1893. Smashed the previous 94-year-old record by 2 degrees. We bound out of the house and off to visit the local Dairy and Cheesery. The way was paved to try out some new delicacies. The aged Gouda was my favourite. At last some real cheese. They also made their own special variety, a combination of two Dutch styles, Maasdammer and Gouda, cleverly called Mazuda. Great taste. Afterwards we ventured into a barn, straight off the pages of Charlotte's Web. Cats gazed down from lofty vantages, eyeing rat sized cracks in the wall. We did glimpse a couple dart across the dirt floor. No wonder the cat was fat. Small pens lined one wall, each with a very young calf. Some lay in the fresh hay not old enough to stand for long periods. Tongues stabbing the air ready to lick whatever they could reach. All had those wonderful bright, honest eyes and loved our pats almost as much as we enjoyed giving them. It was something very new and wonderful for Imogen. On the other side of the barn a Mumma cow looked like she would calve at any moment. Poor thing was exhausted. Large cobwebs spanned the old timber rafters. Silent killers in the form of sticky fly traps dangled innocuously from rusty nails, hundreds of flies tared to the surface. Some animals would see the fate of their own kind and flee, but not the fly. Next, we picnicked at the end of the wharf. For the first time the lake was fully thawed. We overheard an older couple discussing how they had never seen it so low. By two p.m. the sun had burnt off as much of the cold it could manage allowing me to convince the girls to come to Sunnybrae for a bush walk. Imogen was reluctant but really enjoyed following the creek through Herald Provincial Park to the Lake. The very large campground was still closed until April and allowed a peaceful stroll. On the way back we noticed curious timber ladders and stairs clinging to the rock face on the land side of the track. Across the road on the lake's edge there were small, roughly built decks, stilted above the water and literally centimeters off the bitumen. Most were covered on three sides, no doubt to block the wind and onlookers. Some even had sun lounges, chairs and side tables. Sun worshipping British Columbian style. They are optimistic souls. Dirt roads ran off the main drag at intervals, leading to little enclaves with self-proclaimed private beaches and pontoon jetties. Bluffing can get you a long way and a private beach it would seem.

This day was the impetus for, what I later referred to as the "Clothesline Fiasco". Hopeful for sunshine and warmer weather, I rushed down to the hardware store and grabbed a length of cord to string up down the side of the house. I even found a long-forked sapling in the forest to prop it up in the middle. It was a bit wonky but how great it would be to have our clothes flapping about in the sun, or so I thought. The next day I put the washing on early and had it out on the line by eight. Alas, when I checked in the late afternoon the clothes were still damp and had to go into the dryer. The rain and cloud kept the poor forlorn structure bare for most of the next nine months. I did try whenever the sun came out, but it always ended in a walk of shame back to the dryer. This apparatus is as common as double plugger thongs and board shorts in Australia but unheard of in Canada for reasons that became very apparent. Nobody ever asked what the hell I was doing but I am sure there were plenty of raised eyebrows and quizzical looks. Come to think of it there may have been an increased amount of traffic down our road in the following weeks. Sightseers?

Ever looking for something to fill our weekends we found a children's theatre, down the track in Kelowna, who were putting on a performance of the "Flower Ball". We were greeted at the door by the young actors in costume and character, who whisked Imogen over to a craft table to make a crepe flower to be used in the performance. This little hole in the wall, part of a block of repurposed warehouse spaces was the smallest theatre I have even seen. Imogen's face followed each character, clinging to every word. The playwright must have market researched his target audience well, as it had the obligatory Princess and castle. Unbeknown to us, the show coincided with the hockey playoffs in the stadium next door, so parking was at a premium. Luckily, we found an establishment close by that allowed us to park as a reward for our patronage. The Old Train Station Pub was a real gem. Built in the original station, it had great food, decor and service. A pumped-up hockey crowd contributed to the ambience.

The following morning, we visited a small Japanese garden just behind Bernard Street. A few small birds, a crow and a cheeky black squirrel skipped around the melting snow, pouncing on the easy food offerings of pre-Spring. Buds had exploded out of many trees, some the colour and texture of a newborn fawn while others a distinctive hot pink. I suspect the later were Cherry trees. On the way back to Salmon Arm we took the alternate route from Vernon via the Salmon River road. What a picturesque drive with wineries, a dairy and various farms dotted along the way. Farmers and their families were out in force getting the fields ready to plant, feeding livestock and no doubt excited by all the hope that Spring brings to someone on the land.

One could easily fill a coffee table photobook with the plethora of barns, sheds and outhouses found along the way. Some red, many raw timbered and ramshackled. Dutch gables with second story barn doors. Some had large red stars, a nod to the Pennsylvania Amish. Stacked with hay and hedged with a menagerie of loitering farm animals.

The 13th of March, a step closer to Spring and another milestone, the start of Daylight Saving. Clocks were wound forward an hour by we traditionalists who still wear a timepiece as opposed to relying on their phone. This change should have meant more light in the afternoons to get out and about, if only the overcast skies cleared. It also meant 17 hours difference to the eastern seaboard of Australia, home. Alberta changed their clocks on the same day meaning they remained an hour ahead of BC. There was still frost on the grass each morning and a thin sheet of ice skinned the roadside drains. Groups of teenagers sleepily slouched around bus stops, in a way only teenagers can. Clad in seriously unseasonal clothing in the name of being cool and individual. For goodness sake some of the girls were wearing summer dresses and it was 5 degrees with a light breeze blowing across the lake. It made me cold looking at them. When I picked my girls up from school, the sun was peeking through the cloud but before we got too far down the road it started to ...? well I was not sure what to call it. These tiny balls of snow fell from the sky. Not the typical flakes. A bit of research revealed this weather phenomenon is called Graupel, adopted from the Germans. I wonder how many Canadians know that. It is described as soft hail. This country produces every type of precipitation known to man and then some.

To be sure, to be sure! it was St Patrick's Day and another dress up opportunity for the kids at Sorrento Elementary. At the dollar shop Imogen spotted a Viking helmet, green with gold horns, complete with emblazoned shamrock. She had to have one. Since the Vikings didn't make an appearance on Irish shores for some 300 years after St. Patrick in 795 AD and that when they did, they first raided the monasteries, I failed to see the symbolism. I doubted whether Patrick would have approved or that the Irish would want to remember a hostile invader on their special day. Strangely enough St Patrick himself had been captured in England by Irish pirates as a boy and taken back to the Emerald Isle as a slave to work the land before escaping and becoming a holy man. Anyway, in the morning she sorted through her clothes and put on everything green she owned and then pranced out for breakfast happy as a leprechaun who had just found a four leafed clover. Later on, she looked in deep thought, so I asked what was wrong. "Well Dad! my friend Moira is going to have a hard time this morning because every piece of clothing she owns is pink." I assured her that her Mummy would work it out. Isn't it amazing the empathy they have at six. During the day, she went up to her Mum and said, "Those boys are calling me a Viking but I'm a Leprechaun." You have got to love kids! I didn't know my Great Grandfather but from all reports he was a stocky, barrel chested Scotchman with greying red hair. Mum always said she thought he looked like the illustrations of Vikings she had seen in history books. The fact that his east coast village in Scotland was only some 450 kilometers from Norway would suggest he may indeed have had Norse pirate blood. He was just one of my eight Great Grandparents that I am so thankful for. All from different parts of the world, they chose to live in beautiful North Queensland. I have never wanted to live permanently anywhere else. All Great Grandparents settled on the ocean and all hailed from coastal parts of their mother lands. So saltwater is in my blood and now I really know what it feels like to be removed from one's instinctual habitat.

Love it, hate it, resent it, admire its beauty. It was an up and down start to our exchange. Our initial enthusiasm fueled unwillingness to accept the possibility that a satellite community of a small town, may be a major change of pace, soon caused some angst. Forge on into the unknown we did.

Sociology Observation Report of sample group "S" - The shock of a sudden 40-degree change in temperature resulted in several physiological and behavioural outcomes. All participants quickly developed the habit of wearing multiple layers of clothing and gravitated to heat sources like a moth to a flame. Local traditions were embraced with vigour and outdoor pursuits were engaged in, until the cold could no longer be tolerated. Male subject found the climatic and social adjustments most difficult; we attribute this to regular stints of isolation. The group adopted several new indoor pursuits to create mental stimulation. Trying to climb the walls was an involuntary response.

PART THREE

Unlike Australia, Canada uses the astronomical equinox to signal in the change of season. In 2016, Spring officially began on the 20th of March and just as importantly the official start of winter was not until December the 21st. We knew by then we would be on a beach in Sydney soaking up the sunshine. Even though the first quarter had many highlights we were of the belief that we had done the hard yards. I hope that the narrative thus far has been balanced and not merely the rantings of a sunshine deprived, vitamin D deficient bloke from down under with a severe case of cabin fever. It was timely to take stock before continuing into the new season.

Now Winter, yes we were warned. We researched the historical temperatures, saw photos of the region in snow, spent a previous Christmas in Colorado and had spoken to past exchangees. Did it prepare us? Well clothes and car choice, yes. Mentally and physically, no. Once the euphoria of travel and having a White Christmas had passed, the realities of living in a snow bound country set in. It hit like a sledgehammer. But I think the weather would have been tolerable if we were in a much larger centre, with more to do close by. Human interaction, or lack of it was a big deal. We had at times been irritable, not sleeping properly, frustrated by many aspects of our new environment. We responded with a stiff upper lip and reassured each other that it would all be all worthwhile. They say that you need to get out of your comfort zone to enable growth. We must all have grown a great deal.

As the temperature rose slightly, I forced myself outside to walk each day. There was just so much more to observe and absorb with the snow receding. Eagle Bay road was picturesque, and some lakeside businesses started to show signs of life. The golf course in Blind Bay looked inviting so I drove up to the clubhouse and walked the greens. Many well-appointed houses bordered the course. It was certainly in good shape, almost ready to open for the season despite the remnant snow. An elderly man stopped his buggy for a chat. His broad weathered smile made me feel good even before he spoke. He assumed I was a golfer and I played along with it because he was such a friendly chap. I thought I may have found myself a golf buddy. I love listening to people's life stories especially older folk. I was fortunate to have both Grandads until I was in my twenties and I could sit, listen and learn for hours. Boats were getting wet again and pontoons were rolled back into the Lake, ready to make more memories. Oh, it would be great to get out on that lake. Boating, creeks, rivers and the ocean have been one constant of my life. I whole-heartedly agree with Kenneth Grahame's Rat who so eloquently declared in **Wind in the Willows** "Believe me, my young friend, there is nothing —

absolutely nothing — half so much worth doing as simply messing about in boats."

Before long, the last day of term was upon us. Just after class on the Friday, the father of a boy in Anna's class came up and enthusiastically thanked her for choosing to come to Canada and the positive impact she had on his son. It is nice to get affirmations from the parents, acknowledging your hard work and professionalism. I was very proud when she told me the story and it was evident that those few words had touched her.

The first Sunday of the Spring Break. Full of anticipation, we rose early and were off on our long five-hour drive to the coast. This involved reacquainting ourselves with the Coquihalla Pass. Although it had recently snowed in the high country, we knew it would be in far better condition than our first meeting. A young man we had met at the cross-country skiing, caught a ride with us to the Vancouver Airport for a fortnight in Mexico to visit his mother and get some sun. His Mum seemed to have it all sorted out. She lives from April to October on Vancouver Island at Cowichan. As soon as it starts to get a bit cool, they move down to their condo in Arizona, she then rents it out from mid-December and moves down further to Mexico to follow the sun. It was nice to have some company for the trip and a chance to ask some questions that have been churning over for some time. He told a tale of recently spotting a pack of four wolves walking in the misty edge of the road near Celista on his way to work. They did not appear shy and as he slowed down, they wandered out in front of the car as if it wasn't there. What an experience with these elusive canines.

Destination Vancouver Island. For convenience, we stayed overnight in the Coast Tsawwassen Inn on the seaside outskirts of the city near the barge terminal. We had not planned to eat out, but the attached restaurant was very well priced and at the end of a full day of driving, a comfortable chair, a glass of wine and a nice environment were too much to pass up. We were greeted at the front door by a glass roofed sunroom with invitingly warm ceiling heaters and the beat of great music from my youth. Filled with casually well-dressed patrons who all appearing to be in high spirits. We took a couple of photos of the interior as an idea for our new deck at home. This is our kind of place and a really nice evening to start our journey. A much more familiar environment than the past three months and we celebrated with a couple of glasses of BC Sav Blanc to support the local economy. A sip revealed they had taken their own path and avoided copying the much sweeter offerings from south of the border. We ate pan seared tuna encrusted with sesame seed and served with wasabi mayonnaise. Fantastic. Imogen turned a shared dessert into a contact sport. The chocolate caramel brownie and ice-cream didn't stand a chance. At one stage she scrapped the food off my spoon and into her mouth without batting an eyelid. She will never starve that girl of mine.

Tsawwassen itself was a quaint little village by the sea, with well-manicured lawns all dressed in new spring attire. A real oasis from the burbs of Vancouver. The main road came to an abrupt stop at the US border crossing, at Point Roberts. A peninsula and anomaly indiscriminately chopped off by the 49th parallel. A tiny outpost of Uncle Sam's, only twelve square kilometres in area. Home to thirteen hundred permanent residents. If com-mon sense prevailed it would have been given over to Canada long ago, saving both countries a heap of money on border crossing management. As it turned out, this community was a convenience to us. We needed to cross the border out of Canada every three months to restart the clock on our allowance for foreign driver's license use. The trip through customs was far from smooth and left me wondering why we bothered. We got the fifty questions treatment and then they tried to confuse us and suggest we were contradicting ourselves. They had a job to do but surely these confrontational tactics were not necessary. They finally sent us on our way. The family in front of us had their whole car searched, so I suppose we got off lightly. Point Roberts was a real beauty, a little slice of Cape Cod on the West Coast. Modern beachy chic houses dotted amongst wonderfully ocean weathered homes. Shoulder to shoulder along the windswept coast and redwood forest. An impressive marina sat in a natural harbour, lined with impressive vessels that were afforded close cruising options to the Anacortes and San Juan Islands. The rest of Washington State lied just across the Strait of Georgia only some fifteen kilometers away. The residents completed the relaxed feel with driftwood sculptures, bespoke letter boxes, hand painted characters on distinctly US style fire hydrants and strings of fisherman's floats strung along fences. Pleased with our unexpected side trip we headed back over the border, but not before a lecture from the Canadian border control because our visas were not stapled into our passports. If that was a requirement, why didn't they do it at the airport when we arrived as is done in other countries.

    We drove aboard the ferry at Horseshoe Bay, choosing the recommended Tsawwassen to Sidney route. It wove its way through the picturesque Channel Islands. Pebbly shores strewn with sun bleached logs. The waters of the Salish Sea are a deep and sullen green under the morning cloud. A sliver of blue sky sat buoyantly on the horizon, a glimpse of promise for the day ahead. We cruised briefly into US waters before re-entering Canada, not an obnoxious border guard in sight. Many of the heavily wooded islands were dotted with cabins and more substantial houses. I pondered their owner's existence in such a remote place. Maybe they are summer retreats? They must all own boats to access the main island for supplies and a taste of humanity. Some are large enough to have their own community like Salt Spring Island, home to ten thousand permanent residents. Disembarking the ferry was like the start of the Bathurst 500, just without rules. Cars, trucks and buses sped off the top and bottom ramps with no thought of the speed limit. Although the sky had now turned grey, it was not raining and that was a blessing. We drove straight to the world renowned Butchart Gardens, located only some fifteen minutes away. Quickly getting off the highway and traveling past old growth redwood forests, farms with stately homesteads and cabins covered in moss, full of character. Just before the gardens we came across the village of Brentwood Bay. A very new, spick and span look about it, probably a pleasant place to live, just outside Victoria's city limits. My Mum and neighbours have visited the gardens and raved about them. Although I love gardens, I wasn't sure it would be my style. I had the impression of charming English cottage gardens, which I can appreciate but don't really go for. I should not have been concerned. The garden originally started in the old quarry, a dream made into reality by Jennie Butchart, the wife of the Limestone Quarry owner. It was first planted out some one hundred and twelve years ago with a vision of transforming the ugly pit into a place of beauty. Her success was obvious, her vision unique. The rim of the quarry allows aerial views of the meticulously cared for beds of bulbs and annuals which gave a supporting role to the larger trees and dominant rock landscape. Imogen was enthralled and dragged us along with map in hand. She led us onto the carousel and then to the Italian, Rose and finally the Japanese sections. The latter, I can controversially say, was as good if not better than any I saw on our recent visit to Japan. Tiny shimmering hummingbirds buzzed about their daily chores amongst the technicoloured flora. A grey squirrel bulldozed through the blooms looking for morsels of food. A nice hot soup lunch in the adjoining café was welcome. After spending three hours taking in all the delights, we headed out to our accommodation for the next three nights but not before spotting a young black tailed deer just outside the entrance. Did I mention it never climbed above 5 degrees with overcast skies and a bit of drizzle.

A glance at the map revealed the highway from the Province Capital, Victoria, through to Departure Bay at Nanaimo. It had the Maple leaf symbol depicting the Trans-Canada Highway. We were once again hitting the iconic route. This thick yellow line on the map is one of the longest in the world and incorporates roads and seaways. It stretches from Victoria BC on the Pacific Ocean all the way across this vast country to St. John's, Newfoundland on the Atlantic.

After spending many of our travels trying to cram in as much as possible, we decided to base ourselves in a couple of places and do the surrounds properly. I found a really cool Houseboat permanently moored in Cowichan Bay. Once I saw the photo on the internet, I knew it was exactly the type of quirky digs we were after. The bonus was that this part of the island had a micro climate and fertile soil conducive to growing an array of fruits, including grapes. The French would say the land has a special "Terroir". Meaning the geographical influence that produces sought after characteristics in the fruit and in turn the wine. Chance had it that there were about twenty wineries within a stone's throw of our Float Home. The Coastal Salish First Nations people have gathered roots, herbs and berries from this land for centuries and obviously knew a thing or two about choosing a prime position. We drove around Saanich Inlet to Cowichan Bay through the mountains, reminding me of the canopy cloaked road from Cairns to the Kuranda rainforest. A collage of every shade of green. Our houseboat was permanently moored on the aptly named Blue Nose Jetty, right in the middle of this thriving beach community. We had planned this trip whilst still in Australia, so finally arriving and rolling our gear down the gangplank was almost surreal. Her name was Sadhana, a Sanskrit word which loosely means – "heightening your awareness to the possibilities of every moment of your life". Wordy I known but profound it was, undoubtedly. Standing out from the others, she wore a turquoise slip with exposed cedar shingles up her shoulders. Burnt red and washed out ochre highlights completed the look. The lower story was the lounge and gallery, upstairs revealed two bedrooms and a bathroom. Porthole windows, but of course. She had this wabi sabi thing going on. Perfect imperfection. Patina and history in every plank and nail. A small stern deck completed the deal. The introductory letter warned not to be alarmed by bay seals that regularly slip onboard without captain's permission. Any bad smells during our stay was blamed on the seals. We cranked up the heater and sat back in the bar stools with views out across the estuary and the comings and goings along the shore. All very excited and pleased with ourselves for finding such a place. Imogen took us upstairs for a tour, she absolutely loved it. A floating cubby house. Late in the afternoon the sun burst through the clouds for a short visit, basking the patient inhabitants in all its glory. Not to let a chance go by, I dragged the girls out for a walk along the street behind the docks. We had seen some impressive bird houses, but the ones assembled on old pylons would have to be the best. Intricate structures of recycled timber, iron, copper and more, weathered by salt and sun, it looked more like a sea gypsy fairy commune. Maybe it was.

After dinner we all collapsed into bed early. The breeze dropped out leaving the bay a glassy slate. The very gentle rocking of the tide was cathartic and before long we all drifted off. I may have dreamt of Buccaneers, pirates and a damsel in distress, such was the setting, but I could not recall my adventures in the morning. A quick check revealed no evident flesh wounds to tweak my memory. The bonus of Sadhana was that it came with kayaks and bikes! We made plans to give them a go when the weather improved. I didn't tell my girls I saw a photo of two Killer Whales cruising in that very bay. If we see anything while kayaking, I'll just say that the tuna grow extra-large in these latitudes. Of course, neither of them would believe me. We came with no real plans but to soak up the ambiance, enjoy what hidden gems we stumbled upon and roll with the punches of early Spring's variable weather. This traditional Salish land was given the name Quwútsun, the "the warm land" and is officially the mildest place to live in the whole of Canada. But that didn't mean it was warm by Australian standards.

Tuesday brought sunny skies and a chance to experience the Kinsol Trestle Bridge walk. Our excursion took us west through the thick overhanging forest to the edge of Shawnigan Lake then along a narrow road to the start of the hike. The historic timber structure, now used by hikers and bike riders, was built in 1911 for the rail line to cross the gorge. Constructed of timber, this curved bridge is a true engineering feat. Sitting some 44 metres above the Koksilah River and 187 metres long. Several other families were out enjoying the Easter break in the outdoors.

In the afternoon we milled around the shops in Cowichan. A plethora of seafarer themed cafes, boutiques and galleries. Anna had a nice time trying on clothes and contributing to the local economy. In one store we met a young salesman who had grown up on the island. When we told him we were from Australia, he revealed a serious case of warm climate envy. We told him how beautiful his island was, but he couldn't get past the cold issue. The resident Potter's showroom was closed, and her sign read "Mondays and Tuesday – Open by Chance". Now that is a relaxed attitude, no stress here! In fact, Cowichan was part of a worldwide group of towns who have embraced the slow food movement called Cittaslow. Basically, it promotes slowing down and enjoying the moment, the antithesis of fast food and the modern lifestyle that comes with it.

A stroll down a partially covered jetty, nestled between shopfronts, brought us to the maritime museum. As part of its collection, there were traditionally built timber canoes, tenders and small speed boats in the Italian Riva style. A restored Seagull outboard engine caught my eye. One of the earliest companies to manufacture this "new" technology and bring it to Australian waters. My Grandad bought one for Dad when he was about fifteen. What a thrill to not have to row everywhere to go fishing. These little engines were very basic with few things to go wrong, dangling there on the back of old heavy bond wood dinghies. They were a common sight when I was young. The community board was full of boats for sale and we couldn't help to notice how cheap they were. There must be an oversupply of secondhand vessels. One would sure look good moored back in Port Hinchinbrook.

I picked up a local newspaper and was surprised to read that over the last few years the Island had experienced drought. Hard to believe in a place where every roof is covered in moss, streams a plenty cut through the landscape and Larch trees draped in Spanish moss, normally associated with the Louisiana bayou. I know I am here in the rainy season and witnessing the snow melt flow in the creeks but would never have guessed there could be water supply issues. The council was so concerned they had passed a law to ban above ground spray irrigation. The extended dry during El Nino years in Townsville is hard on our garden and I sometimes wish we were fifty kilometres up the road in the Wet Tropics. Somehow knowing that this lush island also has problems with water supply makes me feel a bit better about my lot.

A calmness pervaded the morning, Anna did the laundry in a little shed perched on the pontoon just outside our dock. If you have to do chores this certainly was the place with the gentle roll of the tide a pleasant distraction. Back on the good ship Sadhana, Imogen and I sat in the warmth of the bay window and gazed out at the raindrops creating hypnotic ripple patterns on the narrow strip of water between the mooring and the shore. It was low tide and the derelict pylons told the story of the ocean's ebb and flow. A crusting of mussels and green slime ringed the tell tail high tide mark. Our nature watch was rewarded with a visit by a proud bird with a midnight blue crest, similar in shape to the red headpiece of a woodpecker. She had a long, strong looking beak, perfect for catching her prey. We later identified it to be a Belted Kingfisher and before long she lived up to her name by darting down from her lookout to pick up inch long baitfish. Before swallowing she gave the fish that trademark smack on the pylon. A familiar action by our Aussie Kingfishers and Kookaburras. The latter which catch plenty of lizards, frogs and insects before dispatching them on a branch of the big old paper bark in our front yard.

The side road from Cowichan to Duncan went through low salt pans up into rolling hills. As we came around one corner, we were surprised to find an old church on the rise. Its graveyard flowing down the hill in front. A scene out of rural England or Switzerland. Neat and tidy homes with manicured gardens juxtaposed by dwellings in disrepair, surrounded with rubbish. No singular social group have a mortgage on cleanliness or pride, so it leaves me wondering why oh why. Duncan had a busy CBD with cherry blossoms lining the main street in all their glory. Totem poles were dispersed around town, a unique experience. Anna spotted a Vietnamese restaurant on the main street which lured us in to escape the cold and rain. Pho was our choice and very soon three massive bowls of noodle soup came out with accompanying lime quarters, Vietnamese mint, sliced chili and loads of bean sprout. It was as good as the street food in Saigon, very authentic. There was so much leftover that we took a large container back to the boat for dinner. The meal was finished with a traditional Vietnamese iced coffee; an opportunity hard to pass up. The glass came to the table with about fifteen milliliters of condensed milk in the bottom and a stainless-steel contraption fitted over the top, dripping coffee. When it finishes filtering through the beans, the mixture is poured over a glass of ice. When you think about it, this is a classic example of adaptation. The French ruled Vietnam for over a century and brought many foods with them, including coffee. Due to a lack of fresh milk they compromised with the sweet canned stuff. It is these unexpected little delights that can change the whole day.

We popped into several stores with great local art on display but pondered where we could hang it on our already art cluttered walls back home. In one store Imogen got to roll a beeswax candle and found out that pioneers in British Columbia discovered an endemic fish could be dried, a wick inserted in its mouth and used like a candle due to its high fat content. It is not too hard to imagine a discovery scenario, a Newtonian moment when a prospector chasing gold, camping in the wilderness, catches a couple of fish and puts them over the flames to cook. He gets up to answer the call of nature and notices a bright glow over his shoulder and can't wait to tell his mates. Not only would the camp be illuminated but it would smell good. I suppose you would be able to see the bears coming in following the aroma. Likewise, in Northern Australia there is a native tree called the Candle Nut that was used by early settlers in the same fashion.

We returned to Duncan that night for a children's theatre production with life sized costumes of popular television cartoon characters of which I knew not one. Silly Daddy! What a delight though, to sit and watch a group of kids totally engaged with the story. It is hard not to be pulled into the whirlpool of dance, song and colourful costumes, but mostly the smiles of the little ones. A sign in front of the ten-pin bowling alley read "Sick of gumboots? Come and put on some bowling shoes". A clear sign that they have had enough of the wet weather and would soon be building an Ark. On a side note, it was Federal Government Budget day. I haven't read through it and probably won't, but I hope they have allocated a sizeable portion to fluorescent line marking paint and roadside reflectors. These small but ever so important elements to road safety, that we take for granted in Australia, are sadly missing on many roads. I am used to turning on the car lights and seeing crisp white markings illuminate the way. Maybe it is like that in the east of the country but not in BC. Driving back from Duncan later that night in the rain was nothing short of dangerous. Ok off the soapbox now.

It was our fourth day in the Bay, and it had been a much needed change of perspective mixing it up with different people with a positive and carefree holiday outlook. Relaxation had enveloped the Scott family for the first time since we left home. I had a feeling that being reunited with the sea helped as well. The three of us have lived on the coast all our lives, the salt gets into your blood. Instead of being on the other side of the world, we now felt that we were only on the other side of the Pacific Ocean, although pure semantics, it was comforting. The previous days meanderings took us through countryside, interspersed with Tudor style cottages, farms and forest. Chemainus, a small seaside village to the north, afforded a vantage point to watch tugboats towing payloads of logs, some trailing at least three hundred meters. Going in the opposite direction were barges full of woodchip. Who knows where they were headed, a paper factory, compressed fibre board production or off to China? We conveniently arrived at morning tea and stepped straight into a store where a very pleasant hostess ushered us to a table conveniently warmed through the glass by the sun. We were entertained by the local gossip from the table next to ours. You know how it is! We weren't eavesdropping, they were just talking loudly about interesting stuff. A lemon curd tart topped with Chinese gooseberries soon landed on our table and brought back memories of my Grandma's cooking and Auntie Vera's gooseberry trellis in Brisbane. I visited with my Grandma to see the State Exhibition when I was eleven and it was my first time on a plane. I was thoroughly indulged by the sisters, who hired a minibus to explore the south east of our State. We picked strawberries, visited the Big Pineapple, Lone Pine Animal Sanctuary and many other places. A lot to take in for a country boy who only went to town once a week. I remember the tall buildings and escalators being a novelty. Mum and Dad had told me that I would come home with a sun burnt roof of my mouth from looking up so much. A common old saying that I never hear these days.

Down main street Chemainus, a hot pink Rhino head protruding from an old shop front. Large, lifelike and unapologetically proud to be different. Who could resist? We had to check this out. Clothes, jewellery, household knick knacks. Some very quirky shop fittings had us gawking every which way. Old timber dining chairs and life size bronze hands were screwed to the walls, providing ready-made shelves and hangers for a range of equally cool merchandise. The friendly shopkeeper liked a chat. She was clearly British and had come to visit her husband's Godmother for a holiday five years before and hadn't left. She recalled the familiar challenge of trying to meet people and integrate in the community. She would walk the streets in the afternoon just hoping to find someone outside who was up for a conversation. Now that sounds familiar. Humans are certainly not solitary beasts.

Following the theme of attention seeking, of course I am referring to one pink African animal and not the lovely Pommie lass, the distinctive Cherry Blossoms raucously demanded attention as we drove the back road. It was however the wonderfully oversized purple Magnolia flowers that caught my eye, along with the almost fluorescent Tulips which seemed to grow like weeds.

The distinctly patchy bark of the Arbutus reminded me of the Leopard tree in my front yard. Here they look almost at odds with their surroundings but still a delight. I surmised they may even be Australian natives, but some research revealed they were endemic to Spain and Portugal, which made more sense. Albert Namatjira, if given the chance, would have loved painting these motley orange and deep red, loud and proud crowd stoppers. On to Maple Bay, lined with homes reaching right down to the water. Million-dollar views and a safe harbour. In the absence of a park, we stopped at the jetty car park for a picnic of sorts. Crammed into the hatch back of the car to escape the frigid winds. Down the road, Crofton looked quaint as well, but the main street was dug up for repairs and closed off, so we drove around the backstreets until we found a small beach access to the wide estuary boardwalk. Nice.

Tofino, it just rolls of the tongue like some Italian salutation. The time had come. We had read a lot about the place and were sure the effort to get there would be worth it. The drive to the wild west coast took about five hours, with a brief stop in the bizarre little village of Coombs. A paddle steamer was parked on the grass alongside several log buildings, maybe they were expecting forty days and forty nights of rain. The vendors sold wares you would expect to find in a South East Asian flea market, carvings, necklaces, sarongs. The courtyard was strewn with large stone carvings, presumably for sale, however they were being utilised as a unique climbing gym by a group of kids devoid of parent supervision. No one seemed to care that little Jimmy was about to fall three metres from Ganesha's marble trunk. The grocery market had a deep green coat of grass on its roof where they regularly let out the resident goats to graze. A strange sight indeed. They had not appeared for the day but the goat's eerie was in clear view and looked like an illustration from a children's book come to life. Further west we came to Port Alberni, a larger centre sitting at the foot of Mount Arrowsmith, on a long inlet from the ocean. I would have loved to have gone on the day cruise out to the ocean, but time didn't permit. It was Good Friday and a very significant anniversary for the region. Fifty-two years to the day a massive earthquake hit the coast of Alaska lifting the ocean floor by up to fifteen meters. I know it is hard to imagine that kind of force. The resulting tsunami boasted waves up to an astounding sixty-seven meters hitting part of the Alaskan coast to the north. One hundred and nineteen people were killed. Four hours later, in the middle of the night and with little warning, a fifteen-metre wave travelled thirty-three kilometres from the coast, funneled up the valley. By the time it hit the town it was six metres tall and travelling fast. It extensively damaging the lower lying regions but surprisingly no one was killed. We stopped for morning tea and sat next to a table of retired fellows having their morning chat. Sounds like the start of a joke but there really was a German, two Scotsman and a Canadian who walked into this coffee shop. I couldn't help to overhear their entire conversation due to our proximity and the volume they chose to converse at. They were asking the German what the past tense of a certain German word was. Then continued the linguistic theme by discussing accents, in particular the difference between a Yank and a Canadian. The Scotsman pointed out that despite being built by the Romans in 122 A.D. and in various states of disrepair, Hadrian's Wall seemed to still have a strong effect on accent. The Scotland – England border is north of this ancient divider, but he reported that accents were loyal to history. North of the wall have strong Scottish accents and on the other side, distinctly different. I was intrigued by this, due partly to my heritage and the knowledge that there is no love lost between the Scots and English. Finally, one said if they didn't hurry up and finish their brew the Tsunami would wash them away. But his mate promptly countered "I have checked the projected town heights and they say we are safe here. So, I might stay all day". We got to stretch our legs, get a coffee, a laugh and an education, all in a well utilised half an hour.

The coastal town of Ucluelet, just south of Tofino, became a perfect place to stop for a late picnic lunch at the marina. It was filled with tourist and fishing boats. A large sign read "Don't feed the Sea Lions" but unfortunately, they were nowhere to be found. I was not prepared for the pared back beauty of Ucluelet, separated from its more well-known cousin, by the beaches and rainforest of the Pacific Rim National Park. The lady at the Tourist information centre informed us that some areas of the park were closed due to a large sinkhole that opened up in January. As we were informed, not uncommon in this area due to the marine clay base and plenty of rain. Not to worry there was more than enough for us to visit and get a real feel for the ecosystem. Canada's version of "where the rainforest meets the reef" a far North Queensland slogan. Very different, but equally wild and alluring. Since the sun was shining, we grabbed the opportunity to walk the Wild Pacific Trail on an outcrop of land connected by an isthmus to the rest of the town. Talk about diverse, the sign at the trailhead read "Warning Wolf, Bear and Cougar Habitat". We didn't see any, but they probably saw us. Anna stood in a large turd which may have belonged to one of the three. It was nice and fresh and stuck to her shoe, the aroma followed us for some time and probably reduced our likelihood of a wildlife encounter. Views of the exposed coastline and tiny tree lined islands were the type of images you see in travel documentaries and kept our shutters busy. The rainforest was lush and framed the ocean at endless points along the track. Near the lighthouse we spotted several whale spouts followed by glossy black backs rolling through the surf. They were much smaller than Humpbacks so I assumed they might be Orcas. Shortly after Anna confirmed this by seeing the telltale dorsal fin rise out. How good is that, tick another animal off our list. Imogen saw the craggy rocks around the lighthouse and decided they needed closer investigation, so we all climbed around looking for the endemic bright red, blue and green starfish. She just loves climbing and is fiercely independent, refusing to take a helpful hand. Half of me wanted to protect her and make sure she didn't fall, but I know that I used to do the same thing and quickly learnt to be careful. The alternative is painful. There were several car parks nestled into the forest and we exited the trail at the wrong one. Without a map we were unsure which way to go and back tracking wasn't appealing, especially with Imogen's little legs wanting a rest. I stopped a group of people to ask directions. They were very friendly. We found out they were also exchangees from Finland. The male was a visiting Professor with a yearlong fellowship at the University of Victoria. They had only arrived in January and so we enjoyed sharing notes of our common experiences. They loved Vancouver Island but were also looking forward to Summer when their family was coming to visit. His wife was very interested in where we were based and said how lonely she has been even though they were based in a city. They acknowledged that we were both separated from our tribes. Very nice people, it was a shame they weren't based closer,

I had a feeling we could have become friends. My Dad grew up living close to several Finn families who owned neighbouring sugar cane plantations. They made an impression on him and he always said how friendly they were. We finally found our car and grabbed some supplies in town. The girl in front of me in the queue was talking about the Easter long weekend with the check-out assistant. She remarked how uncanny it was that every time a long break came around, the sun came out as well. She figured it was the power of a collective consciousness, willing on the weather. Noetic science amongst the rainforest? I will let you ponder that one. A faded card pinned to the community board outside read "Handyman and Chakra Cleansing - fix your house and your soul!" This truly is a funkier version of civilisation!

With a permanent population of only around 2000, Tofino is situated on the exposed western coast of the island. Named by the Spanish, this little utopia is now famous for its surfing, fishing, untouched wilderness and wildlife. Our stay coincided with Easter and the annual Whale Festival. Although there was at least one Church in town, I got a sense that most of the population are more into nature than religion. The beach, islands and ocean are their Church and Mother Nature the preacher. They gather to take part in outdoor pursuits and to learn from their environment, what it needs and in turn what they need to be in harmony with it. The world needs more places and people like this.

Books and the internet are cluttered with various descriptions of the term, Fringe dweller, many versions focus on the marginalised but I find this description narrow and negative. I see Fringe Dwellers as communities living off the beaten track, the end of the road, an outpost town where a group of people choose to live amongst nature on the edge of civilisation. There is something about these types of places that fosters quirky people, unusual ways of getting the job done and a rugged independence. A mix of adventurers who never left, tree or sea changers, hippies and those whose family name have graced the pages of the local paper for many a generation. There is often an honesty devoid of political correctness, shaped by the facts and not what the do-gooders thousands of miles away in the cities think is right. How refreshing is that. I find myself drawn to these places, maybe not to live long term but to soak up some of their genuine outlook to get me through life back in the mainstream rat race. So, as you can now appreciate, I for one was very glad to be in Tofino for four nights amongst these eccentric bohemians who choose to live on the fringe. In Australia, places like Cooktown, Broome, Weipa and Thursday Island come to mind as being of a similar Ilk. Of course, most of Australia's interior, what we call the Outback, is made up of fringe dweller communities.

Tourism is the mainstay of this community with kayak, seaplane and boat tours a plenty. Draped over the railings of many dwellings are wetsuits, a cue to the favourite pastime of surfing. I felt like I had entered some parallel universe where surfing in 9 degrees water was the norm and not the exception. Was this a case of fearless or feelingless? I know that people all over the world try to get in on the surf culture vibe, no matter how removed from the Tropics they are, but I would have thought a hoodie with a Surf logo embroidered on it may have been distinctly more appropriate than dropping one's self into water many degrees below human core body temp. Unnatural and unnecessary I thought, sitting snugly behind a large picture window sipping a half decent brew. We stayed at the Sand Dollar Inn, very close to town. It was actually a converted downstairs room of a private house. Very neat and tiny, just perfect for our needs. The walls were covered in maps of the region. A clear glass coffee table with divided display sections sat in the lounge. Each section had a piece of flotsam and jetsam. Imogen quickly spotted a sand dollar which she told me was Mermaid money. In the next space there was a peculiar shaped specimen that had the appearance of seaweed. The label said it was a Mermaid purse, more scientifically known as a Skate, or stingray egg case. Not pretty but interesting.

On Easter Saturday, after checking out the downtown shops and galleries we headed for the Botanic Gardens, which we make a habit of doing wherever we are in the world. It was drizzling rain, so we joined the locals and donned our rain jackets, which they call Tofino tuxedos in these parts. This was like no other, part outdoor art gallery, partly planted and the rest left untouched rainforest, dissected by boardwalks. Each led to a curious find. An old timber shack with maps carved in the walls, a human sized shingled, pointed roof Pixie house, found timber viewing platforms and Oregon decks overlooking the sound. One track led to a memorial for those affected by the Japanese tsunami in 2011. There is no land mass between Fukushima and Tofino, so an endless array of curious finds continues to wash up on the local beaches. In the garden a large section of blue fishing net had been strung up between trees. At various points, these beachcombing finds were attached. Pretty powerful stuff if you take the time to reflect what it would have been like for those people. There are Tsunami evacuation signs all through this part of the island. So, it is a threat close to home. The garden is kid friendly with realistic timber carvings of animals hanging in the trees. We even encountered a big fat Banana Slug to show Imogen and tick off our list.

It was the last day of the Whale Festival and the final event was a lecture by a biologist who had worked as a National Geographic photographer for over twenty-five years. To accompany his incredible photos, he spoke about environmental issues facing the planet, the role of photojournalism in spreading the word to the general public and the trials and tribulations of working with wildlife. He had dived in the arctic with leopard seals, so close that they wrapped their jaws around his lens. He came within arms distance of an enormous bull walrus and photographed whales underneath the ice shelf. I learnt many new facts about these animals and things that are going on environmentally in some parts of the world that are simply wrong. The majestic Narwhal, the Unicorn of the sea, are being indiscriminately killed. Many are shot and sink before they can be towed to shore. A lot of the time, only the tusk and skin are taken. The world knows about the poaching of elephant and rhino, but few know about the Narwhal. Although it finished a bit late for Imogen, I am glad she sat through and watched intently. In the not too distant future, her generation will be the ones tasked with preserving nature.

Easter Sunday. The girls had a bit of a sleep in, afterwards the chocolate eggs were discovered in the makeshift torn newspaper nest. Later in the morning we drove down to Ucluelet for the community Easter Egg hunt at the imaginatively named Big Beach. What a beautiful spot. The sun came out as we picnicked on the foreshore while waiting for the main event. Ten degrees and a breeze that nearly blew the bark off the trees. We huddled behind a windbreak hedge keen for proceedings to begin. The couple sheltering beside us were lamenting about their attempts at keeping chickens. "If the bloody bears don't get them, the Raccoons do. I'm just giving them live feed!" I personally don't keep chooks because they bring in the rats which bring in the snakes but bears, I do not have to worry about.

All of a sudden, like flies to a Sunday roast, kids came out of the woodwork and lined up at the starting ribbon. Not knowing the protocol or wanting to push or shove, we stood back. Anna was afraid our Princess would trip over in the stampede or miss out on an egg, but she was out of the blocks fast and nailed twelve of the blighters before we could catch up with her. Never stand between an Aussie girl and her chocolate. Once down on the beach we were sheltered by the headland and it was very pleasant. The tide was low, and we rock hopped out exploring the pools. There were plenty of elegant Pacific Green Anemone dancing in harmony with the waves. Little crabs slid further down crevices, believing we didn't spot them. Small clumps of pink soft coral added spots of vivid colour. The beach was a fine, greyish black sand and the high tide mark was strewn with logs, beautifully smoothed and bleached by the elements. We hopped over the rocks for over an hour enjoying being part of the community in a spectacular setting.

With chocolate fueled enthusiasm down to the town wharf we went, greeted by galleries and an unexpected aquarium housed in a custom-built stunning piece of architecture. A wave inspired roofline sat on oversize Oregon beams, all supported by massive raw tree trunk columns. The centre and jewel of the CBD. Its small size disguised impressive displays punching way above its weight. Imogen loved the place and spent almost two hours working through the Detective search sheet and tickling the creatures in the touch tanks. After joining in for some time I spotted an inviting lounge chair beside a full-length window facing out to the wharf and estuary. I watched the fishing boats come and go and an elegant heron stalk its prey before a grey and white splotchy seal broke the surface right below and proceeded to entertain us with its water aerobics. I'm sure it was showing off and proving to us that it was far more interesting than watching boats or birds. On the drive back to Tofino we couldn't suppress the urge for a walk on Long Beach to giggle at the antics of the mad surfers. A group of young women were getting suited up for a lesson, they looked so cold in the brisk afternoon breeze but not as cold as they would be in a few minutes when they hit the water. Something to tell their children about in years to come. The crazy things Mummy did when she was younger. In the car park behind the dune, several young blokes sat around their vans, surfboards strewn here and there. They were severely underdressed for the weather, just boardshorts, lily white skin, blue tinged lips. They stared back at me with those silly smiles, no doubt halfway through some chemical daydream. Or maybe I am being a little too presumptuous, they could have just been high on the salt air. I held back the urge to throw them a blanket to slow the hyperthermia.

Tofino juts out into Clayoquot Sound amongst an archipelago containing deliciously named Islands that just roll off the tongue like Wickaninnish and Saranac. The much smaller Strawberry Island sits just off the coast and is very distinctive in a cartoon kind of way, like the farcical Gilligan's Island. It had an old timber yacht raised on stilts above the tide line which had been converted into a house. Attached to the shore, a string of pontoon houseboats reach out into the bay. Floatplanes glided in and out, along with tour boats full of passengers in puffy orange dry suits like escapees from prison. We tried to book a kayak trip out around the islands but the company would not go with just one family so we missed out, the long consolation walk along the foreshore at low tide was a great way to spend a morning.

With snowcapped mountains in the distance we drove through evergreen rainforest. Passed blue lakes and craggy rock faces, back towards the Island's east coast. The road was incredibly windy and as the driver, I didn't really get to appreciate all the scenery, but I don't think I would have been able to hold on to my breakfast if I was a passenger. Our apartment was situated on Fisgard Street, right in the centre of Chinatown and only a few blocks walk to anywhere in the city of Victoria. Next door was Fan Tan alley, which drew us off the street and down its narrow-cobbled path circa 1885. Once housing gambling clubs, opium dens and Chinese goods and chattel dealers, it had retained much of its old-world charm if not the characters who frequented it. Strings of coloured lights draped with Chinese lanterns, scarred brick walls cut by tiny keyhole shops, worn staircases and back alley doors. The diminishing afternoon light added to the feel of intrigue and hint of yesteryear, far removed from the relatively modern streetscape at either end. Without much styling it could easily have been used in a Hollywood period film. I am thinking wizards and the like.

Few that have visited this compact capitol city of British Columbia would argue its beauty. Set on a picturesque harbour at the southern end of the Island, Victoria has that bit of sophistication mixed with history and natural beauty. People were noticeably well dressed, and a trendy café culture kept the pulse of the city humming. Repurposed factories and warehouses have now become shop fronts and loft housing, giving the place its own unique ambiance. Patinated signs of yesteryear whisper, "Cuban Cigars for Sale" and sit effortlessly alongside trendy boutiques and high-end department stores. We headed off on foot along Government Street, taking in the old town atmosphere before cutting across to Wharf Street to enjoy views of the streetscape, gardens and harbour. The large, blue green verdigris stained roofs of the Legislature Building dominated the view to the east and made a strong statement about the very British heritage. Horse drawn carriages plied their trade along the strip for the tourists. I loved watching the huge Clydesdales plod effortlessly. So strong, so gentle and so calm. Imogen however was not too keen on the smell of their droppings. Across the road sat the Royal Museum of BC. Within lay a very impressive and kid friendly historical displays with the attention to detail of a Disney theme park. We walked through gold mines, first nations camps, saloons, a salmon cannery and so much more. Lunch was found at a row of food trucks where we were fortunate to be introduced to the Northern European pasta dumpling dish of Perogies. We picnicked in the grounds and Imogen used up all her extra energy chasing a chipmunk who she eventually patted on the head. I know it was bad parenting to let her touch the wildlife but who in their right mind would have expected her to tenaciously wear this ball of fluff into submission? Back in the building we took in a US national parks film at the *IMAX* theatre. It was great to hear the 'Wows' coming out of Imogen as she watched images of the parks, wildlife and various outdoor adventurers at play. It confirmed that she likes similar things to her Mum and Dad and that is fine with me. We followed the bay foreshore west to Fisherman's Wharf. A permanent community of vibrantly coloured houseboats moored to finger wharfs. Some had flower boxes, all had their own special design features and charm. Several food outlets had also set up shop, a great place to eat out on a sunny day. A river otter darted effortlessly close to shore as we walked down the gangplank. Distinctly different from sea otters, shorter fur, longer and thinner. It was the harbour seals, however, that stole the show. Imogen bought some sardines from the fish shop and fed them. Some even came up and took them straight out of people's hands. They are so much like dogs and very clever, splashing their flippers to get your attention. A ferry ride from the Wharf back downtown passed vessels of all shapes, sizes and functions. We spotted a moored sailing boat proudly displaying the name of its home port, Hobart Tasmania. Good to see another Australian.

The following day we walked through the city to Beacon Hill Park for an appointment with the petting zoo. Baby goats frolicked in between delighted children, all too happy to find a soft lap to nap on. The old goats sat contented on the periphery watching all the attention afforded the young. Their eyes so beautifully clear and wise. I would give more than a penny for their thoughts. It was no secret however that they enjoyed the warm sun on their face, some even had their eyes closed in meditation. They were that calm that Anna went up and played with their long goatee beards and even started to plait one. A very, very fat pigmy pig called Sweet Pea slowly scoured her pen for anything resembling food. Tired of being asked if she was pregnant, the attendants had placed a sign stating that she was indeed "Not" in the motherly way and just really likes her food. Peacocks squawked from their perch on high, feathers shimmering in the sun. Female Ducks were scattering every which way, chased determinedly by male suitors, it must be spring. I was amazed at their rough house tactics. Certainly not gentleman ducks in this park. They were employing the not so subtle Cave-man approach to romance or should I say procreation. In the small bird enclosure Imogen sat quietly on a bench, holding out a finger. When we asked what she was doing she said she was waiting for the little birds to sit down and say hello. Beautiful! Just beautiful.

Before boarding the return ferry, we stopped off at Sidney, a small village on the coast facing back towards the mainland. Sailing boats plied the bay between the Channel Islands. Washington State's snowcapped mountains as their backdrop. It's a good thing that the trip back across the bay was peaceful because the thirty kilometre drive from the wharf to Kitsilano Beach took ninety minutes in heavy commuter traffic. Another reason why we love living in Townsville and not an oversized city. Our accommodation was on older end of the spectrum. A nondescript set of units in need of a significant renovation. It was drab but right on Cornwall Street and across the road from the beach. No need to move the car until we left town. Perfect! Due to the unseasonably good weather and Friday afternoon mix, the place was pumping with enthusiasm for the weekend. People out walking, kids playing in the park and a multitude of volleyball matches on the beach. We walked to Granville Island Markets to stock up on Parmesan cheese and a large bottle of anchovies for our Friday night homemade pizza tradition. Both commodities which have proved to be rare and expensive in the interior. Street performers provided the artistic soundtrack for the seagull's acrobatic food fights. I saw one poor gull swallow a large cardboard tub of mayonnaise before its unsuspecting owner could toss it into a bin. Now that is going to be an eye watering moment on the way out. By the sound of the surrounding accents there were more foreigners enjoying the day than locals. Back at the main beach we mucked around on the playground equipment then sat and watched a beach volleyball match. It was certainly fun to see all the twenty somethings fight for attention from the opposite sex. One bloke would take his shirt off, the rest would follow, then a young lady would remove her shorts to play in bikini bottoms, the rest would do the same. After all it was spring and a game on the beach beats butting heads like the elk or longhorn sheep. But interesting sociology all the same.

We didn't want to leave the coast but that was the deal, the holidays were drawing to an end. The Coquihalla was postcard perfect on our drive back and a pitstop at the park in Hope allowed us to take in the beauty of the little town. Adding to the attraction, we found that Sly Stallone filmed First Blood there in the early eighties. A friend back home had exchanged to Hope some time back and said the locals had been so welcoming and supportive throughout their year abroad. But all small towns are different.

The first stop in Blind Bay was the post box to see if my heavily anticipated Visa permission to teach had arrived. Sure, enough the brown envelope with a government emblem was there and sensing it was important, Imogen asked to open it. To my despair they were not allowing me to teach. This was a kick in the guts. I didn't want to talk about it for a while. I had told so many people that I would soon have my working visa and be ready to get into the classrooms of Canada. Now I would have to be content to watch from the sidelines. Whatever will be will be, I suppose.

After enjoying a fortnight continually with the girls, the tick of the clock and the drip in the downpipe were the only interruption to the deafening silence. I walked the streets in the hope that someone would be out in their front yard to have a chat with or just to see another human. No luck. Of course, my temporary boredom and loneliness is not really an issue compared with the hardships people endure around the world. This morning on the drive back from dropping the girls at school, I saw a man dressed in road control gear, hard hat and fluorescent vest. He was missing a leg and had no prosthetic limb, just a crude stick with a rubber stopper on the end. He was doing his job and had a smile on his face. I will never know this man's story but his triumph over adversity was inspiring. Just watching him limp along made me reflect on the resilience of mankind. A little further down the road, a father waited with his children at the bus stop. He was in the same spot every morning and I later found he had recently immigrated from South Africa. I pondered just how much the freedom and safety that rural Canada must provide and allow him to relax and breath. He must have to pinch himself every time he lets his children out to play in the neighbourhood without worry or the fact his family no longer live in a fenced off compound with armed guards patrolling the boundary. We are so fortunate in Australian but spend so little time being thankful for something or someone in our lives. A good habit to get into! As they say in Bhutan, the gross national happiness would rise exponentially.

Something that became glaringly obvious to me was the extent to which a nation's climate and geography shapes its people. I suppose it is obvious but for the first time in my life it was slapping me in the face. Being a tourist is so different than living somewhere. Even though Australians have similarities to Canadians, we are very different people. In this high-tech age where the popular media paradigm is focused on issues like driverless cars and drone postal services, few take the time out to reflect on what has shaped us as a race. What has made us unique. Sure, we know about the indigenous Australians, the British colonists and the prisoners, the European immigrants, the harsh and beautiful geography and our glorious weather. But we should not underestimate the influence and huge benefits of having no land borders and our relative isolation out in the middle of the South Pacific. I think collectively we are aware of all of these things but take it all for granted, as if our national identity just appeared out of thin air.

I had no idea that the majority of North Americans think Australia is that little country wedged between Italy and Germany where Mozart composed classics and Schwarzenegger started lifting weights. Or alternatively a desert island with lots of dangerous beasties poised to kill. This became apparent very early in the piece and was reinforced in conversations, media and text. To many Canadians we are still Terra Australis Incognita, the Unknown Southern Land. The fact that we have lakes, rivers, snow clad mountains, deep rainforest jungles and everything in between, has somehow not crossed the Pacific. Likewise, there are many unexpected differences between Australians and the people who call Canada home. If I had to choose two defining cultural determinants, the first would be that Canadians have a very, very diverse mix of ethnic groups with reasonably large population percentages. Australia is a multicultural society but in comparison to Canada, our subcultures are small minorities. Without delving too deep into the statistics, it is safe to say that around ninety percent of Australians have descended from the British Isles while only around thirty percent of Canadians. The U.S and French influence cannot be understated. The other intriguing discovery is that the very dominant French population are similar in size to Scottish and Irish with Germans not far behind. It begs many questions of why the French are so dominant and explains some of the internal tensions.

By April 6, I had joined the earth on 50 revolutions of the Sun. So, time to reflect. The son of a third-generation sugar cane farmer, it does sadden me that I was the one who moved away from the family profession and that intrinsic connection to the land. Deep down I knew that farming wasn't for me, although I loved many aspects of the lifestyle. The family farm had sustained us. I love the genuine honesty of it all and how it contributed overwhelmingly to my upbringing. I had the privilege of growing up with Grandparents on both sides of the family and could not image my childhood without them. Maybe it was because I was a good listener, curious and eager to learn, that I gained so much from our relationships. Each Grandparent brought something special to the table and very few days go by without remembering them. Growing up having a stable family life is also something I took for granted, as a normal. Of course, in our world it is increasingly not the case. Mum and Dad did everything for us kids and we had the most wonderful free, salt encrusted, sun drenched childhood living between the beach and the farm. Camping, fishing, music, sport, art and loads of playmates. Many have now passed on, our family is very small and dispersed, which leaves a hole that cannot be repaired just lived with. I am blessed with my own family. My girls are the focus of almost everything I do.

Sensing that fifty was a big number, Imogen innocently said "I hope you never grow old Mummy and Daddy". I felt like saying "Don't we all wish that sweetheart" but as a tear welled in my eye, I left it at that. I know each moment together is precious, from the highs and great adventures to the everyday. A friend sent me an email that said, with all the advances to science and medicine, fifty is the new thirty-five. Now I like the sound of that. I am optimistic about the future and, like my Dad, am intrigued by each discovery and advancement.

Over the years I have very much enjoyed the radio snapshot of what happened this day in history. Especially on my Birthday. It always brings a smile to my face to know I have something in common with others and historical events. I share birthdays with the famous escape artist Harry Houdini and the US outlaw Butch Cassidy, who is exactly 100 years older than I (although his birthdate fluctuates a few days either side of the 6th depending on the source). The Scottish produced the Declaration of Arbroath on this day in 1320 proclaiming independence and an attempt to get rid of the influence of the feudal English Norman Kings, this battle continues today. Something I previously did not know, was that on the exact year and date of my birth, Australia had its most prominent UFO encounter. Over 200 students, teachers and general public in and around the Westall High School witnessed an unexplained ship land and take off on the oval in broad daylight. The events that followed were intriguing and included an attempted cover up by the school and RAAF which involved alleged threats to teachers to keep quiet. When I was in trouble as a boy, Mum would often say "I don't know where we found you" well now we may have an answer. I might just be a piece of lost cargo from when that silver orb made a hasty getaway?

Uncannily, the local radio station ran a story on the 2015 UFO sightings data and reported that there had been a large increase in the previous twelve months. This piqued my curiosity and a search revealed recounts of some local activity. I found a story about a sleepless man, living in the neighbouring village of Vernon. He got more than he bargained for when looking for the Northern Lights. He was outside in his yard facing north when two bright orbs appeared low on the horizon. They were flying in his direction then all of a sudden swerved to make a sharp 90 degree turn and sped off. I have an open mind to such things, but I did make a mental note that we are living in a renowned wine region and it was late at night. Another story was about a young couple from Kamloops reporting a sighting of a Boomerang shaped object with illuminated edges. It flew above their home and then with a flash disappeared over the horizon. I thought to myself "Boomerang shaped? Might be some government incorporating age old Australian technology into a new high-tech jet?"

By 11a.m. I gave up waiting for the sunshine, donned several layers of clothing and ventured out for a walk. Finally, the local restaurant was open for business and the ten-minute walk there meant easy access. I decided to book a table for Friday night so I could celebrate with the girls and have a night off cooking. The lady who took my reservation noticed the 1966 ending to my mobile phone number and commented it was a good year. I figured she might be around my age so acknowledged that it was and revealed that it was indeed my birthday. We were equally pleased with our common ground; she was also an April baby and wished me a happy birthday. Nothing like a bit of positive human contact to lift the spirits, I left with a bit of a spring in my step. When Friday evening rolled around, our friends Tori and Aiden joined us for a meal at the restaurant down the road. Great setting and friendly staff. After the meal we were invited around for a bonfire. It was a cool night, but the large fire quickly chased it off. We had marshmallows and the traditional Canadian treat S'mores, which consist of two crackers (biscuits) with a piece of chocolate and a molten marshmallow in between. Now there is a calorie laden sandwich which a nutritionist has never prescribed.

Less than an hour drives down the highway, towards Kamloops, is the BC Wildlife Park. On our visit we saw many of the animals on our list. A glimpse in the wild is wonderful and memorable but a zoo affords you the time to just sit and observe. An added bonus were the cheeky chipmunks and marmots zipping in and out of enclosures and the picnic tables making sure they avoided the bear cage. Cute and not silly. The Raccoons are still one of our favourites, they posed for the camera and pushed each other off benches. One caused a kerfuffle when he sat on his roommates while he was fast asleep. The coyote, wolf, lynx and bobcat were great to see but the elegant and arrogant cougar prowling around demanded more attention. The moose and bison sheer size always stops me for an extended look. The pure white mountain goat and long horn sheep lazed in the sun. Late in the day, after a ride on the train, we walked back past the Grizzly enclosure. No one else was around and as we passed, one of these enormous creatures walked right up to us and sat down about a meter away, with only a weld mesh cage and thin railing between. He looked us in the eye as we spoke to him quietly and seemed to be enjoying the encounter as much as we were. He mouthed some gentle noises then snarled and snapping his fangs at a bee that buzzed around him. Then lashed out with a paw, swatted it to the ground and through it down his gob, before returning to his calm pose. What a special experience.

On the Sunday we headed across the river to Roderick Haig-Brown Provincial Park which runs along the banks of the Adams river before it collides with Shuswap Lake. The last time I drove into the carpark, it was covered in ice and I wondered how well my winter tyres would work as I spun them desperately not wanting to become stranded in the subzero temps. Along the road we spotted a professional looking sign which advertised a "Float Boat Show". Now if the boat doesn't float, you've got problems. I am sure the locals know what the sign means but it gave us a good laugh. After a picnic lunch sitting in the glorious full sun, something no one does in Queensland, we hiked over the lower section of the trails. It cut through dense forest then followed the rapids of the Adams River past viewing platforms and secluded park benches. Thousands of visitors flock here each October to view one of North America's most impressive and important salmon runs. At the entrance to the trail a sign reminded us that we are in cougar country along with a temporary sign screwed to a post warning of recent bear sightings. The locals have not been too concerned or forthcoming about protocol only to say, "try not to startle them". We did see another garter snake, but this time a western version with different colouring, and a rather large, dashingly dressed, Northern Leopard Frog. The ever-present Canadian Geese wandered around the banks, honking loudly to warn us away from their eggs. Many of the trees near the river were wrapped in chicken mesh, no doubt to deter determined beaver. What surprised me was that even very large trees with a diameter of over two meters were covered. I wonder how long that would take our bucky friends to gnaw through? On the drive back we stopped to check out a herd of deer on the roadside and took some photos of the Spring wildflowers.

Each day brought on more delights of Spring. On Sunday the lake was void of wind and lay glassy within its banks. Equipt with Kayaks, kindly lent to us by Richard and Petra, we drove down to

Reedman point. Nice and close to our house and more importantly the closest point on the south bank of the Shuswap to Copper Island. There were a few boats trailing fishing lines, slowly crisscrossing the bay and the odd Canadian goose honking its delight at the warmer weather. Imogen sat in the front of my kayak and leaned back on my legs for a comfortable ride. I remember boating as a kid, sitting up the front of Dad's, half cabin cruiser. I loved looking at the bottom on those calm days, the water was clear revealing all types of marine life. Copper Island is 1.3 kilometer off the coast, and I had not intended to go all the way out, but the kayaks were well balanced and seemed to cut through the water well. Before we knew it, we were halfway across and it seemed the girls had already decided that we were going all the way. We landed on a small rocky beach on the east side of the island. Having taken no footwear, we only did a short hike. The moss-covered rocks and large tree canopy provided a pleasant landscape with views out to various points on the north shore. The signs said that bears often swim out to the island for part of the year, so we made sure we kept up the noise. Not hard to do with a very vocal six-year-old. We had morning tea back at the kayaks and then headed back. Halfway across we stopped to watch a happy angler reel in a decent sized trout.

Excited about the possibilities opened up by the kayaks I set about working out a safer way to strap them onto the roof racks to allow trips further afield. After visiting all the hardware stores in the district, I finally found a removalists trolley. A quick remodeling with a cutting disc on the angle grinder and we had our own kayak wheels, making access to the shore less of an issue and avoiding having our arms stretched out of our shoulder sockets. A set of new straps completed the outfitting. When recounting our adventure back at work the next day, Anna was told how silly we were to go out when the water was still so cold, that it would have been dangerous to capsize. My goodness this place is hard to engage with. Maybe we should all take up knitting in front of the fire.

Tori and Aiden came over for dinner and we had a great night. They are really nice people and their willingness to engage with us was thoroughly appreciated. They seemed to have similar interests and views on life. It is nice to be making some friends. They invited us down to their parent's lake house near the US border which will be really nice. They also came with a boot load of dry firewood which I will put to good use. All the talk in town has been about the unseasonably warm weather. Hasn't been this warm since early 1900's and they don't seem prepared for it. Even though most of the snow had melted from the surrounding peaks it was still very cool during the day. A lot of the sporting groups start up after May and most have truly wound up within sixteen weeks by the end of August. I think it would take me several lifetimes to get use to this restrictive climate. If you choose to go away for the Summer break you cannot participate in many of the sporting opportunities.

Turtle Valley Donkey refuge had an open day on the weekend. They were raising funds selling plants and aged donkey manure. I should have bought a bag to accompany Imogen in the back seat. Then she would have something tangible to complain about. On our way we spotted some furry little animals scurrying across the road at the edge of Phillips Lake. They were only about two hundred millimetres long and ran on all fours, unlike chipmunks and squirrels, who hop around. It was too small for a Marmot, so we had a mystery. Back at work Anna asked her aide who suggested a Hedgehog but when we checked a photo it was nothing like our mystery beast. We started to research. Too small to be a Badger, not quite a Marten or a Stoat weasel. It sure looked like a Groundhog but wasn't large enough. Too big for a Vole. Not a Fisher or a Mink and definitely not a Mole. Gee they have plenty of little furry things around here. We were happy to add another animal sighting but couldn't quite identify it.

    I ventured into the local outdoors store in town to get some safety gear for the kayak. I thought safety had gone slightly over the top in Australia but making an adult wear a lifejacket and carry a bailing container, whistle and recovery rope on a lake seemed to be over the top. I had also heard that I needed a license to fish so I asked the lady at the cashier station. She said, "well there are different rates, sounds like you are an Alien so it will cost $80 for one year." I smiled and told her that I was feeling particularly Alien that day and may even have developed a green tinge on my skin. I'm not sure she got the joke but did find out that kids under fifteen don't need a license so I figured I would trail a line out the back and tell the Fisheries officer I am just helping Imogen reel in the fish. She told me that a cougar was spotted last week at Cedar Heights, close to the house we are staying in. I wonder what the protocol is from the authorities. Do they trap and release when predators are close to built up communities or just warn people and leave them be? There are a lot of young children playing around in their backyards and a playground not far from the sighting. It is a worry. I stayed to browse for a while and found a hunter's picture chart with all BC's fur critters. Inadvertently I solved my mystery mammal quandary. Staring back at me with its motley furred face was a muskrat.

Not far from Blind Bay, across the highway, down some back roads toward the garbage dump, Recline Ridge winery sits aptly beside rows of vines which were just starting to show the blush of new buds. To our surprise, it was open, and a steady stream passed through the cellar door. This small-scale boutique winery offered us the most comprehensive tasting I have ever had. Six white, six red and two desert whites. Being one of the most northern latitude wineries in the world they have been forced to grow cold hardy grapes, most varieties of which I had never heard. Almost all were to our liking, no we are not alcoholics. Of particular note was the Ortega, a blend of two Madeleine varieties and a Rose blended from Pinot Noir and Marechal Foch grapes. We grabbed a few bottles and since it was sunny, indulged in a glass of wine and slab of local smoked cheese on the patio. I just sat back and soaked in my surroundings, surely the mountains and sunbathed vineyards made a good wine taste better. Some of my best travel memories are sitting back in stunning locations having a drink to celebrate a great day's adventure. Like in a rocking chair on the front porch of Roosevelt Lodge in Yellowstone sipping a Mountain Mist. We still have the serviette that Anna scribbled down the cocktail recipe. Monterey wharf and that concoction that hit us like a sledgehammer, don't remember too much after that. Something about tasting all the free clam chowder that was shoved in our hands by eager restaurateurs. This left me to ponder why I had never heard of Canadian wines or seen them for sale anywhere else in the world. Back home we have a very strong domestic wine industry that produces a very high-quality product. But that doesn't mean we don't try anything else. There is of course a proliferation of very good New Zealand wine and we have had the occasional curious foray into both Chilean and South African wines, but no Canadian. When in the U.S we seek Italian offerings because we find the local drop far too sweet but thankfully there is change in the air. Some years back, I mentioned this to an Australian wine-maker plying his trade in the Sonoma region in California, he was giving us a rather nice tasting at his cellar door and was matching each wine with a small hors d'oeuvre which to my surprise really enhanced the taste. But when I mentioned the wines were much sweeter than the same varieties elsewhere, he gave me a look that would make a bunch of grapes shrivel up and fall off the vine. Maybe he had just swallowed a bad olive. On arrival I was very keen to compare Canadian wines and it was a pleasant surprise to find out we would be living next to the Okanagan Valley, the premier wine growing region in the country.

Yes, I like a glass or two in the evening, that may be part of the DNA from Dad, only he preferred Beer and my dislike for it must have been a bit confronting to him. On the occasion that Dad had a few too many he was a happy drunk. The best type to be. I vividly recall one Friday night when I was around nine or ten, my Mum, sister and I were watching some TV and we heard Dad's old truck roll up the driveway. Moments later a frozen chook came rolling through the door, skidding across the tiles. He had won it in a spin the wheel raffle at the pub and stayed on longer than expected. The frozen fowl had dual purpose, both peace offering and an advance party rolled into one. Something to gauge whether the inhabitants were hostile or not and grease their palms to ensure safe passage. Dad followed not long after with a big grin.

Chase was the next village, west along the Trans Canada. A small community perched between the highway and the

Thompson River had a railway slicing through its centre. Like so many small towns in North America and Australia for that matter, it appeared to be down on its luck and in decline. Businesses were closed. For Sale signs plastered across shop fronts and a general look of deterioration pervaded. Old timers sauntered around the streets. But I did not come for the town itself. Twenty-two shades of grey, at least that is what the hiking group I joined for the day should have been called. I met a small group of fellow hikers on the Pine Street Bridge. They were parked waiting for our fearless leader Al, who I had only spoken to on the phone. Soon enough he pulled up in the middle of the road, as one does in these parts, and ushered us to follow the convoy of some thirteen cars already in tow. This was starting to look serious. They pulled up at the Adams River Secwepemc First Nations Band office to pay the Chief for the privilege to access the meadow beyond. Al appeared from his large 4wd, clad in a knee brace for each leg and a padded sling protecting his broken arm, complements of a recent fall. Al was seventy-five years young and a real trooper. He welcomed all, told us the plan and went through the safety considerations. This was my first foray into Adams River Indian Band land and what struck me first were the street signs in both English and Secwepemc Nation language. Next to the Band office was Chief Atahm School which I had phoned regarding a visit some months back. It is a native language immersion school catering for children from prep through to Year Twelve. It was run by parents, elders and some teaching staff who deliver several pathways. The hiking group consisted of mainly over sixty-five-year olds, all seemed to be happy and many welcomed me with a chat. We then drove to the Neskonlith Hills which were ablaze with the large, corn cob yellow flowering Arrowleaf

Balsamroot which only bloom for a short time at the start of Spring. I took many photos, but the composition of three bands of colour, the grass, the flowers and the sky provided the most special graphic memento. The walk was only gentle, which suited me fine as I had the opportunity to chat with several people along the way, all with their own story and their very welcome bits of travel advice. One of the ladies mentioned that she had a friend who moved to Melbourne and was shocked that her house was infested with cockroaches. I had to smile, yes we do have bugs and the further up into the tropics you go the more bugs you will encounter, but if you are infested with roaches anywhere in the world, it is a good bet that you need to look at your own hygiene and set some traps. Nice of her to say though! I had noticed more stink beetles in the house over here than cockroaches back home.

Mobile phones. Cell phones to North Americans. I am proud to say I held off owning one for a long time and have really only carried one for the last few years. I still see it as an optional accessory and often leave it at home. No, I certainly do not suffer from FOMO. However, since being abroad I have been slightly better at checking the missed calls box, primarily because I was hoping someone would call with something exciting to do rather than my cooking, washing and cleaning regime. As it happened on that rainy Friday, buoyed by the anticipation of another weekend adventuring with the girls, I sat sipping a macchiato at the mall after the grocery run. I hadn't turned the volume up from the previous night so was surprised to find two missed calls. Now I didn't know too many people and less knew my number. Two calls in short order probably ruled out telemarketers so I figured they really wanted to talk to me. I called back. It was Richard who answered, he had been out for a walk and was asked by a neighbour if he could recommend anyone to rebuild her deck. She had acquired a quote from a builder and didn't want to part with an arm and a leg. I was keen for a project and some extra cash, so jumped straight in the car. We went around to check out the deck, meet the client and measure up. Bridget was a sweet old lady and very happy when I agreed to do the job for half the labour costs as her previous quote, as long as it was cash. I am not sure why, but when Richard yelled out measurements in feet and inches, I just wrote them down on my sketch. It took me quite some time to transpose to metric later. Richard also kindly lent me his Ford F-150 and the tools I needed for the deck job. Driving that beast back took a bit of getting used to but his act of generosity was not lost on me.

A visit to the hardware store was an exercise in patience and an opportunity to smile through adversity, confusion and translation difficulties. It made me wonder how comical things could get doing the same task in a country that didn't speak English. Charades for tradesman! But back to Canada. If I have to work in imperial beyond twelve inches it becomes tedious and they didn't comprehend or acknowledge metric as a mode of measurement at all, even though the country became metric in 1970! There is much resistance to metric and that US influence of course. The planks came in 16-foot lengths and the screws are sold in pounds weight not in quantity. As chance would have it, they had sixty length of an end of production decking they were almost giving away at cost. I zipped back to the house to work out the quantities and purchased the timber before someone else did.

I arrived at Bridget's early the following morning wearing every coat I could find including a big old jacket I found hanging up in the garage. It was three sizes too big and covered in dust. I was ready for the demolition phase equipped with an 8-pound fireman's hammer and crowbar. I like to have heavy artillery because I think the nails come out easier when they are intimidated. I found Bridget out in her garden planting Dahlias. She explained that they are the large "Dinner Plate" type and come out in August through to October. I will have to drive by and have a look. The demolition went to plan except for a couple of bearers that needed replacing and the fact that the handrail was installed after the deck meant that all the bordering deck timber was skew nailed or concealed under the posts. In fact, the handrail was in very bad shape and only being held together by several multicoloured coats of paint, wood filler and good luck. I mentioned this to Bridget, and she agreed to rip it down. I think she knew that it may have had to be replaced. I left that for the next day and headed to the dump with the overloaded ute, crossing my fingers that I wouldn't get caught and fined. Bridget was eighty and had built and lived in the house for over twenty-five years. She told me of her emigration from England as a ten-year-old just after the war and her love for gardening. It was indeed an impressive one surrounding her home. I asked if I could bring my girls over for a look. The house was built in the late eighties and would fit in anywhere today, a timeless design. A real feat. It incorporated many angles and interesting roof lines. I complimented her on her house, and she revealed that they hired a young architect from Calgary who came and camped on the sight for a week to get a feel of the block and how the elements would affect his design. She loved it but feared it may be hard to sell because it was so different. I doubt she will have a problem.

On Saturday we attended a sixth birthday party. Games, lollies and happy kids playing in the sun. Sorrento park was hidden away down a side road. Bordered by a stream running across the back and circled by mountains in almost every direction. Sunday was an equally beautiful day. We met Richard and Petra on their pontoon boat at the marina. Talk about luxury, surrounded with padded seats, bimini cover and a relatively quiet outboard, we cruised out of Blind Bay checking out the flash homes from our mariner's vantage point. Many are only lived in a few months of the year and certainly have great outlooks. The lake had risen at least a metre over the previous fortnight and the beach where we launched the kayaks a few weeks back looked so different, filled with people delighted to break out their summer clothes and togs. The lake is at its highest toward the end of Spring due to the massive snow melt and drops gradually over Summer and Fall. We motored around to a clearing on Copper Island and did the circumnavigation hike, which took a leisurely hour. Richard asked Imogen to take the lead which she thought was great. She yelled out track reports for her followers "Narrow section! Steep!". We played a game to see how many different wildflowers she could find and was particularly fond of the orange tipped Indian Paintbrushes. To our delight we came across wild strawberries and blueberries growing along the path. What a different dynamic does to a kid's outlook. When she is alone with us, she complains at the suggestion of a hike. She raced ahead and would have happily gone around again. Back at the house we tried to identify the birds we encountered and discovered the ruddy brown chested birds we constantly admired in the backyard were Robins. Curiously they catch their prey then stand erect to attention, as if to show it off. The other smaller ones were Chickadees.

On the way to school the next day we were talking about our great weekend and our hike over Copper Island. Imogen said, "What hike, we were just looking for flowers!"

A nice surprise for the girls when Samantha asked if Imogen would like to go hiking with Hannah's Scout group up to the White Lake lookout. Both mum and daughter jumped at the opportunity. White Lake has been underwater filmed by National Geographic due to it being one of the top three lakes in North America for water clarity. The lake was named after its stunning white clay base that anecdotally was used by the National Air Force as a bearing at night, especially when the moon made it glow. Despite this, the fishing and water clarity had diminished over the last few decades and local conservation groups were banding together to remove noxious vegetation. They also have found that feeder creek flow has been reduced by beaver dams which in turn has affected fish spawning. Those critters are just too efficient. The authorities are starting to lower the dams, I wonder what the beaver make of all this? The girls reported that the hike was steep, and both enjoyed the all-girl outing.

The local free newspaper had a heading which read "Start of Bear Jam season". Before I could read further my brain started to visualise what this unusual combination of the words could possibly mean. Was it something you spread on toast or a strange preserved bear meat or even a bear bone marrow stock perfect for next year's winter soups? I have seen far stranger things eaten. When I read further, it explained that in Spring, the black bear population frequents the sides of the highway eating the nice green grass and wild berries. Thrilled commuters often hit the brakes and stop in the middle of the road to get a happy snap. An impromptu roadblock without warning! We experienced this some years back in Yellowstone National Park. The cars in front would hit the brakes and all jump out of the vehicle feverishly clicking their cameras. But in their defense, it was in a fifty kilometre zone and to be expected in that famous park. That newspaper was certainly informative and entertaining. One aging contributor relayed in her weekly column that herself and several of her friends were looking forward to the upcoming legalisation of Marijuana. A liberal thinking Grandma indeed.

During my visits to town I started to spot women and girls dressed in old fashioned pilgrim style attire. Hems to the ankle, white aprons and bonnet. I suspected some religious order but was not sure. Maybe they were members of a local theatre company drumming up support for their coming production of Oklahoma? It certainly wasn't a new fashion trend. Stories and visuals of the Amish have always intrigued me. In particular, their well-known rejection of modern technology. On my previous visits to the continent I have always wanted to visit a community to satisfy my curiosity, but the stars haven't aligned, and it has not been practical to our itinerary. A few weeks later I came across the same attire at a market stall in town selling honey and jams under a Mennonite Church banner. With that puzzle solved I wanted to know more about them. The Mennonite and Amish originated from the same Anabaptists of Europe but formed splinter groups in 1693. I was not sure what the local community customs were. Did they live in a separate community or integrated? Did they shun technology?

Mother's Day was upon us, so we treated Anna to a weekend at Nakusp Hot Springs. A three-hour drive southeast including a ferry trip across Arrow Lake. It had been booked several weeks in advance and we had all been excited about the journey as well as the destination. I picked the girls up straight after school and told them to make sure they had all the necessaries in order as we needed to catch the 5pm ferry or sit on the bank until 6. The sun was not setting until half past eight at that time of the year, which was a bonus. Our route headed east towards Revelstoke as we crisscrossed the rail line. Back home we are not impacted much by trains but in Canada interruptions are a big gripe and when in company, someone invariably brings up the topic of crossing wait length and no wonder. They seemed to go on forever and some research revealed we were not imagining it. In the 1990's some rail executive decided that longer trains would increase efficiency. Now the average, not the longest, train is over one and a half kilometres. It is not uncommon to see them stretch over four kilometers. Now that is enough time to play a game of cards and order a pizza while waiting at the crossing.

We turned right just before Revelstoke and rushed headlong through wild mountain passes, arriving with ten minutes to spare before boarding the ferry from Shelter Bay to Galena. The free twenty-five-minute cruise allowed time to stretch our legs and take in views of Arrow Lake and surrounding craggy peaks. There was much more residual snow at this higher altitude. The wind had a chill from its encounter with said peaks, but strategically positioned behind the wheelhouse, bathed in the afternoon sun, all was good. Several fellow travellers wore singlets and boardshorts, which had me reminiscing Friday afternoon ferry crossings of Cleveland Bay to Magnetic Island, one of our favourite places just off the coast of our hometown. As nice as the Rocky Mountains beckon, there was part of sun worshipper in me that wished I was heading to Maggie for the weekend, dinner at

Bungalow Bay and two days on the beach. But I knew that would be a reality soon enough.

The well paved road to Nakusp, hugged the mountains. Several deer were out enjoying new shoots of grass on the edges. Before checking in, we strolled down to the foreshore for a look. Heavily flowering shrubs encroached the path, their heady scent pervading the promenade which perched on a steep bank yielding uninterrupted lake views. The vast body of water was spotted with organic, ever changing patterns created by clusters of floating logs, at the will of the wind. Its beauty stopped us in our tracks. A group of teenage girls giggled and splashed at the water's edge. They were a part of the Province Girls Soccer tournament to be help over the weekend. The motor inn facade was typical 50's bland box architecture. Weathered boards and little to no landscaping or aesthetic appeal, but we had read reviews. This was the best in town, and it was very reasonably priced. Inside had obviously been through a recent refurbishment. It was spacious and clean with a little kitchen. The girls were happy and like the saying goes "Happy wife, happy life".

Built in the 60's, the council run Nakusp Hot Springs had two pools which bubbled away at 38 and 41 degrees respectively. These crystal-clear ponds were wrapped in a semi-circular building, a wonderful feel of yesteryear. Clad in boards washed in a kind of faded military green, creosote hue. Sun bleached cerulean blue Adirondack chairs and sun loungers lined the perimeter with a backdrop of deep green fir. Pan pipes drifted on the breeze, just audible above the gurgling nearby creek and the frenzied chatter of a dozen tiny hummingbirds on a sugar high. Sounds like a set for an over exuberant movie director, but it was real. The lady at the front desk said she topped up the bird feeders twice a day.

Must be good stuff. I think if I had to flap my arms fifty times a second, I would need a constant stream of sucrose as well. While changed into hiking shoes in the carpark, two SUV's pulled up. Each emptied out young men with long bushranger beards and modern casual clothing. You could have mistaken them for Hipsters until their female companions emerged. They wore elaborate head scarfs, the type one associates with Queen Guinevere and the medieval period. A roll of fabric formed a crown from which a bright purple cloth draped over their necks. Skirts to the ankle completed the look. Hmm, I pondered the transport and clothing. It did not match Amish or Mennonite ideals. Earlier I had seen a poster in town advertising a Medieval weekend in July, but surely people don't visit the springs in costume two months early. I was later told they may have been from the Hutterite community, another Anabaptist offshoot. This was certainly becoming an education in the diversity of religion. As part of the Hutterite teachings, all married men are required to grow beards and although scarfs are normally black or black and white polka dot, I did see some colourful versions online. I mean every club has its trendsetters. A track led off the car park and along the creek to a solid timber covered bridge with views of the river foaming and bashing its way downstream. Further on we followed a zigzag path up the mountain to the original hot springs. Donkeys once ferried the patrons but now the forest is quiet except for the chirp of chipmunks and the wind.

    We spent the afternoon back in downtown Nakusp. Despite it being Mother's Day weekend, we almost had the place to ourselves, so dawdled through interesting shops and strolled along the lakefront path. A float plane taxied then dashed east over the snow frosted peaks. I drifted off in thought wondering what they were doing, where they were going and how great the view would be up there. Onwards down the steep concreted embankment to the solitary sandy strip below. It had been some time since we had sand between our toes. Imogen beachcombed the jet black and ivory white polished river stones. From our vantage point we spotted an old tavern perched in prime position; its large deck had unobstructed lake views. Impressive! We promptly booked a table for dinner. The Leland Hotel was built in 1899 and is now the oldest standing hotel in Canada. The building techniques and style of architecture leave no doubt about its British colonial past. It should have been no surprise, I mean if you are a fresh Pom tasked with building a Pub on a lake, it is probably going to mimic the style of the mother country's watering holes. Surprisingly the only dry white wine on the list was from New Zealand's Marlborough region, one of our favourites. A band in the public bar belted out some well-known tunes, the music drifting out to the deck. As we were leaving the main street "Broadway" was eerily quiet, it resembled an old western town from the movies where the locals were all hiding prior to a gunfight. But there were no cowboy's in Nakusp on that Saturday night. No one at all.

The draw of another dip in a hot spring was too great on Sunday morning so we backtracked to Halcyon. A modern resort with accommodation and a restaurant, but less history and patina than Nakusp. The pools were similar temperatures to the previous day but easier to linger longer due to the cooler overcast weather. Flamenco music complimented the scene for the family-oriented crowd. As I did my best hippopotamus impersonation in the sparsely populated warmer of the two pools, I watched Anna jump into the ice bath then scurry back to the warm pool. Brave or crazy? I still haven't worked it out, but she did it a second time and tried to coerce me to follow suit. Yeah right! The altitude was not high enough that I could conclude oxygen deprivation. Afterwards we travelled south and crossed the lake via the short Fauquier ferry ride. The drive through the Monashee Mountains to Vernon was very windy but offered great views of roadside rivers and spring blooms. Snow still congregated in patches along our path and we were fortunate to spot a vibrantly coloured Ring Necked Pheasant waddling along the roadside. They are the ones you see in European artwork, strung up in kitchens ready for the pot. These fancy game birds no doubt found their way to North America with Europeans, however they originate from Asia. They have lived in these woods for so long that many think they are a native species.

Imogen took a liking to the proliferation of garden snails with their distinctive mustard and caramel, swirled shells. They appeared in the gardens and school grounds in unison with the Dandelions and other spring life. When visiting me at my construction project, she found a tiny one in Bridget's garden and kept it in a little pink basket overnight before its excursion to school the next day to be shown off to her friends. Twinkle, as she affectionately dubbed the invertebrate, made it through class time, recess and big lunch, but during library time he absconded and was now reading his way through the entire horticultural section while avoiding the French culinary collection. To say that Imogen was displeased would be an understatement, as she dragged me around the back yard after school in search of a replacement specimen. For some unknown reason they had vanished. I suspect that news had got out that this poor male snail was being tortured. Given the name Twinkle, placed in a hot pink basket and humiliated in front of all the year two girls screaming

"Oh yuck I can't touch that". Enough to give any animal the will to grow a backbone and get the hell out of there.

I finally completed Bridget's deck and was very happy with the outcome. So was she. The neighbourhood had been watching my progress for the last three weeks, no doubt something to talk about. I thought maybe I would get some more work, the deck being a good advertisement. The job ended up being twice the size of the original quote but will now last for many years to come. Functioning within the Canadian system was an ever-present challenge. Most things are different in varying degrees. Dumping requires meticulous separation of timber, metal and general waste. I don't think too many builders back home would put up with it. Time is money and it took too much time. The tools, I had been so lucky to have access to, were different to what I would use at home and this meant compromise and adaptation which kept me thinking. As mentioned, forays to the hardware store became a comical diversion to the day. Before I entered, I would jot down my list, convert it to imperial and consider the size of the timber before it was dressed all round. Curiously they don't sell timber at what size it is, but what it used to be, before it was dressed? Like buying a fish at the weight it used to be before it was gutted. I also filled my head with several alternate words that could be quickly interchanged to describe what I needed so when I got the predictable blank look, I could spit out the other descriptions until the shop assistant called BINGO. Well not quite, but we had the most wonderful conversations, which regularly resembled a Monty Python skit. One day I walked in and asked for some treated 2 x 4-inch boards. The nice man gave me a confused look and after a prolonged silence he said, "we have 4 x 2's?" I said, "well that will do just fine, I will have some of them instead". We were both smiling at this stage. He because he has been helpful, me because, well you just have to smile in those situations. While I waited for the order to be processed, a box on the counter caught my eye. It was a Mole trap which looked nasty with the word "KILL" in large red letters across the top of the box leaving no confusion about its purpose. I thought to myself, I would hate to have the gruesome task of removing the dead mole. Better that than being the mole I suppose! The device resembled one of those full body torture traps called an Iron Maiden. Gruesome indeed. At home we have a much more peaceful strategy. Just the smell of our Beagle, Coco, in the yard is enough to keep the Bandicoots from digging up the lawn and the Possums out of the Pawpaw trees. If only they knew she was deaf and slept through the night like a log.

This carpentry job had been good for my headspace and wallet. Great to get out and about, meet people and get active. I hoped there would be more opportunities. By 2.30 that Friday, I had returned Bridget's place to how I found it, taken a few pictures to show the folks at home and was out of there. In a hurry to wind everything up before the weekend, I had skipped lunch and morning tea, so when the girls picked me up, we headed straight to the Marina Grill on the bay down from the house. We sat on the deck quaffing the local vino and appeased Imogen with a bowl of hot chips. She wanted to go and play. We had a great chat with the waitress about our two countries while watching the table next to ours knock down frozen margaritas with short upturned bottles of Corona beer jammed into the icy top. When I enquired, the manager said they were called Bull's Horns and, with a smile, told me not to introduce them to Australia. As if they didn't pinch them from south of the border down Mexico way!

Following an advert in the paper, the next day we drove out to the local Heritage Village with a promise of a pancake breakfast on the opening day. Well it was very quiet indeed, nothing special was happening and with only one other family there, it was a bit of a ghost town. The displays were good and in particular the school house brought back memories of my early years of education in a one teacher school. The individual timber desks, wide bare timber floors and words to "God save the Queen" written neatly on the blackboard, showing the conformity of Colonial British outposts.

On Sunday we took the kayaks to Skmana Lake, north of Chase. Having traveled through Skylax and down a dirt logging road, for about forty minutes, we were glad to see the small unobtrusive sign on the right leading to a pristine lake setting. The type of visual you see in outdoors magazines and wish there was a place name in the fine print so you can track it down. Well that's what I would do anyway. A group of friendly campers had prime position at water's edge. A fire smoked away on which one woman cooked bannock wrapped around a metal fork. They offered to help unload the kayaks, but I proudly had it under control with the DIY trolley, things went very smoothly. We pushed off from the bank in no time at all. The still morning air and glass flat lake allowed the mountains to stand back and admire their own beauty. Our craft slid along at an easy pace, on the lookout for wildlife above and below. Each drip off our paddles created ever increasing circular ripples. Before long a family of shy Western Painted Turtles came into view, lined up on a log and gave brief glimpses of their red under carapace as they plopped into the cool waters. We cruised over three large beaver lodges, the clear water allowing us an extensive view. Very impressive and something we will never forget. The sheer volume and size of the trees used must be one of mother nature's most impression architectural feats. Further on we startled a mother duck and her brood. She let us know in no uncertain terms that she was plenty displeased with us scaring her young. The ducklings swam every which way and took quite a while to herd. Sorry Duck but it was great to watch a good mother at work. We paddled through a narrow lane between the reeds which opened to the larger of the two lakes. A Common Loon entertained us with its beautiful black and white plume and diving skills. On a smaller scale, but no less spectacular, we watched blue dragonflies swoop down and pluck tadpoles from the lake surface. I had no idea this was part of the food chain.

Feeling very happy with our mornings nature immersion we paddled back to the car. On the way to Blind Bay we deciding to take an alternate route via Chase and took the opportunity to turnoff to Neskonlith Lake for a picnic lunch. Campers were dispersed along the northern shore in various levels of sophistication, all seemed to be having a good time. It was a much larger lake with steep banks and plenty of open water. The wild roses were blooming, their simple, delicate, pink flowers popping against the dense green forest understory. Lupins of white, blue and pink appeared spasmodically, as did various other colourful specimens we could not yet identify. Back in Chase I remembered reading about a walk which started from the grocery store and went under the highway via a drainage tunnel. We pulled up just in time to see two women disappear into the drain so quickly followed. Another adventure beckoned. Usually I am prepared for our walks complete with map, distance and trail notes but we decided to just wing it. Once through the tunnel, a small sign on a timber stake heralded "Welcome to Fairy Laneway- Please enjoy the treasures and magic that has been placed along this path. We, the Fairy Believers, ask that you look with your eyes and touch with your heart". This unexpected treat came out of the blue and Imogen crept along for half an hour, spotting all things fairy. Little houses embedded in moss covered rocks, tiny fairy clothing lying in the underbrush. Feathers dyed in brilliant colours hung from prime spots and painted river stones wedged in crevices. The trees seemed to lean in, enjoying the proceedings as much as we were and adding to the atmosphere. On cue, several butterflies danced along the path with us. One even stopped on a bracken frond and allowed us to gently brush its wings. I half expected a unicorn to shyly peak at us through the greenery. We never found the track to the waterfall and none of us seemed to care at all.

Since our encounter with the majestic Loon at Skmana, I had been thinking about this iconic bird gracefully emblazoned on the one-dollar coin, which in turn has taken on its name. Yes, this gold piece of legal tender is universally referred to as a "Loonie" and despite or because of the Canadian two-dollar coin depicting two polar bears, it is cleverly called a "Toonie". The Australian one-dollar coin has five Kangaroos and the two has an Aboriginal Elder sporting a long Ned Kelly beard. Do we need a nickname, I think not. But if we did what could it be? Speaking currency nicknames, with the exchange rate between Canada and the US greatly diminished in recent months, it is interesting to see a newspaper cheekily referring to its own currency as the "P eh so" a reference to their national tendency of ending a sentence with "Eh" and the eternally low exchange rate of the Mexican Peso.

Monday morning, bright and early I heard Imogen chattering up the hall. It was just before 6am and long before she usually made an appearance. It was no coincidence that her class was going on an excursion and I got to tag along as a parent helper. We were off to five pin bowling. No not a type error, five pin bowling seems to be the norm in rural Canada. I don't know why and have never heard of such a thing. Later when I asked the teachers about it, they looked at me as if it were the only form. Ah to be the outsider in a foreign land. Our little princess bathed and even ate breakfast without having to be threatened with no play that afternoon or something similarly horrible. As soon as she was ready, she started to herd up her parents like an over excited cattle dog. As a bonus the whole Scott family got to ride on the big, yellow, smelly bus. If you have ever travelled with school kids, you will know what I mean. About a decade ago I had a year eight student vomit down the back of my neck from the seat behind. We were halfway up the range to the Atherton Tablelands with no running water to clean up properly. That girl grew up to be a comedian and I often wonder if she has used that tale at one of her performances. The bowling was fun and great for kids, the balls were about the size of a softball. As if the day wasn't exciting enough, that afternoon was Imogen's first yoga lesson at Sorrento. Ten other happy little faces were at the studio when I dropped her off. Great to start them off young, looking after their mind and body. She loved it.

A new Art Studio opened in a neighbouring town early in the Spring. I had read about their exhibits and decided to visit. The owners were a lovely couple who had just moved to town from the far northern oil fields. Neil was a self-taught artist, who worked primarily in the impressionist alla prima or wet on wet method of oil painting. They ran kids' classes in the afternoon and adult ones at night. Imogen was very keen, so we both signed up. In Imogen's first class she painted an impressionist still life of the bunch of Peony flowers freshly picked from Neil's garden. I sat and watched for a while as she intently listened to instructions and meticulously mixed and applied the paint. At my first class we learnt about tones, values and how to build an image from dark to light. No mucking around with this bloke, on week two we were tasked with painting our own choice of subject onto a large canvas. I spent a fair bit of time over the weekend deciding what to do, sketching up options to scale and thinking about colours. When I arrived we got straight into it. Neil started painting a picture of a native man he had recently met. It was great to see how he laid down broad brush strokes in unconventional colours. The proof of an eventful life showed in the wrinkles that began to leap off the page. Neil gave bits of advice as he painted but mainly taught by example and osmosis. After three hours we both had made a lot of progress and I was really pleased with what I had put down. During the lesson, visitors came in off the street to look at the art on the walls and observe our progress. I had some positive comments and kind of felt like a real artist sitting their dabbing away. A surreal experience I thought I would never have. Chalk another one up.

The school sports carnival came around next. It was run and organised by the Parents which was also new to us. They did it partly due to goodwill and partly because there are no Sports teachers in British Columbia elementary schools. I have been at schools which treat the day like a mini Olympics and others where it was pure fun. This was the latter, with egg and spoon relays and sack races. The criteria of success was happy smiling faces out in the fresh air, running around. They passed with flying colours. The stray dog that was always lurking around the school seemed to be in her element. It looked like a cross between a wolf and a border collie, had a bit of age on her and clearly meant no harm. When I asked what is the story with the stray, Imogen became quite indignant and said "that's Abbey the school dog and she belongs to the kids!" I assume Abbey came from one of the nearby houses and returned home only when she was full of lunch scraps and sufficiently pampered.

Drives into Salmon Arm became more frequent as did our sightings of many and varied little critters standing up on their back legs patrolling their patch. At first, in my peripheral vision, I thought they were pop up sprinkler heads. I only saw them in one specific spot on the highway, just before the Salmon River bend. This distinctive stance, to my limited North American field identification abilities, said Gopher or Prairie Dog. Both are found in the region, but size became the discerning factor. Prairie Dogs are from thirty to forty centimeters long and the fifteen centimeters average size of the Gopher was a perfect match. I wondered if these little burrowing rodents ever terrorised the local golf course. Unlike Prairie dogs, who have a complex social life, kissing, hugging, preening and generally playing around, the Gopher is solitary outside of the breeding season. They are larder hoarders and their full name, Pocket Gopher, refers not to their size, but cleverly designed cheek pouches where they stuff food to take back their burrow. The pouches are fur lined, extend well back onto their shoulders and can be turned inside out. Not sure how they manage that, a good party trick indeed. We still wanted to see a Prairie Dog in the wild. Maybe in Alberta?

21st May - Victoria Day long weekend beckoned as we jumped in the loaded-up Chevy and headed East again, towards Golden on the British Columbia and Alberta border. The holiday is Canada's version of the Queen's Birthday holiday in Australia and a special one it was with the Queen turning ninety. First stop up the highway was Glacier National Park. The Giant Cedar Trail was a well-constructed boardwalk through old growth Red Cedar forest. Many of these sentinels of nature were over five hundred years old and, as the interpretive sign highlighted, would have been seedlings when Chris Columbus first made shore on the New World. Although not showing themselves that day, many trees bore the distinctive holes of the Pileated Woodpecker, who are endemic to this part of the rainforest. There are several varieties, but the large red crested bird is the one Disney used as an inspiration for their Woody Woodpecker character, fondly remembered by many people around my age. The three of us, each with our own camera clicking away, spent a good hour discovering unusual flowers and fungi. The light bounced off the foliage to create wonderful and unique snapshots of nature. Our art teacher had just finished a painting looking up into the bows of cedars on a one and a half metre canvas. It was good to see his inspiration. We pointed out the Skunk Cabbage and Bear Bread fungus along the path and explained to a curious Imogen that the bears use the former as a laxative at the end of hibernation and the latter as a plug moving into winter. As we left a tour bus rolled in, disgorging its noisy contents into the park. We all agreed how nice it was for our little family to experience this special place without the herd. Independent travelling takes a lot of work but has plenty of rewards.

The stream of "Flatlander" prairie people heading towards the coast was relentless. All motoring towards the Pacific for their hit of coastal life and the clean salty air. When we arrived at the Hemlock Grove trail, a couple in the car park said they had just seen a bear along the track. We headed into the elevated boardwalk hopeful to see one at a safe distance, but it was not to be. The ice melt seemed to have created a swamp with little crystal-clear streams running around the distinctive buttresses of Hemlock. The word Hemlock evokes thoughts of caldron ingredients, crooked black hats and broomsticks conjured up from literary tales and the cinema. But these were references to the European Hemlock, which has long been associated with Witchcraft. One and the same active ingredient used in the death potion that the Greeks administered to one of their greatest minds. The fellow was called Socrates, you may have heard of him. These Eastern Hemlock trees however are coniferous, tall and very long lived. Along the path we came across a Blue Heeler Cattle dog, an Australian breed. Both Anna and I looked at each other and simultaneously thought, "there isn't too many breeds of dog that resembles that shape and colour". The owners told us that they are a popular in Canada. Well who would have thought. Nice to meet another Aussie, a long way from home. Further up the road was a flashing sign which read "Bears on the highway" but again they had moved on before we passed.

With wild west names like Kicking Horse River cutting through the centre of town, it was hard not to picture cowboys of the past sauntering through the landscape. Six shooter strapped to their hip, upon a trusty steed. Alberta is modern cowboy country and the town of Golden is about as close as you get before entering the landlocked Province. The town has even adopted

"Mountain Time", in line with Alberta, a separation of sorts from British Columbia. Our motel in Golden was mediocre with tired decor but had unobstructed views out across the Alps which included the onsite restaurant where we treated ourselves to dinner, sat back and drank in the surroundings. Gophers played on the lawn just outside the picture window, seeming to enjoy each other's company and not the solitary animal described in the field guide.

Wow, wow, wow! What a day. A day that Anna and I will be telling our Grandkids about and Imogen telling hers. It started with the, true to form, last minute change to the weather forecast. Instead of raining and thirteen degrees it was going to be mostly fine and nineteen degrees. You will take that any day of the week in Canada. After breakfast we decided to drive straight through to Emerald Lake. The winding road led us through some of the most glorious landscape on the planet. We spat out far too many adjectives while highlighting to each other what we were witnessing. At that altitude the Dandelions were still out in force, blanketing the edges of the highway. All the peaks had residual snow. We passed many frozen waterfalls on the cusp of awakening. The numerous tunnels and nature bridges punctuated the endless craggy peaks. By chance it was the first day of the year that the parks opened to the public. Early due to the unseasonably warm Spring. Once again fortune favoured the Scott's on this point. After only half an hour, we took the turnoff to Emerald Lake, stopping for a jaw dropping exploration of the Natural Bridge. A rock formation in the middle of a glacial blue, pumping river. A pedestrian bridge gave access to more viewpoints. Enough photo opportunities to fill several rolls of film, if you were partial to using a camera that belonged in a museum. These lakes on the

Rockies are glacially fed. Their distinctive colour due to the refraction of light by the rock flour. Turquoise, aquamarine, electric blue. The hue changed with the position of the sun and clouds. It reminded me of my mother's pottery, in particular her favourite glaze colour, the washed out, cloudy Sea Blue Green. Yoho National Park meaning "place of awe" in the language of the Cree Indian. An accurate description.

Further along the track was Emerald Lake, a scene that took our cumulative breaths away. The deep blue green of the lake, the fluorescent white of surrounding ice, the fire engine red canoes and the pretty as a picture, stone restaurant, accessed by a matching footbridge. The walk around the lake, through thick green forest and glacial overflow, took about two hours. We found Banana slugs and were joined by Columbian ground squirrels, which are the size of a chipmunk but have distinctive markings down their flanks. Little, purple slipper like blooms, sat beside five pointed, faded yellow, pixie caps nodding up top of delicate green stems. A colourful curiosity which made us stop and discuss how fairy folks could gather their wardrobe in that forest. Driving back to the highway, a car hit their brakes and flashed their headlights as we passed. I watched in my rear vision mirror as they did a rapid u-turn and drove back towards us. My first thought was an unmarked police car going to pull me up for driving three k's over the fifty speed limit. My confusion rapidly dissipated, but pulse sped up. As we rounded the corner a Moose confronted us. Only some three metres from the car stood this anomaly of nature. Gangly, disproportionately long legs. It seemed very uneasy about being exposed on the roads edge, like a woman who has answered the front door in her night dress and hair in curlers. Unlike the healthy, shiny coated moose with full set of antlers, we had the fortune to see at close quarters in Alaska, this poor fellow looked like he needed a good feed and a course of multivitamins. He must have had a hard winter. Clumps of malting fur hung awkwardly from his torso. We were able to sit for some time, quietly observing the beast. Excitement that is hard to explain to the outdoors challenged, just basking in the ephemeral grandeur of nature. A fleeting experience that will last forever, like dragging your hand through an inky night ocean full of efflorescence. So beautiful that sometimes the memories seem unreal. The reddish-brown velvet stubs of its new season antlers were only about two hundred millimetres long, a fifth of the size they would eventually grow. The antlers are very soft at this stage of Spring and will grow deformed if damaged. Since the females have no antlers, we knew this was a male or bull Moose, which on average grow to weigh over half a tonne. Some have been recorded as heavy as seven hundred kilos. Due to their size, they have few natural predators except bears. Notoriously reclusive, rarely seen in the wild. We had heard about their unpredictable and sometimes aggressive nature, glad to be in the relative safety of our car. How fortunate. We truly struck the jackpot, seeing one of Canada's big five. The retractable sunroof had become very handy for photography. Imogen took advantage of standing up through the opening and checking out the wildlife. She absolutely loves her best view in the house.

We eventually moved on to the tiny village of Field perched on the edge of a wide glacial river delta in a high mountain landscape. With a history dominated by rail, mountaineering and now tourism, this pretty dot on the map benefits greatly from its proximity to the wonders of the Rockies, the winter ski action and the desperate need for accommodation. We found a ramshackled store which seemed to provide most of the life sustaining ingredients for the community. Good coffee, great brownies, booze, hippy clothes and jewellery. The double shot Americano with almond milk was the closest I could get to a flat white, it was good and pepped me up for the afternoon, while the girls tried on nice shiny things from the display. It was around one thirty when we stepped out. Considering we were only twenty minutes away from Lake Louise a vote of two to one saw us heading eastwards, up the range towards one of the most visited lakes in the world. Upwards of three million people visit this section of the Rocky Mountains each year, the majority over the three months of Summer. Imogen wanted to go back to the chlorine haze of the motel's indoor pool in Golden. She will thank us one day.

There are certain vistas one has the fortune to experience in life, that you will never forget. For me the timeless view from the rooftop bar of the Majestic Hotel in Ho Chi Minh city at night looking out across the Saigon River. I felt like I had been transported back in time a hundred years. Sailing the deepest blue waters of Oro Bay on the Isle of Pines, waking to the view of tiny scattered Islands in Sitka Harbour Alaska and hiking through Monument Valley are up the pointy end of my list. But as we hit the car park near the Chateau, I had no idea that this would be another of those experiences that permanently etched themselves into one's psyche. I thought to myself that I would hate to negotiate the car park on a busy day, but fortunately we found a spot and cantered down the short path to view this icon of Canada. The far end revealed sharply rising bare stone cliffs, partially covered by glacial ice. The white tongue extended to the water's edge. The sides of the lake transitioned to thick forest until reaching the clearing for the hotel grounds. I love photography and this digital age lets me click with abandon, but I have observed that some fellow snappers have turned it into a competitive sport such was the crush at water's edge. We tried to imagine what the lake would be like in winter with skaters strutting their stuff but agreed that we were fortunate to enjoy our day in the sun. To the side of the path, up on a mound of remnant snow, sat a bird I had never seen before. He wore a rather formal grey suit with black trim and a sharp black beak. I suspected this serious fellow may have been a relative of the flamboyant north American Magpie that we had come across earlier in the day prancing about with its long iridescent blue tail. Conveniently just down the track a small sign had a picture of our new friend and identified him as a Clark's Nutcracker. I never knew there was such a bird and a clever one at that. It uses its sharp beak to rip the seeds out of pinecones and transports them in a pouch under its tongue. Ingenious. A survivor in these parts needs a trick or two. After noting some trails for our stay in August, we moved on to explore the Fairmont Chateau. Originally built in 1890, by the 1920's it had become a favoured location for Hollywood, both for filming and vacationing. The mountain climbing and ski fields ultimately turned it into a yearlong operation. Leaving later than expected we drove back towards Golden. Not too far into our trip we came across several cars parked just off the side of the highway and had enough time to pull in behind them anticipating another wildlife encounter. A large black bear sat ambivalently munching dandelions. Unlike the moose, this bear was relaxed and had a wise, knowing look in his eyes. The jet-black coat juxtaposed with the sun drenched, yellow blooms made it all the more surreal. Imogen opened the sunroof and popped out again, in an almost reflex action. Anna had her window down getting some great headshots of the furry native. Strangely enough I had a feeling when we left Lake Louise that our great day of discovery was not over yet. Rare alpine air, mountains, rivers, glaciers and wildlife, sure produced some potent endorphin enriched cocktail of happiness. It made our budget alfresco dinner consisting of chicken and pineapple jaffles accompanied by wine in a paper cup, taste almost extravagant. The view of the snow-capped Rockies from the Motel bedroom window didn't hurt either.

Sunday came in wet, cold and windy, but after the previous day I dared not complain. We braved the horrid conditions and drove around Golden to find shelter in a coffee shop then trudged the streets around to Spirit Square, with its wonderful timber covered footbridge over the Kicking Horse River. The waitress had made a big deal about us being Australian and waxed lyrical about how good Australian coffee is. She said she would do her best, but it wouldn't be as good as home. Slightly embarrassed I assured her it would be just fine. I knew we had good coffee but was unaware that Australia had a reputation for it. We checked out the Art Gallery across the road and considered driving to Radium Hot Springs, but the forecast said it was raining there as well so we spent the afternoon watching TV and teaching Imogen how to sketch. On the news that night reports came in of heavy snow in Calgary. We felt relieved to have narrowly avoided the worst of it and there were no road closures. The weather broke Monday morning as we sidetracked into the Wolf Education and Refuge Centre on the outskirts of town. They had several grey wolves of various ages and one wolf-dog cross which had started life as a pet before several wolf instinct related mishaps convinced the owners to hand it in. The guide said they had taken the crossbreed to an off-leash area and a Chihuahua went missing. I think she may have been pulling our leg, but maybe not. She spoke for at least half an hour explaining the many attributes and misnomers while the wolves roamed their compound nearby. She said the best food for the animals was roadkill, because they eat the fur, bones, organs, the lot. Curiously the local government, instead of being happy the roads are being cleared for free, charges sixty dollars per beast for the privilege of scraping them off the road. Now that is one crazy nonsensical law. We drove back along the seemingly endless stretch of oxidised licorice through the greens, slate greys and ochres of the countryside, rolling into Blind Bay by late afternoon having experienced much more than expected, which is always a good feeling.

When we eventually downloaded the photos from our weekend in the Rockies I came across, what I thought was my best ever wildlife shots and it was a fluke. We startled some bird life near the shore at Emerald Lake. By the time they had landed on the lake, they were out of range to identify. I attempted to use my telescopic lens to sneak a look but couldn't get it still enough to focus so while I had the general direction of the bird, I just breathed out slowly and snapped a speculative shot. What evolved was a perfectly focused image of a Hooded Merganser Duck. This debonair gentleman of the bird world resplendently dressed in a classic suit of black and fawn brown with accents of white. Its head tilted perfectly and the light breeze on the lake combined with the subdued sunlight created thousands of tiny dabs of white on the glacier blue lake. What a beauty!

Tuesday morning, getting back to school was a bit of a grind for the girls. I had backed the car out on the driveway, packed the school bags and checked under the bonnet for the cause of our lack of power steering we encountered the day before. When I finally got them in and reversed down the drive, a full-grown Black Bear stepped around the corner, only a few meters away. It sniffed around the front of the house then realising that we were watching tried to climb the embankment with no luck. Eventually it absconded up across the road. I noticed the neighbour, Luke, out front of his house crouching down behind a hedge. We assumed he was hiding so gave him a smile and a big wave. Apparently, he was pulling weeds and oblivious to our visitor and not too happy later when he found out. A mother bear and two cubs had just been put down in Salmon Arm because they were hanging around a school and homes looking for easy food. I hope our bear doesn't suffer the same fate. When it comes to interactions with wildlife, we seem to have an uncanny knack of being at the right place at the right time. A former colleague reckoned "the animals can see you are kind, so choose to let you see them". I am not sure it works like that, but it was nice of him saying. I recalled another memorable encounter when we were eyeballed by a Humpback Whale and her calf as they cruised up to our boat anchored between Great Palm and Phantom Island. We didn't have time or the inclination to pull anchor and motor away. The mother ever so gently dived under us and surfaced alongside within a meter of the hull. At one point rolling its head to the side so to get a better look. This massive creature dwarfed our boat but was so gentle, duck diving with only millimetres to spare. We just sat in awe. In our urban dominated world, how many people on this earth have had the opportunity to experience nature in its rawest, unpredictable, elegant self.

No one else seems to have spotted a bear in our street before. Great experience, but I became uneasy when the girls were out playing in the yard from that point on. Later in the week Anna was driving out when the lady from the corner house said she just saw a Black Bear disappear down the side of our house. I received an urgent phone call to shut the carport and get the girl's inside. Thankfully Imogen and her little friend were playing dress ups upstairs and none of us saw the bear. Not long after I heard, what sounded like a shotgun go off. When I went out to investigate, the neighbours said it was probably a bear banger. A handheld device that is designed to startle a bear. The young woman across the road told me she asked her boyfriend for a bear banger for her birthday to take hiking. Not something that was ever requested by my dear wife.

Wednesday offered another opportunity to go on an excursion with the school. The salmon embryo, that had been growing in a fish tank at school, were now seven months old and about fifty millimeters long. Ready to start their journey to the sea and back, which takes four years on average. Harvested last October, on the Thanksgiving weekend, they were placed back in the same river system so their natural instincts could take over, directing their homecoming through sense of smell, which is ten thousand times more sensitive than our own. The spot on the Shuswap River was out from Enderby toward Mabel lake. A small community hidden away off the highway. Along the way someone had stenciled wings on each deer alert road sign. A nice little touch. Proceedings got underway fairly quickly with each child given a bucket with a tiny Chinook Salmon fry. They were told to give it a name, wish it luck and warn it of all the dangers to avoid on its journey. Imogen called hers Squishy and carefully released it in a backwater near the fast-moving river. The rest of the day was taken up with environmental bushwalks and river organism identification, which the kids just loved.

The cool weather continued into the weekend with rain and temps in the low teens. It even snowed heavily on the Coquihalla Pass creating mayhem on the highway with plenty of accidents and some serious injuries. It was almost the end of May and I had not expected the cold rainy weather to drag on so long. Maybe the caravan park down the road knew better. Believe it or not, they only opened their gates on the weekend, and I suspect they would close sometime in October. Not sure what they do for the rest of the year, but I bet it includes a passport, beach and sunshine. I know it is none of my business, but I still can't fathom how you can make enough money in a few short months to sustain a family for a whole year. Thinking of friends and family, we decided to cook up a batch of **ANZAC** biscuits. We had to substitute golden syrup with maple syrup due to the local quartermaster's supplies, but the biscuits turned out just right. Chewy not crunchy. We were a bit late for **ANZAC** day, but it is never a wrong time to think of home.

June 4th

The Boy's weekend fishing trip - We travelled to Kamloops and then south for almost three hours towards Princeton. The girls dropped me off at Chase earlier that afternoon, where I caught a lift with Aiden and his colleague Tony. A forgettable stop in Merritt for groceries and my first piece of fast food in over a decade. The burger was bad and almost nine dollars, it will likely be another decade before I try one again. Maybe the bikie dressed in full leathers in front of me in the cue or the disinterested kid taking my order should have told me that this was not my type of place. Anywhere that asks, "would you like the combo with that?" is not for me. Even though it was after seven, the sun was still high in the sky as we rattled up the dirt driveway to the cabin. Aidan and his mate had bought the land and built the dwelling years back when they were bachelors. Rustic it was not, with all the luxuries of a regular house, even a marble kitchen benchtop. It was located near a chain of three lakes in the ever so sleepy village of Bankier, actually more a cluster of cabins than a village. Some of the other lads had arrived early and the campfire was blazing away. Following our male instincts, we unpacked in minutes. A simple process of dumping all our belongings on our allocated bunk and positioning the ice box within easy access from our fold out chair near the fire. After initial introductions and recitals of Crocodile Dundee quotes in a bad Australian accent, we settled in for a few after dinner drinks and star gazing. The others knew each other quite well and the banter flowed thick and fast. Being of a similar age and having the fortune of being a young man in the wonderful 80's, it became clear that this would be the social glue that kept the conversation going. We had a lot of pop culture fueled experiences in common. We reminisced about favourite bands, movies and fondly remembered the crushes we had on young Hollywood starlets of the period. They moved on to ask about the differences between Canada and home, apart from driving on the other side of the road and being inundated with "things that can kill you". After light heartedly pointing out the inefficiencies of their toilet design, long story, and trying to find out why they still teach imperial in school, it came back to the weather and how it makes our lifestyles and outlook totally different. They seemed to be curious, so I hope I didn't offend.

We are however, connected through our common British heritage. With time to ponder the formation and evolution of our people, it is fascinating how each Nation has developed and gone in different and diverse directions. Our coordinates on the planet, climate and neighbours are significantly different. Australia, remote in comparison and a big player in the Asia Pacific. Canada bordering the USA, the biggest player in the world. But back to the British influence. At the centre of this historical connection is a British sailor named Captain James Cook, a household name and central to any primary school history class in Australia, but strangely far less known in these parts. Early in his career he was sent to, what was then the British base of Nova Scotia to assist the cause in the Seven Year War (1756-1763) against France. He then took part in the blockade of Louisbourg and capturing the French stronghold of Quebec. Cook studied surveying and chart making whilst on assignment. He honed his new skills mapping the St. Lawrence River and the coast of Newfoundland before becoming a Captain. After discovering the east coast of Australia in 1770 and claiming the continent for Great Britain, he was sent to look for the Northwest Passage and spent time at Nootka Sound on Vancouver Island in 1778. George Vancouver, from whom the vibrant city and beautiful Island were named, sailed with Cook on some of his voyages of discovery. He then went back to the West coast and carried out significant mapping through to Alaska. On an earlier visit I was surprised to find the easily identifiable, large, bronze sculpture of James Cook on the Anchorage foreshore. This man's influence has opened up the new world territories and having Canada, Australia, New Zealand and Hawaii on his list, James certainly could find a beautiful location. I could not help thinking about that Seven Year War and how The British must have been having a really good day when they allowed the French to stay after they emerged the victor. This act of kindness has had an indelible effect on Canada's development as a nation.

At one point in the discussion around the campfire I referred the British as Poms for which I got blank looks and questions. Although by now I was accustomed with such reactions, I had thought the term universal, at least in former British colonies. It is certainly used by the English themselves even if they don't like it. It has been around a very long time and few Australians would ever think about its origins. It is so ingrained in our slang. Some suggest that it is an acronym of "Prisoners of His Majesty" referring to the reason why many of my countryman gained free transportation to the great land of ours. It is more than a little ironic that most British would now love to live or visit Australia. Another version explains that when the lily white, chubby, little English got off the boats in Australia their faces turned red from the heat and were given the nickname Pommie, short for the fat red Pomegranate. All jokes aside, it had never really occurred to me how much we had in common to the British until I lived in Canada. We are our own people but share a sense of humour, determination and larrikinism.

The boys hit the grog hard but by midnight were definitely slowing down. I worked out a while back that hangovers are simply not my thing, so adopted the slow and steady approach. As I fell asleep, I reminisced about the shared house living of my early twenties, the food disputes, lack of hygiene and regularly finding a random soul asleep on the lounge chair in the morning. The snoring from the bunk below broke me from my dream but a shake of the bed post seemed to disrupt the perpetrator and I eventually fell back to sleep. The following morning's breakfast consisted of enough oily bacon and eggs to clog up the arteries of an army, so I willingly copped a bit of flak for eating my cereal and banana knowing I would feel much better for it later in the day. After breakfast I took the chance to borrow some lures for the day. Like all fishermen, everyone had a favourite, but the general consensus was either a feathered fly or a spinning metal rig they called a "Pumpkin Head". I managed to score one of each, Tony then went about explaining the intricacies of catching trout, hands waving about like only an Italian can do. The rest of the party arrived mid-morning, having driven up from the coastal, lower mainland. By eleven we were boarding the raft, tied up in front of a lakeside log cabin. The owner had been bribed with a bottle of Rye for the use of his good ship. His cabin had various outhouses clad in vintage signs and slowly decaying memorability including snowshoes, gardening implements and even a road sign from Butchart Gardens. Aiden suggested we peek through the window of one outhouse. It was common to see an elk carcass hanging on a butcher's hook, aging in the cool air. Unfortunately, no elk. The raft was not the Huck Finn-esque, rope tethered log caricature I had expected. This beast had aluminium barrels and frame beneath a hardwood timber deck. A small fabricated transom pod held a 6-horsepower outboard, so there was no need for my imagined Mississippi push pole, to ply these languid waters. Folding chairs, fishing poles and ice boxes were tossed about as the ten intrepid fishermen jockeyed for prime positions. An old upholstered lounge chair with a wonky leg and a raffia laden beach umbrella proved very popular. Osprey Lake, at an altitude of 1098 meters, was almost three times higher than the Shuswap at Blind Bay. It was flanked by campgrounds and cabins on the west bank with the Kettle Valley Railway walking trail on the other. After an hour and a bit of trolling and fly flicking, I was fortunate enough to get the first strike. A thirty-centimetre trout surfaced, its pink luminescent skin glimmering in the sunlight, although it flicked off as I was trying to find the landing net, I was happy to start the ball rolling. I should have just reefed it onboard but was not sure of the local protocol. A steady stream of fish were caught over the next two hours. By this time everybody was ready to get back to the cabin, several still suffering from the effects of partying the night before. Most retired for a siesta and resurfaced around six for a few games of Bocce. The commentary of a Blue Jays baseball match blared from the outdoor speakers. What an experience.

Breeze rustled through the oval leaves of the Aspens lining the driveway, reminiscent of shell wind chimes. The silver leaves contrasting with the distinctive white bark, a pleasant change from the deep greens of the firs. Swallows swooped for insects; embers crackled awaiting the night when they would rise again to take centre stage. Large bumble bees raided the wild rose nectar bounty while nearby a chipmunk and a family of gophers played hide and seek around the wood pile. Hard to imagine a more quintessential Canadian scene. I feel sorry for the city dwellers who never experience their country. Tony is a hunter and brought along some homemade sausages. I tried the Black Bear laced with jalapeno and the Elk with cheese. They were ok but more like a Kabana. Finely ground and tightly packed. I think a coarse minced version, like the Italian sausages they make in Ingham, would let you taste the meat better. His wife warned him not to bring any sausages back home as the deep freeze was already full of game, including two full bear skins with heads attached. He explained that unlike most game which is lean and needs to be mixed with pork fat, the Black Bear has a thick layer which he described as "Nature's gift to man" it can be rendered down and used to fry in. A bit like goose fat I suppose.

Another member of our group was also a hunter and told about his dream to bag a Bison up in Vanderhoof way up north near the Alaskan border. I was surprised that licenses are given for Bison but apparently numbers are thriving up there. A ballot is run each year and a very limited amount of license tags are allocated to shoot on Indian land. Both seemed very responsible about their pastime and attitude to conservation quotas. As the cans of beer kept on coming, I noticed some were topping theirs up with a reddish liquid. Now I know lime wedges are common and have seen ginger wine added to an ale but when they told me it was a mixture of clam and tomato juice; well I was lost for words. It was one of those things that you would not believe unless your saw it for yourself. Some research revealed that the concoction was created in the States in the sixties and used as a mixer for spirit cocktails. Somewhat similar to a Bloody Mary. The Mexican's have embraced it as well, but what made the Canadians think it would taste good with beer? The fellows explained that when the beer strike hit in the eighties, an influx of bad tasting beer crossed the border. It was so bad that they tried to find something to mask the taste. Somehow this red juice became popular. When beer supplies went back to normal, the country's drinkers had the taste and wanted more. One beer company even makes a pre-mixed version. There is also a beef and tomato juice cocktail mixer on the market. Stranger than fiction. They all seemed to have a story about getting very sick from it due to using juice past its best. Mustn't have been too bad because they were all guzzling it down. Later on, we were all relaxed, sitting back around the fire when one bloke held up, what looked like an oversize firecracker. With a grin as big as a dog in a butcher shop, he simultaneously threw it into the fire and ran. The reaction was instant. Chairs, drinks and expletives flew in every direction during the retreat chased by a deafening boom. The explosion blew out the fire. Chunks of glowing charcoal flew over the lip of the ring landing metres away. That was one supercharged firecracker. Who does this kind of stuff? An interesting hobby indeed. He later told us how last Halloween he made a Jack-O-Lantern and filmed it exploding in slow motion for a season greeting email to his friends. Things had only just settled down when someone emerged from the shadows with a short length of four-inch pipe and inserted it into the reassembled fire. A can of kidney beans appeared out of the ether, as if someone had one in their back pocket just in case. The self-proclaimed artillery officer loaded the legumes and while the anticipation rose, I slowly edged out of my chair, a casual but strategic repositioning of my body behind other members of the group. A human wall, of sorts. I mean what could go wrong! As I searched my memory for first aid procedures, a few crackling expansion noises broke the silence. Then Bang! She flies, the can a silver streak, beans spraying into the night air like confetti. I sat beside the oldest member of our party, a retired logger well into his eighties, who had sat calmly through the night's entertainment puffing away on a fat cigar. The heady smell of bay leaf and cloves wafting through camp. No doubt he had seen it all before in some shape or form. I will never forget this weekend, the laughs, the scenery, the friendships and fishing, but most of all the generosity of Aiden for inviting me. I would like to have the opportunity to return the favour one day. You never know. After our farewells the following morning we arrived back at the Bay by mid-afternoon. Aiden dropped me off at the park where the girls were attending another birthday party. They were pleased to see me but had a good weekend down on the lake with Tori and her kids. Imogen had a great time and learnt how to paddle a kid's size kayak. They both complained of the water-borne duck itch in the evening and were scratching away at a nasty rash.

June the 10th, off again for the weekend on a discovery mission to the lower Okanagan district. After a rainy drive south, we checked into our two-star motel right on the esplanade at Penticton, just across the road from the lake. It was clean, had a kitchen and location, location, location. To our surprise the skies cleared at about eight pm. The sun shone through giving us a glimpse of what must be the latest evening rainbow event on the planet. Even though it was past bedtime for our little one, we bent the rule book and went for a walk along the lake. Many others appeared to have the same idea as it was strewn with dogs, prams, walkers and joggers, all making hay while the sun shone. On Saturday morning we checked out the main street markets. This town had soul. It was more alive and happening than any we had come across in the interior. The market had it all, street performers, all types of produce and craft. We picked up some yellow stemmed chard to try, but mainly just enjoyed the energy and familiarity of the market scene. The chocolate ganache tarts didn't hurt either. A thunderstorm midmorning did nothing to dampen our spirits. We spent much of the downpour waiting for Anna to try on some hippy clothes. After lunch the scenic Naramata Bench, running along the east bank of the lake, lured us with its orchards, wineries and unexpected discoveries like a wander through a Lavender farm. Cherries were loaded on branches waiting to be relieved of their crimson delights. We picked up some from a roadside stall and then on to the wineries. It just happened to be the day the Canadian National Wine Awards were announced, and a jovial mood emanated from the victors. Three of the four businesses we visited, had picked up a medal, not a bad strike rate for a random visit. Of particular note was Terra Vista winery which grew, along with Viognier and Marsanne, some interesting Portuguese grape varieties. Namely Alberino and Verdejo, which were zingy and interesting. Very different to New Zealand Sav Blancs but I reckon you could drink them with similar foods. A very nice surprise find. The fellow offering the tastings owned the vineyard, his wife was the vintner. They had a high-tech setup housed in an architectural gem constructed of concrete slabs with an angular skillion roof. I commented to Anna that we could easily deck it out as a house with some internal dividers. It would suit the tropics well and double as a cyclone shelter. We joined three other couples for a great informal chat about the wine and the region. I hoped to come back when my sister visits. Sunday morning was warm and allowed us to slowly meander our way back north stopping for the markets in Summerland and Peachland for a sip of Lake culture at its best. Bands played on the sidewalks and people were out enjoying the sunshine. We could have easily stayed much longer.

By June 19 it seemed like Imogen had been counting down the days to her 7th birthday since January and finally it was almost upon us, the hype and hoopla were in full swing. For some time, we had been planning to take her to the Enchanted Forest kids park, up near Revelstoke the weekend before the big day. We had assumed it would be warm and sunny by late June. Saturday was cold and showery but with a slightly better forecast for Sunday. With plenty of hope and positive thinking, we set off East. By eleven it was still overcast and only thirteen degrees, so a dip in the hot springs on route seemed the obvious choice. The warm water lifted our spirits, so we rugged up and forged on to this iconic fairyland built by a single family in the late sixties and opening in 1971. The Enchanted Forest had become a mainstay for kids across the nation. It had numerous nursery rhyme settings, complete with wonderfully reconstructed buildings, like the old woman's shoe and the three little pigs' cottages. A fantastic treehouse sat way up an old growth fir tree. The access staircase wrapped its way around the portly trunk. A boardwalk through the marshland meandered past a couple of beaver lodges but the highlight was rowing a small dingy around the lake surrounded with boisterously yellow water lily blooms. I felt like I should have been dressed in a straw boater and pinstriped blazer with matching bowtie, my ladies in long flowing cotton summer frocks. Their wide brim hats held down with a scarf tied under their chin. Yes, this was a quintessentially British pastime. On the trip back we stopped in at Dutchman's Dairy for some homemade ice cream and a walk around the menagerie of animals they kept in cages out front.

Along with wildflowers and wildlife, Spring brought out many interesting behaviours. We observed several people out with pressure hoses cleaning off their street. Obviously, the council only cleans the winter muck off the major roads. I suppose it reduces the dust. Many of the snowbirds (part time residents) had returned with their southern tanned faces and sunny dispositions for 12 weeks of lakeside frivolity. The restaurants opened, portable jetties, boats of all shapes and aquatic rental company's gear all appeared from winter hideouts to bask in the sun. The little beach beside the Bar & Grill was full of people in summer clothes and swimsuits which had been rediscovered in the deep dark recesses of their dresser drawers. The snow melt came early and rapidly consumed the muddy marshland flats leaving only a sliver of sand on the water's edge. The twice daily tides we are accustomed to on the seaside, are replaced here by one year long incoming and outgoing cycle. Snow was replaced with Cotton Tree jetsam and Dandelion floss swirling to the will the wind. It moved through the landscape uninhibited, like the remnants of some colossal pillow fight in the sky. I even herd about a Kelowna radio station running a competition with a Spring garden makeover as the prize. A well-known garden designer comes and sits cross legged, in meditation pose, eyes closed, in the middle of your garden. He returns a few days later with landscaping plans ready to go. Now that, I would like to see but onward into Summer we went.

PART FOUR

Summer

June the 20th, the first day of Summer. We had made it. The time of the year that countless locals had told us to wait for. When it was not raining, our walks around the neighbourhood had become much more interesting. Flowers and manicured lawns were at their best. We witnessed Hummingbirds zooming around gathering nectar and had the fortune of meeting an old man Raccoon. He waddled across the road in front of me like an old dog without a care in the world. Two crows chased him from above making all kinds of racket, none of which seemed to have any impact. I suspect he had just raided the eggs from their nest. The Spring lead up had been great, but we were now expecting some weather that didn't involve long pants and a jumper. The days were longer and the anticipation of spending more time outside exciting our senses. Warm Days + Great Outdoors = Very Happy Scott Family. Having left home in early December, we had been away for 196 days. There were many more adventures to dive into with only 157 days to go. No time to waste.

June 21st - Imogen's Birthday eve. Now I like to cook, in fact I cook almost every day, but cakes are not really my thing. A more rustic approach in the kitchen suits me and often I don't follow a recipe. This, I have been told, is unsuitable to baking, so usually I leave this to the fairer members of the family. Having now provided the disclosure statement, I was approached by my dear wife (who was fully aware of said disclosure) to bake a birthday cake. Happy to have something to do I jumped at the challenge. I had already planned to cook up Imogen's favourite fish, cheese and pasta bake, but figured what's one more item, I could do them at the same time. I think women call that multitasking, but it just comes so natural to men that we don't even bother giving it a name. Now more disclosure, it is only fair to point out that this is not our kitchen and it is a bit limited and unfamiliar. There were no kitchen scales or cake tins, so Anna diligently found a bread baking pan and converted a recipe from weight to cup quantities for me. The directions were not particularly clear, I am sure they were for her, but I thought "this is a good thing, if it comes out wrong I can just say I followed the instructions and filled in the gaps the best I could". I call it the art of covering one's backside. A disaster plan of sorts, it may not have been a good plan and I hoped I wouldn't have to use it, but it was a plan. On another cold morn I walked down to the store in the rain to gather the ingredients. The scribbled recipe instructed to heat the chocolate and sugar together until it was smooth. Having burnt chocolate in a pan in the past I figured it was a good time to put in the butter. Proud of my improvisation, I started to assemble the dry ingredients and beat the eggs and milk. At this point it dawned on me that my Mum and Grandma always creamed the butter and sugar then adding the eggs one at a time. Too late, the butter was already melted in the chocolate. I summoned my experience as a teacher dealing daily with teenagers. THINK COMPROMISE ADAPT BLUFF. No worries, the butter is only a lubricant and it shouldn't matter when it goes in, as long is in. Right? If I believed that last statement all would be ok. Into the dry mix went the beaten milk and eggs. I paused to pat myself on the back for remembering to stir it through before adding the hot chocolate, so I didn't cook the eggs. I didn't want a chocolate omelet. I preheated the oven and poured the mixture into the lined bread tin. In it went for two hours at 150 degrees. In between all this excitement I had managed to boil the pasta, make the white sauce and grate the cheese and zucchini. I am a messy cook but, I assume, so are the best. The only reason they look good on TV is because they have so many lackeys cleaning up after them. Anyway, I had earlier spilt some sauce on the hot plate here and there. It had smoked up a bit before I hurriedly cleaned it off. Later when I started to get a whiff a burning smell, I just put it down to the smokiness lingering longer than expected. The alarms didn't complain so it must not have been too bad. I ignored it and busily finishing off the pasta bake. The smell was still there so I decided to peek into the oven. Not a happy moment indeed! The mixture had risen over the top of the tin and pooled in the bottom of the oven like a lava flow. It swelled enough in height to be permanently in contact with the electric coil. Hence the burning. Now I had been ready just to sit down, have a coffee and be quietly proud of my morning's achievements. This was not in the plan. Sometime during the next 20 minutes while cleaning up the mess, I recalled that there was in fact baking powder and baking soda in the recipe. So even a rudimentary understanding of science should have screamed at me to not fill the pan so high. But I only had a bit left in the mixing bowl and was brought up not to waste good food.

Decision time! I tasted the partially cooked cake to determine any smoky flavour, which may be desirable in some foods but not in cake. My girls can find a problem with the taste of my cooking from thirty metres away. I needed to make sure. Thankfully it was OK. Now what to do? There was still too much in the pan, the excess batter had to go somewhere. There was good chocolate in there, I wasn't going to throw it away. In desperation, after finding absolutely nothing to bake it in, I scooped the brew into an oversize coffee mug and cautiously zapped it in the microwave until it became solid. I had seen mug cake gift boxes for sale in the shops so it must be legitimate? I leveled out the top of the original cake and put it back in for another hour at which time it popped out onto the platter easily. It probably didn't want to be tortured any further. If only the rest of the process had gone so smoothly. It looked good but I decided to coat it in a thick layer of industrial strength Ganache. You simply can't ever have too much chocolate ganache and if someone, by chance, doesn't like the cake they can quietly eat the topping and tell me how lovely it all was. In comparison the ganache making went without a hitch and as I troweled it on with glee, I pondered whether to tell my tale before or after consumption. At least it looked good and had a wonderful story all of its own. Thank goodness I didn't attempt the three-dimensional Raccoon cake Imogen wanted. I will leave that for Mummy to bake next year.

Finally the birthday had arrived. Present opening at breakfast and a little party at school. In the evening we went to the restaurant down the road and sat on the deck with views of the lake. Imogen insisted we all colour in the kid's menu with the pastels provided. This entertained the birthday girl as well as the other patrons and wait staff. Our little girl was seven and I have had flashbacks today of that special Monday morning, dressed in full operating theatre garb, hair net, elasticised plastic booties, the lot. I stood at the end of the bed talking to Anna while Doc was at the business end. A mixture of excitement and concern was finally replaced with uncontrollable joy. After a few worrying moments, when the doctors face showed concern as he quickly removed the cord from around her throat, I had hold of my own flesh and blood. Seven years and the ride continues with this beautiful, headstrong girl, which we have the honour of guiding through life. What a wicked sense of humour and dry comedic timing she has. Imogen was becoming more independent by the day and making a real effort with her knife and fork although she did have a mishap recently with a mischievous piece of spaghetti which absconded during dinner. We all had a laugh and I thought a poem was in order.

EATING WITH MY MOUTH SHUT

It swirled around my pink tongue
It bounced off my left cheek
And when I opened up my mouth
It took a little peek

It must have liked what it had seen
And found a missing tooth
For you to know what came next
You need not be a sleuth

Now it took, its only chance
This tube spaghetti fled
Across the clean white tablecloth
It trailed it sauce of red

It looked at Mum, it looked at Dad
It side stepped past the salt
Then shimmied round a saucer
Ending with a somersault

It did not see me coming
It did not have a chance
I raised my fork into the air
And stabbed it with my lance

Now as I rubbed my tummy
I smiled a little smile
I will eat with my mouth shut, I thought
At least for a little while.

The school had a day at the waterpark for their end of school year celebrations. I went along for the ride. The sun came out and the kids had a whale of a time. Imogen was easy to spot as she was the only kid with a hat and had her arms wrapped around herself as she quickly maneuvered from the cold slide water to the hot tub. The hot tub looked like soup by the end of the day. Thank goodness for chlorine.

June 25th - The school year was over. We drove through Kamloops to Sun Peaks mountain resort, taking in some new sights on route. As a bit of a treat we booked a couple of nights at a nice hotel in the village. It had a large picture window facing a grassed courtyard which allowed us close views of a gopher family, a squirrel and several robins, going about daily life. We repositioned the sofa towards the window and were thoroughly entertained. A bit like one of those high-priced suites facing the lion's den in a zoo only our creatures were much cuter, and I had the feeling that the inspiration for a children's novel lay just beyond the pane of glass. I'm sure if our stay was longer, we would have given them all names. The room had no obvious beds, so we quickly figured out the sofa was one. Then went to investigate the wall cupboard which unexpectedly pivoted at the base to reveal a double bed. Nice use of space. We discovered it was called a murphy bed. The legend has it that the inventor was courting a woman but couldn't invite her around because he had a one bedroom flat. In the early 1900's moral conventions made it impossible for lady friends to be entertained in a man's bedroom, so he invented a hidden, pivoting bed. When folded away he called the room a parlour, which was an acceptable place to greet a woman. Love finds a way! Sun Peaks is a skiing mecca in the season. In summer it is frequented by mountain bikers who enjoy the various jumps and trails. There were some pretty expensive looking bikes with equally impressive body armour on their owners. We even saw one fellow riding with a set of crutches in his backpack. Was he anticipating the worst, already injured or misinterpreting the idea of a first aid kit? We sat and enjoyed a band playing to a meagre audience in the court, before jumping in the hot tub back in the hotel.

After a mid-morning foray down through the village, a visit to the jumping castle and bungee jumping trampoline, we boarded the chairlift. It afforded unrestricted views of the valley and bike track below. Moments before Anna spotted a full-grown bear strolling around the slopes about three hundred meters up. An unexpected bonus. As soon as we reached the summit a swarm of hungry oversized mosquitoes from hell took a liking to our exotic blood. We sprayed and quickly headed out on a couple of intermediate hikes, enjoying the afternoon walking through fields of wildflowers and stands of forest in between the ski runs. Amongst the mass of orange, blue, purple and white carpet of flowers, we spotted a mule deer and enjoyed following its prints on the muddy trail. Ravens resplendent in their glossy, jet black trench coats, pecked around the under growth and proudly strutted around. The sun glistened off their backs like jewels cast in a field of green. It is no surprise many cultures have these mystical avians entwined within their legends, folklore and spiritual beliefs. On a rocky embankment, we came across a family of marmot, long haired from their alpine existence. Imogen and I quietly climbed down to get a better peek at their hiding spots and took some great photos. Lots of fun for the little Scott. Back down to the village we found the only spot that seemed to be alive. A pub with a beer garden facing the mountain. The music was good, a mix of

80's and 90's hits, and the drinks were cold. We were equally entertained by the gophers and the mud splattered mountain bikers at the next table, relaying their afternoon feats with gusto and plenty of gesticulations.

The hour and a half drive north to Clearwater along the banks of the North Thompson river was striking, with blue waters and forested banks of green cutting through the arid hills. The river looked so inviting, I'm sure we all considered ditching our four wheels for a kayak and getting in amongst it. The further north we travelled the greener it got, reminding me of the Atherton Tablelands back home. The town of Clearwater was very spread out. From the highway one could easily dismiss it as just another speck on the map but a little more investigation, driving down roads not knowing where they would lead, revealed the lower section of the township and the beautiful Dutch lake. We checked in at Wells-Grey National Park information centre, adorned by a gruesome array of taxidermy, an oversize bronze moose sculpture and a Teepee out front. Our afternoon was spent investigating several hikes to view magnificent and vastly different waterfalls. An added bonus was the family of bears on the roadside, deer and squirrels prancing around. At one of the falls we noticed something fly across our view which did not move like a bird. We watched it move closer then drop down into the gorge before passing into the mouth of the cave, shrouded behind a curtain waterfall. It was a drone. Wow what a great use and safe way to bow to your curiosity. I too wanted to know what the inside of that cave looked like. Maybe it led to a land that time forgot or a tropical oasis. That night we had dinner on a picnic table out front of the motel, near the pool. Nice mountain view, shame about the highway in between. The girls couldn't miss the opportunity to combine two US traditions, Dairy Queen icecream while swinging in an old whitewashed porch chair. Happy days!

Our room was wedged in between two older couples who were sitting outside their own in the evening. They seemed nice and we exchanged hellos but once we were inside, they struck up a conversation across the space, which was our doorway. They seemed to have a lot in common and not the least was their hearing loss. We now know lots about both families, their jobs, children, where they went to school and a plethora of ailments they were dealing with and how to ease them. The joys of motel living! We turned up the TV volume, but the walls were thin.

Early start the next morning, heading north to the small highway township of Blue River, Population 260 hearty souls. We joined a safari which had set up base camp on a barge in the river. It had a small cafe, booking office and boat dock which would not have looked out of place in similarly exotic places like Africa or deep dark South East Asia. The online ratings for this trip were off the planet so we didn't mind the long drive and were full of anticipation for our Bear seeking adventure through the wilderness. Imogen strutted across the small gangplank and onto the dock like the seasoned traveller she is. Lucky girl! I pondered how much more accessible air travel had become since I were a kid. She has been on planes since she was eighteen months old and has made all of our experiences all the more special.

Our young guides were a fellow from New Zealand who had spent a year living on Magnetic Island, just a twenty-minute ferry ride from our home in Australia. His partner was a Canadian born Australian girl who had been living in Perth down under for over half her life. Therefore, we felt an instant connection, pleased to have people from the Southern Hemisphere to talk to. After a short cruise past grassy sandbanks and thick forested shores, under the ever-present watch of snow-clad mountain, we slowed down and were told to scour the bank for bear. We were soon rewarded as four of them crashed out of the undergrowth and put on a display only some fifteen metres away on shore. They playfully climbed trees and played tiggy around the bank. The larger ginger tipped one came in for a swim. Magnificent experience. My camera ran hot and the look on Imogen's face was priceless. The guide said that it was the best viewing he had seen in his two years with the outfit and it was uncharacteristically sunny to boot. Pleased with our morning activities we had a lazy lunch at the town lake at Blue River, then drove back to Clearwater. That night on the Vancouver news they showed a car that had parked outside in the driveway overnight. The owner had left a loaf of bread in the back seat and a bear had ripped it open like some enormous can opener. The interior was shredded and covered in a telltale coating of fur and drool. This was not a cabin in the sticks but a residence in West Vancouver. Another woman in the U.S, running a marathon, came over a ridge and startled a mother bear and her cubs. The bear attacked, hitting her across the face leaving a nasty gash. She pretended to be dead and the bear eventually wandered off. Despite all this we still managed to have sweet dreams of gentle little teddy bears. Well I did anyway.

Canada Day at Blind Bay was a special experience with the parade marshalling in our street then progressing down to the community park right on the bay. A riot of colourful floats, vintage cars and even a couple of Mounted Police in full traditional regalia. At the park, there were market stalls and live performances for most of the day. Many locals were complaining that the overcast skies and 22 degrees were a bit too steamy for them. Then it rained. Good weather for ducks. That night Imogen and I stuffed and baked cannelloni for dinner. Not traditional Canadian tucker but still a real treat. After dinner we walked back down to the lake and joined our neighbours to watch the fireworks from their boat.

A few days later, we headed off, taking a new route south, clinging to the west bank of the lake from Vernon. We spotted longhorn sheep clambering up a mountain close to the road. The blue chicory flowers had made an appearance and dominated sections of the carriageway. In one particular bay sat hundreds of floating logs corralled and waiting to be transported to the lumber yard. We made it to the Peachland Sunday Markets, on the foreshore, for a lunch break and appeased our seven-year-old with some time on the swings and a Princess balloon made by a very happy clown. Onward via the east shore of Skaha Lake, Okanagan Falls and Oliver, passing endless fruit orchards and winery tasting rooms. Finally, we arrived at our simple accommodation on the shores of Osoyoos Lake.

Breakfast in America on the 4th of July. Independence Day! Rising early, anticipating a lot of traffic at the border crossing, we drove the few kilometres south. It was quiet and the pleasant security guards made the process simple. Not much was open due to the public holiday, so we found ourselves in the Oroville grocery store grabbing a simple breakfast. Moving on through sage bush of the Columbia plateau that transitioned into intensive apple orchard farming on our way to Wenatchee. It certainly was an unfamiliar scene. No wonder it is the self-appointed "Apple Capital of the World". Got some great photos of gnarly old timber apple crates with faded, stenciled, red branding. They were stacked at the edge of orchards, some several stories high. On the outskirts of Brewster an unexpected scene caught my eye. Up on a plateau sat several enormous satellite dishes, like giant mushrooms. Many people suspect it is some hushed up government facility coordinating confidential operations, but the official spiel suggests it is a COMSAT Earth station built in 1965. It is the largest grouping of communication dishes in the Western Hemisphere and at last count there were forty of them. It has far reaching applications from air traffic control, foreign corporations, news. Most things that use trans-pacific satellite communication. Now not being cynical at all, but one web poster pointed out the very close proximity to an NSA "Training Facility" at Yakima only some one hundred miles south. Some believe the location is no coincidence. Intriguing. Not far down the highway, we came across a photo worthy anomaly. An end loader parked on the edge of the road was holding up an electricity pole fully wired to the grid. I assume the whistle blew for knock off time for the long weekend and they figured it could stay there hanging for a few days. Bizarre really. If the hydraulics slipped, half the district would be without power.

We rolled into the small Bavarian style village of Leavenworth around lunch, amongst busy traffic. The main street was closed for Independence Day celebrations. What a special place! Although kitschy, we had a lot of fun dressing up as a cowboy and show girls for a wild west photo shoot. We joined the throng of revelers to enjoy the festivities, checked out all the market stalls and quaint shops on a lovely sunny afternoon. That evening, as we sat at an Italian rooftop restaurant, we reflected on our very cosmopolitan fourth of July. This little Aussie family had woken up in Canada, drove on through the United States to a Bavarian styled village and had Italian for dinner. Not bad, not bad at all.

After dinner, enjoying the extended twilight, we strolled down to the river park, admired the wild cherry trees and came across a bicycle bump station where several kids were having a great time riding the tight circuit constructed of rubber soft fall. Something new, I hope it comes down under soon. Or maybe it already has.

 The next morning, we followed Highway 2 through the Cascade Mountains toward the Pacific Ocean. It would have to be the most beautifully bewitching stretch of road we travelled on our year abroad. Up there with Cairns to Cape Tribulation and Te Anau to Milford Sound. The distinctive white pines clung precariously by the tips of their toes to the banks of the Skykomish and Wenatchee rivers. Torrents of snow melt raced down streams, rounding and polishing boulders of all sizes as it had for eons. Welcome and very unexpected roadside espresso bars and stalls selling dried salmon appeared intermittently. As did quirky little villages hiding around bends and outposts wedged into the undergrowth, almost invisible through thick layers of moss. The many unsubtle signage references to Bigfoot enhanced the journey. We coasted through the pleasant northern, seemingly affluent, Seattle suburbs of Bothell and Mountlake Terrace, on route to the Edmonds-Kingston ferry for our journey across the bay to Bainbridge Island in Puget Sound. Such was the vista from top deck we agreed our ride was too fleeting. Before we knew it, we had disembarked our good ship and were driving across the Agate Pass Bridge to a heavily forested island. An immediate delight, sometimes you just know you're going to love a place before you even get there. Bainbridge Island would turn out to be one of our favourite places on the West Coast. We followed our bearings to Winslow Way, the island's main street, to gather supplies for the next five days and see what else it had to offer. What a lovely place in an idyllic setting. I bet the real estate here is worth a quid. Of course, we were seeing it at its summer best. Anna and Imogen found a kid's clothing store which had a resident white rabbit running around inside. Fortunately, the owner did not wear a mad hat or invite us for tea. She was very friendly though, handing out maps and advice. The little rabbit, who had an access all areas pass, intrigued Imogen. Anna had a hard time getting her attention to try on some clothes. We browsed through a number of art galleries and stores, with some interesting wares, before heading off to find our much-anticipated digs. Our loft apartment above the owner's garage on Point White Drive faced the channel between Bainbridge Island and Waterman Point. A finger jutting out from the mainland. The owners had lived there while the main house was being built. It was very well appointed with a kitchen and balcony facing their garden. The ocean only some fifteen metres away. We enjoyed the rhythmic passing of the ferry through the narrow passage at all times of the day. Sun, rain and heavy fog. Its horn grabbed us from whatever we were doing, summonsing us to the deck for a look and a wave to the passengers on route to Seattle or Bremerton. Yes, the green and white tub had some kind of subconscious allure. Who was on board? Where were they going to? Did they have a good day? Is someone waiting for them on the other side?

Over the coming days we saw a black tailed deer with her fawn and raccoons wandering the roadways. However, the most nature driven excitement was had sitting on the deck watching the Red Hummingbirds, Blue Jays and Pileated Woodpeckers with their red caps. Our hosts did not seem to share our enthusiasm for these distinctive natives who apparently cause havoc in the garden boring large holes into trees in search of grubs. On two of our days, we caught the ferry across the bay to Seattle, the Emerald city. A heavy fog had rolled in the previous evening giving the headlands across the channel that gentle grey filter that slowly diminishes in colour and translucency until there is only imagination to draw the outline. I had a restless sleep, wrought with excitement and anticipation of the day ahead. At 5am the ferry foghorn woke me. I quickly rose to peer out the French doors to see the spotlights having little effect on the deep fog that cloaked the bay. There was a fifteen-knot breeze making the stars and stripes dance on the neighbours flagpole. By the time we boarded our ferry the day had cleared significantly, although still very overcast.

A small, but interesting aquarium on the Seattle Docks was first stop. We witnessed a very cool octopus make a rare daytime appearance; she must have known we were coming. "We get bored watching the Puffins fly through the water with ease", said no one ever. Between swims they hopped around the rocky enclosure showing off their classical black and white markings with pops of raucous orange on their feet and beaks. Across the road was the famous Pike Place Market with several floors of wares from fish to flowers, leatherwork to legumes and plenty of souvenirs to boot. We passed by the distinctive and slightly gross Gum Wall, where people constantly change the patterns on the wall by depositing fluro coloured chewing gum. A germophobes nightmare. One entrepreneur sold the eye-catching gum from a nearby store. It was tempting! Now that is an unusual take on public art.

Opened in 1907 Pike Place is one of the oldest community markets in the States. We were fortunate to be on hard when the fishmongers started their daily frivolity by tossing fish several meters across the display cabinets to the waiting hands of their coworker, who wrapped the fish and bagged it for the stunned customer. Real larrikins these blokes. They had a rather ugly halibut fish hanging over the edge of the display cabinet. When people passed by, they yanked the piece of string tied to its tale which invariably provoked jumps, screams or a combination of both. Just outside was a Policeman on his trusty steed. I lifted Imogen up to give this beautiful, calm horse a pat.

We went on a guided tour under the streets of Seattle and learnt about its extraordinary past. How in days gone by the shops were regularly flooded, the location of hidden Speakeasy Bars during Prohibition and how the term skid row was coined from the greasy track used to slide the timber from above Seattle down to the docks. As we descended, I found myself mouthing the immortal words of Alice "it's becoming curiouser and curiouser" as she fell down the rabbit hole. I don't particularly like Lewis Carrol's inventive use of the English language but "more and more curious" might not have fit the scene either. Many interesting characters have called Seattle home at one point or another. One of which was the lawman come gambler, Wyatt Earp of Tombstone fame. Cagey old Wyatt didn't drink, probably a good idea for a gambler to keep his wits about him. But he did splurge on a bowl of ice cream each day. His game of choice was Pharaoh or Faro, a popular card game in the 1700's originating in France.

Washington State is absolutely stunning but Seattle city centre is not the most attractive. What it lacks in aesthetics it gains in colourful history, a life well lived. On our second visit across the sound we were greeted with blue skies and an uninterrupted view of Mt Rainier reaching up towards the heavens. Just south was another very famous mountain. As a kid I vividly remember when Mount St. Helens blew its top. My Dad subscribed to National Geographic magazine and we spent a lot of time looking at the amazing photos and reading about the volcanic eruption. What kid doesn't like a volcano right! A visit to the park would have been great but you can't do everything. Those magazines along with World Book Encyclopedia opened up a world of opportunity to me from an early age. A curiosity and desire to explore that has never waned.

In downtown Seattle we boarded a monorail, built for the 1963 World Expo, and shot out to the Seattle Centre with its many and varied museums and exhibits. For your average futurist with a healthy and nostalgic appreciation of the past and a zest for the present, this place was amazing. We chose the Space Needle first. Imogen got a bit toey while waiting in line but I really enjoyed reading the information under the old black and white photos and construction plans as we inched our way to the elevator. These included a framed napkin on which the original architectural idea had been roughly sketched and a photo of Elvis dining with some glamourous broad at the revolving restaurant up top. After Imogen got over the fact that we arrived by elevator and not teleportation, she had a great time on the observation deck checking out the sights. Back at sea level, we roamed around and found the huge International Fountain, also from the 1960's World Fair, with its waterspouts synchronised to an array of notable music. We couldn't miss the opportunity to join the throng of excited visitors racing around the mist inside the bowl trying to stay clear of the water jets. Lots of fun. The playground was next and proved to be the highlight for Imogen. This was no ordinary playground with wonderful rope climbing towers and tunnel slides all perched beside the magnificent modern architecture of the EMP

Modern Arts Museum with its emphasis on musical popular culture and designed by none other than Frank. O. Gehry. Next stop was the Bill and Melinda Gates Foundation Visitor Centre. Great to see the initiatives this couple have on the go all over the world and how they make sure their investment on improving the planet is maximised.

After another session at the playground we headed back to the waterfront and an early dinner at Ivar's Seafood Restaurant, a Seattle institution since 1938 with a wonderfully rich history. This Ivar Haglund fellow was a real character, entertainer, radio personality and entrepreneur. The kind of person who can set the tone for a whole city to follow. We were shown to a table with views of Puget Sound and entertained through the window by the seagull circus. Passengers streamed on and off the ferry nearby, while cars hurtled along the Alaskan Way viaduct overhead. Humanity in motion. Our final treat for the day was provided by an elegant Heron which stalked its scaly prey beside the boardwalk as we disembarked. A well-dressed assassin indeed.

On our last day on Bainbridge we strolled the beach collecting large sand dollars and taking plenty of photos of the coast line. A fisherman pulled up a nice sole fish off the jetty but there were signs warning not to eat the shellfish, I suspected the water was polluted, what a shame. Later we wandered into a local gallery and got talking to the lady who ran the establishment. She had a French accent and was about my age. One of those people you seldomly meet whom you make an instant connection with, like you have known them your whole life. She had also done an exchange, but as a high school student. She confided that she never really felt that she belonged in France and had returned to the States to complete University. Never went back. We told her our story and she understood, having lived all over the States. She agreed that the climate really shaped the people and it can be very difficult to come into some communities. Unfortunately, I never learnt her name, but she offered us some philosophy as we were leaving "Life has its seasons and this journey has a reason". I undoubtedly believe she was true.

We reluctantly left our seaside loft, heading for Port Angeles. A relatively short drive, or so we had thought. The quirky Norwegian themed village of Poulsbo was our choice for morning tea. Nestled on the banks of Liberty Bay inlet. From here we headed for Hood Canal Bridge to skip across to the Olympic Peninsula and our cabin in the woods. This peculiar floating bridge opened up the region to commerce and tourism. It pivots on a hinge to accommodate the rise and fall of the tide and can be draw away to allow ships and submarines access to the Naval Base at Bangor. On this particular day the bridge had jammed open and after waiting in line for almost an hour, we were told to turn around. The alternative route took more than four hours. The silver lining was that we saw some great countryside along the canal which we would never have explored. Lots of quaint villages and homes bordering on the inlet. It just oozed relaxation. A place where kids would love to grow up and adults retire to. By the time we rolled into our much-anticipated micro cabin in the woods we were all exhausted and in need of some relaxation. The road into the cabin revealed bits of junk randomly strewn amongst the tress and long grass. Sure, the cabin was different, but we expected something a bit more inhabitable for the price we paid. Stepping from the car to stretch our legs, an intense smell of smoke attacked our senses. I made a dash for the outside toilet which unexpectedly was not a long drop, but a civilised porcelain flush variety or so I thought. Then a sign on the wall caught my attention "All used toilet paper to be thrown through the hole" with an arrow pointing to a fist size hole in the corrugated iron wall. Ok we have travelled in South-East Asia and seen our share of stomach churning, nose burning excuses for a toilet, but this was unnecessarily in bad taste, especially when you have paying guests. After inspecting the rather grim and confined cabin interior constructed with a random assortment of recycled materials and roadside finds, our collective sense of humour was hemorrhaging. It is not that we weren't up for an adventure, but it had been a very long day, it was getting late and we were tired and cold. We began to unpack our belongings. By this stage the smoke was really making it hard to breath. Anna suggested it may just be strong incense burning somewhere nearby, but I didn't buy it. She rang the owner who had not previously made an appearance. A woman eventually came and told us that there were no fires on her property, but then she also smelt it. After a brief investigation she whispered in a rather embarrassed tone "Oh (significant pause) it looks like my husband has burnt the bucket where the toilet paper is thrown, and it's been smoldering." I flooded the can with water as the woman scurried off. The smoke stopped but the smell lingered, and I questioned what type of incense my wife had previously smelt because we had been inhaling burning human crap. Not a nice welcome to the woods. As the evening chill descended further upon us, we quickly cooked our dinner on our portable stove, then huddled inside. We were a little dejected but decided to go to bed early and leave a call whether to stay or go until the morning. By 6.30 am the next morning the discussion had happened. The decision unanimous. We quickly packed the car, walking past the life size carving of an Indian

Chief. His eyes seemed to follow us back and forth to the car and the creases in his face seemed to deepen with his disapproving stare. Imogen refused to use the toilet and Anna had been claustrophobic in the mezzanine bunk bed where she hit her head every time she moved. We were out of there! As I drove out the gate, I remembered the French lady's advice from the day before. "Life has its seasons and this journey had a reason" and I smiled. You don't get stories like that sitting on the couch at home.

Since we were already halfway along the Juan De Fuca high way between Port Angeles and the Tongue Point Marine Life Sanctuary, we went for an early morning visit. A magnificent spot. We climbed down cliffs and rock hopped around tide pools, full of sea anemone, starfish, urchins and barnacles. Large kelp forests lay just off the edge and Vancouver Island was visible across the international border, only some sixteen kilometers away. A little further around the Salt Creek campgrounds, we stopped for a picnic lunch and were entertained by two agile raccoons and several chipmunks keen on grabbing any crumbs we dropped. Without going crazy with anthropomorphism, chipmunks are cheerful, they look like they have a permanent self-assured smile. They are the confident stranger who strides up and just starts talking. The epitome of an eccentric, caffeine fueled mover and shaker. The high-powered door to door salesman of the animal kingdom. I half expected him to sidle up to the picnic table and interject "So Pal, what can I sell you today?". My first encounter with a Chipmunk was in Yellowstone NP. I expected a shy animal, hard to catch a glimpse of, but was amazed at how curious and cheeky they are. One climbed up my leg in an attempt to pinch a corn chip out of my hand. Down on the beach we discovered artistically eroded cliffs which looked like a great spot for pirates to hide their treasure. We have missed the beach and the ocean, so took the time to go for a long walk. Back in Port Angeles we found a motel and set out on foot to check out the town. The region had long been inhabited by indigenous communities and the Spanish. At one time it homed a healthy fishing and whaling industry. Relics of this era gave the town its frontier feel.

    After a much better sleep we drove straight out of town and up to Hurricane Ridge. Climbing 1600 meters through patches of remnant snow and ice, it proffered outstanding views in every direction. The wildlife had surely become used to two-legged visitors. We had up close and personal encounters with deer, marmots and chipmunks. After a picnic we went back down the range to Crescent Lake with plans to hire a canoe, the weather had a different idea and came in rainy. The lodge, built in 1916, had all the trimmings of a turn of the century American resort. These solidly built historic venues are a joy to explore. A welcome fire raged in the main lobby, high ceilings, ornate staircase and elegant timber furniture with heavily embroidered cushions. Elk and various other unfortunate beasts' heads looked down at our every move. A perfect place to film a who done it murder mystery episode. I bet these walls could tell some tales of yester-year. The side of the building opened up to a solarium facing the lake. It looked very inviting indeed. I could have easily settled in with a hot drink, maybe laced with something a bit stronger to warm the cockles. A game of cards or perhaps backgammon would be more appropriate. Instead we put on our rain jackets to check out the jetty and cabins. I rarely walk in the rain at home. Maybe I should start, at least it wouldn't be cold.

    From our motel roost up on the hill above this peaceful windswept port town we could see the gulls swooping to feed in the bay, punctuated by fishing vessels and the regular ferry to Vancouver Island. Church bells tolled loud, proud and regularly in Port Angeles. They start at six in the morning, the last around nine at night. Quite quaint really, I closed my eyes and imagined we were in a little European seaside village.

Now I like to travel with a plan, but it is always nice to come across an unexpected treasure and the Olympic Game Farm at Sequim was one of these. For a few dollars we got to drive our vehicle through a well-maintained home to an alphabet soup of free-range animals. We spent several hours visiting the menagerie representing every continent except our own. A beautifully gentle Yak tried to force its rather large head into our car window in an attempt to grab a slice of bread. There were so many highlights, the llama were so curious with their wise eyes, the retired Disney bears were great to watch as they put on little impromptu routines as we drove past. At the entry grid to one section of the compound it stated "Enter at your own risk, keep the vehicle rolling or the animals will scratch and dent your car" we chose to drive through, but not until we summoned enough courage to drive straight at a bison who was standing guard right in the middle of the road. He eventually moved slowly to the side giving the impression that he just felt like it and not because we wished to pass. At the last second, he turned and gave us an arrogant glance. Deer, antelope and a magnificent elk with full set of antlers, ambled around the enclosure.

Next stop, the quaint old town of Port Townsend with its distinctive old buildings balanced on high sandstone cliffs above its safe harbour. Now a popular home for retirees, it was all action back in 1981 when the majority of the movie "An Officer and a Gentleman" was filmed in the town. The site was used because the US government would not allow filming at the real Aviation Officer School in Pensacola Florida. We crossed the bay on another car ferry to Whidbey Island and stumbled upon the charming seaside village of Coupeville. There was some sort of yacht race in the bay and seals glided around in the shallows near the beach. A former frontier seaport sat within a protected bay lined with gracefully aging weatherboard buildings clinging to the pebbly shore in sun faded shades of ochre, rouge and eggshell blue. A splash of restaurants and a jetty to stroll, made it the perfect place on that perfect summer day. It made quite an impression on all of us. We wished we had stayed a few nights but had pre booked Bellingham. We will return one day. On route we passed through the scenic Deception Pass State Park which beaconed to be investigated as well.

After a long day driving, we unpacked the car then I left the girls at the hotel pool and went for a walk. Before long I came across a strong smell of hooch and scanned around in hope of identifying its source. No camper vans with smoke billowing out, no group of teens sitting under a tree smiling at the clouds. Nothing. I walked on forgetting about it. On my return I noticed a small sign, a green marijuana leaf on the fence adjacent to a side road leading to an inconspicuous red brick warehouse behind the main shops. Sure enough, this was where the smell was coming. They must have some good extraction to be pumping it out some sixty meters down the lane. Marijuana legalisation is a big topic in North America and entrepreneurs are rushing to develop legitimate businesses around the laws. Canada was grappling with it during our stay and there were already rumblings back home.

In the morning we crossed the border into Canada ending the U.S. leg of our road trip. This was our third visit to the land of stars and stripes. We always enjoy it immensely and feel very welcome. The people are warm and helpful. We seem to mostly understand each other, and their country is vast and amazingly beautiful. The border crossing went smoothly but we struck very heavy traffic on the southern outskirts of Vancouver which frustratingly endured for the whole journey through to Whistler Ski Resort, up the Sea to Sky highway. Somewhere north of Vancouver we randomly took a side road, needing to rest our legs and ended up in West Vancouver, which is the prettiest suburb we have encountered in the city. It reminded me a bit of the Sunshine Coast in Queensland. Fueled with coffee, we crossed the train tracks and strolled along the beachfront walkway with views back to Stanley Park and the Lions Gate Bridge. Back on the highway we crawled along, sometimes only covering ten kilometers in an hour. Of note, the road signs now had both English and the local first nation language. It was not until we reached Squamish Village for lunch and read about the huge Pemberton Music Festival starting that day, that we realised the reason for the mad midweek traffic.

Accommodation at the year-round resort is expensive so we booked a family room in a hostel. Our first time staying in one of these communal type places, so we were slightly apprehensive, but the facility was new. We had a bathroom in our room and the shared kitchen was never crowded, despite the busy looming weekend. The soup of foreign accents and languages were great for Imogen to witness and later discuss. A large world map allowed guests to pin their hometowns. There were people from New Zealand, Brazil, France, and Lagos in Nigeria to name a few.

The fusion of spices used in the kitchen provided a heady, but pleasant aroma throughout the second level of the building. Short on supplies and locked in by traffic, we grabbed whatever we could from the small convenience store across the road. Who would have known a can of lentil soup mixed with two-minute noodles, cheese and tabasco sauce could taste so good.

Not wanting to endure any more delays with traffic or parking problems, we caught the bus into the main village each day. Along with Vancouver, Whistler was home to the 2010 Winter Olympics. A lot of infrastructure was put in place at that time making it a well-known destination around the world. Obviously snow sports draw the crowds but as I found out from one of my students before leaving Aus, it is arguably one of the best mountain biking trail networks in the world. The village was very commercial but fun. We spent time at the playground, it doesn't take Imogen long to find one. Took photos beside the Olympic rings, did over the shops and caught a movie. At a cafe, we got talking to an Aussie waiter who was spending the last bit of his summer in Whistler after three weeks backpacking in South America and waiting on tables at Hamilton Island in Australia. Not a bad break from University, which he was attending in London. He came from the tiny town of Chinchilla in Queensland. Just goes to show you can do anything if you are willing to dream. We had a chuckle about Canadian quirks, and he told us they call the place Whistralia because forty percentage of the employees are from home. Anna ordered a frozen Bellini and it was so cold out on the deck that it wouldn't melt enough to drink. At dinner that night we sat between a table of Aussies and Kiwis. In fact, it sounded like half the restaurant was from down under. Of course, the Kiwis went straight into talking about their recent dominance of Rugby

Union. I just politely smiled. Not that I follow Rugby Union, but I can remember throughout the 90's when Australia was on the top of that heap. I thought it was a bit much considering I didn't start the conversation with a sheep or gumboot joke, for which there are plenty. Anyway, good people the New Zealanders. Always up for a laugh.

The next morning, I left the girls to sleep in and went for a hike to the Train Wreck of 1959. During our bus trips to the village I first heard a couple of young fellows talking about this landmark and then on the way back in the evening I overheard two waitresses say they were going to do the hike on their day off. There had to be something special about it. It turned out to be a great walk along the Cheakamus River with plenty of photo opportunities. Poorly marked though, everyone I met was asking for me for directions. I must have looked like I knew where I was going. Not sure how I managed that. Over the years, the wreckage had evolved into mish mash of DIY mountain bike obstacles where decades of stunt jump additions, graffiti and decay had transformed the rolled wagons into a surreal scene increasingly consumed by the old growth forest. Part art, part unsanctioned extreme sport facility. Some of the jumps shot off the end of containers potentially directed the rider into thin air several meters above the earth. It made me wish someone had been riding during my visit, but then again it had been a while since I did my last first aide course and the likelihood, I would need it was high.

We headed off the following day, entertained by the roadside antics of the tired, unwashed Music festival punters. Between Whistler and Kamloops, we passed through many small communities in desperate need of some aesthetic cajoling, reaching the township of Lillooet around lunch. I didn't like the look of the town, for some reason it made me feel a bit uneasy but when we saw another young family in a park, I thought it would be ok to stop for a picnic. Not long after we had set up, the family left and a car pulled up unloading two men, one had a large beatbox on his shoulder which was blaring out some unfamiliar din. The shorter of the two started taunting us immediately. I just tried to ignore him but kept him in view. He then proceeded to walk towards us. If this type of thing happened at home, I would have known how to handle it or what to expect but I was not sure what this bloke was capable of and decided it was time to get my family out. As the saying goes, I was going to give him a dirty look but he already had one, so I stood up and walked toward him while Anna and Imogen quickly packed the car. He didn't like my advance and quickly began to retreat while giving me a barrage of abuse. An ugly incident which could have been worse. He could have pulled a knife or gun for all I knew. It left a bad taste in our mouths and we had to explain to Imogen that not everyone in this world is nice. It is best to keep away from trouble if you can. Sometimes people's behaviour is hard to fathom. We drove through several dusty outposts before rolling back into the now familiar greenery of the Shuswap.

Back at Blind Bay for a fortnight. According to the newspaper, the first nineteen days of summer had rained, and the locals were none too happy about it. I don't blame them; this is the time of the year they hang out for. We were keen to see as much as we could while it was not covered in snow, so tried to get out and about each day. White Lake, just to our east was wide and long with a reputation for good fishing. As soon as our kayaks slid into the clear waters, a school of orange fish flashed through the shallows. They looked exotic. I bet someone emptied the contents of their fish tank in the lake and somehow, they survived. A paddle through the tall reeds exposed hordes of blue dragonflies emerging from their casings to take flight for the first time. When it was time to pull ashore, we crossed paths with a family walking their piglet on a leash. This brought a smile to our face and I hoped he wouldn't end up on the Thanksgiving table with an apple in his mouth.

A few days later, we kayaked Gardom Lake, just south of Salmon Arm. This was more our style, smaller with more features to investigate. When most people picture a perfect North American summer lake scene, I bet it looks a lot like that place. It wasn't promoted as a tourist destination or mentioned by the locals as a must see, in fact some of them had never heard of it. Tucked away off the highway, we passed several hillbilly looking, makeshift structures only visible from the access road. No power lines, just living off the grid. Like many lakes in Canada, it is impossible to walk the shore because houses go right down to the water's edge and fence off access, so a kayak provides the best way of taking in the views. Most homes have a private jetty with diving board and Adirondack chairs. Their backyard gardens were on display and ducks frolicked in the relative warmth. Two heavily wooded islands gave us an opportunity to come ashore and stroll around. A young bald eaglet squawked loudly from a tree above, telling its mother it was hungry. Imogen sat on my lap and did some paddling. Great to see she enjoys it. I think I know what to buy her for Christmas.

One day Anna went to town and I planned to do some craft or paint with Imogen, but she had other ideas. "Dad! I need to alter two of my Barbie Dolls dresses. Can you sew?" to which I replied "No". She retorted "Well Dad it will be a good opportunity for you to learn". How could I argue with that logic? There we sat cutting the halter neck straps in two, slicing a bit of the excess Velcro from the back of the dress and sewing on the cut ends. It made her very happy and in turn I was pleased to be able to enjoy some time with her. I hope she remembers because I know I will never forget.

Celista sat just across the river and conveniently had a winery which conducted tours twice a week. Not to miss an opportunity to taste some wine and learn about the process, we gathered one Wednesday morning with a relatively large group of people to walk the property and hear the owner's story. The winery had only been producing the good stuff for a few years but already had won several awards. It was a retirement project for the couple who lived most of their working life up in the icy North West Territory. They only produced small vintages and the room where all the magic happened was only about the size of a double garage. On the way back we saw a young bear scampering down the road then disappearing into the trees. After a picnic on the north shore of the Shuswap we hiked the north bank of the Adams River up to the gorge and were happy to run into a rafting company having a break on the bank. The guide was showing them some native rock art, which was cool. Lucky, he pointed it out, as the red ochre had faded, and the stick drawing deer took some imagination.

The weather smiled again the following day, so we went back to Adams River and hiked the Bear Creek logging flumes trail. The path disappeared into dense woods. It was damp underfoot, a thick layer of emerald green moss covered fallen trees as we forged on under the massive cedar and fir canopy crossing the creek several times before climbing a steep bank. Timber flumes had been constructed to transport the log down a steep incline. I couldn't help thinking how much hard labour would have gone into the project only to be used for a few years while that section of forest was logged. There must have been good money for lumber. This particular flume was built in 1908 to service the newly established Chase Sawmill. They had moved on by 1912 leaving behind history and access to a great hike. On the drive back we searched for an elusive playground tucked away behind houses in Blind Bay. We were beginning to think it was an urban myth. There was no reference to it on maps or signage but by pure luck we turned down a quiet street and saw an access lane. Why a park would be situated down a hatchet block and not on the lake is anyone's guess. While Imogen used the swings, Anna found a sugar plum tree and had a feed of the sweet, juicy fruit.

Having enjoyed the stone fruit, we searched and found a "Pick your own" cherry farm on the outskirts of Salmon Arm. The farmer said he had lost sixty percent of his crop, splitting from the unseasonal rain. He gave us a couple of buckets and said eat as much as you like, so we picked and munched our way through several different varieties. All nice but very distinct flavours. I thought we would never get through two buckets of fruit but over the following week this proved to be a misjudgment. We had them fresh, as well as in a Cobbler which Anna baked. Later that day we sat on the patio pitting the fruit and were entertained by a chipmunk who was raiding the chestnuts to fill his larder. Anna had been keeping an eye on the nuts, waiting for them to come ripe, but within a few days they were all stored away for the winter somewhere up in an old cedar tree. For dinner we had pork and apple pie. After seeing it on the menu board at the pie shop in town, we came up with a recipe using what we had in the cupboard. It went down really well. A future family favourite.

APPLE & PORK PIE

Into a fry pan throw a handful of pork mince and another of beef or leftover pork roast. Fry until brown.

In a separate pan fry two peeled and coarsely chopped apples, celery, onion, bacon, spinach and garlic until apple softens. Add into the mince pan and stir through.

Mix in one teaspoon of mustard and a couple of sage powder, salt & pepper, chicken stock cube dissolved in ½ cup of water and a tablespoon of flour. This should make a thick gravy. Add extra liquid if required.

Bang the mix into a pie tin lined with puff pastry. Place a pastry lid on top.

Bake for 1 hour at 180 degrees - serve with quince or fig jam

Since our kayaking visits to Reedman Point, adjacent to Copper Island on the lake, I had been waiting for good weather to take the girls down for a picnic. We gathered our BBQ and set up camp on the headland. After a stroll along the foreshore and some stone skipping, we settled down and just enjoyed the sun. The picnickers next door had music playing, a welcome ambience for a relaxed meal. The following day we revisited Skimikin Lake. Last visit was on Groundhog Day when we walked the frozen waters and our lips turned blue. We paddled the unusual brown, tannin stained waters and found a beaver's lodge along with an unfamiliar water plant complete with tiny pink flowers. It certainly wasn't a lily. The following few days of warmer weather allowed us to open the windows in the bedrooms. One night I woke to the mournful wolf pack howl. I read in the paper that they had been culling them up near Sicamous in an attempt to save the remaining Moose and Caribou. An imbalance in nature somewhere along the line. The warmth only lasted two days then back to the cool, rainy status quo.

Imogen had a play date with Moira and enthusiastically recounted our woodpecker and blue jay encounters in Washington. Her friend's mother developed a huge grin and told us she had never seen anyone so excited about a bird. Then went on to describe an Australian bird she took a fancy to on her travels down under. It was the much-maligned Ibis, a nice looking bird with its black head and elegantly curved beak, bright red splotches on the underside of black and white wings. They are scavengers and have an unfortunate penchant for congregating in large flocks around local rubbish tips. Hence the nickname "Dump Chook". A fall in grace considering they were sacred to the ancient Egyptians. For me it is hard to go past the majestic Jabiru, our extra-large black and white stork with bright red spindly legs.

Not knowing what to expect or how welcome we would be, we drove over to Kamloops for the annual Pow Wow gathering of First Nations people. This annual event attracts participants from all over North America and is a celebration of their heritage through storytelling, song and dance, woven together in ceremony. The proceedings were housed in a large, log built, round stadium with the roof over the seating creating an oculus type opening over a grassed, circular parade ground. The colour and intricate detail of the costumes, the guttural chanting and rhythmic drumming became somewhat hypnotic. An explosion of the senses leaving us unsure where to look. This was compounded by the need to photograph the event for prosperity. I was a bit tentative at first, aware that some cultures are uneasy about being photographed, but judging by the constant, uncontested clicking of those around me, it seemed to be ok. I must have taken a hundred shots. Thank goodness for digital cameras. We found a great elevated spot to sit and were entertained by the circular dancing of the different tribes/clans/bands with participants of all ages. There were three separate drumming groups, located around the circumference, who took turns supplying the backbeat and vocals for the mass of vibrant bodies seemingly moving to their own individual interpretation of the music. When I closed my eyes, it was easy to visualize a spirited group of warriors on horseback in full paint rushing into battle. Each song was introduced by a slick talking announcer who loved superlatives and may have had a previous life as radio host or auctioneer. Red, white, black, blue and ochre body paint had been masterfully applied as per traditional design. Head dresses and feathered bustles had extraordinary detail, some with taxidermied eagle heads in the centre. Intricate shawls and blankets were wrapped around shoulders and feet clad in ornately decorated moccasins. Bracelets, anklets, rattles and bells added to the many other unfamiliar sights and sounds. We were present for a "welcoming into the tribe" ceremony for a four-year-old boy. It involved a sage bush smoking ritual, waving, dancing and speeches. What a great experience. The best thing was its authenticity. It was all for the people, not staged for tourists.

You know those photos that occasionally appear online of dog owners looking uncannily similar to their pets. Well I rarely give them a second glance and move on but can now report that seeming this anomaly in the flesh is much more comically satisfying. On the now familiar Blind Bay road that follows the shore, I saw many people walking. They are literally hard to miss as there are no paths or even cleared edges, so walkers take their chances on the road. There's one lady who owns a cute white West Highland Terrier, she also has pure white, shoulder length hair controlled by a headband creating a protruded fringe much like her lovable pooch. So along with exercise she unknowingly creates a happy moment for passersby, well at least one. Another observation out on the roads! It would appear there is a correlation between oversize utility trucks and reckless, high speed driving. The personality that yearns to own one of these steroidal chunks of steel and rubber must, on some level match up with a reckless gene. Or to give a Freudian perspective, the truck maybe compensation for something else they are missing in their lives, like blokes who own big, nasty dogs.

Off again on our summer road trip adventure - Part Two. It is said that the Rocky Mountains stitch together the Provinces of British Columbia and Alberta. Whoever was responsible for this rather messy needlework, sure created a jaw droppingly beautiful landscape and home for an array of wonderful wildlife. I stumbled across the Tete Jaune Lodge and campground while looking for affordable accommodation near Jasper. Although it was an hour drive from the township, this spot nestled on the banks of the milky grey Fraser River turned out to be a destination all on its own. Tete Jaune is French for Yellow Head and refers to the blond hair of a pioneering Metis fur trader who discovered a Secwepemc village on the banks of the Frazer. The native people were living well on the abundant fish, wild berries and land mammals. A town named Tete Jaune Cache was built next to the new rail in 1901 and boomed for twenty years. In the first part of the twentieth century paddle steamers plied the waters and it had all the services of an outpost town. Hard to imagine, little more than photographs remain of the town and its infrastructure, but the rugged beauty prevails. We stayed in a log cabin with shared bathrooms not far away and went for walks along the riverbank, bravely stepping up to our ankles in the freezing summer melt flow. One neighbouring camp had kayaks lying beside the tent and two 7mm wetsuits hanging in the breeze. The river sure did look inviting, but it was running fast and the inevitable dunking was not as palatable. On our first night, we acquired some firewood and sat around in the early evening enjoying the setting surrounded by some of the tallest mountains in Canada. A large jumping salmon making its way upstream in the fast-moving water rewarded a serendipitous twilight stroll down to the river. Only the stronger, larger fish make it up this far from the ocean and this one would have fed us for a couple of nights. Further along a lady pointed out a large animal swimming upstream. She declared it to be an otter but on closer inspection we agreed it was a large old man beaver cleverly using the lee of a mid-river sandbank and the power of its paddle tail to take it home. We watched it for at least ten minutes feeling privileged to witness this tenacious critter in the wild.

Earlier in the day we had stopped at Valemont for supplies and picked up a copy of the Rocky Mountain Goat. This local paper was a fascinating read giving insight into small town life in the mountains. Sport, entertainment and opinion painted an idyllic scene. We got to talking to a local out front of the grocery store she said "You are lucky to be here in this weather up until now the summer forecast in the Robson Valley has gone along the lines of "Wet -Very Wet - Cloudy with possible showers - Sun showers" No doubt she was frustrated. After living in Blind Bay for seven months we could empathise.

The following afternoon Imogen dragged me down to the playground where a slightly older girl was hanging out by herself. She immediately started talking Dragons and asked us "who wants to be the keeper of the dungeon?" She went on "Let's pretend you tied me up in the chains of the swing! That's if you want to play on my swings!" Imogen just kept on swinging while quietly sizing up this forward girl. She let her talk and talk, then chose to engage. They spoke about spider webs and all things Dragon. It was just wonderful to watch kids play on that little patch of green, oblivious to the world and immersed in one of their own. For a while I lay back on the bench seat, watched the clouds roll by and joined them in uncomplicated childhood bliss. I think I spotted a Kookaburra shaped cloud, but it quickly flew away.

Thursday 4th August

Jasper township here we come. A fortuitous glance at the petrol gauge showed we were running on empty so a brief stop at Mt Robson servo was in order. It sat beside the National Park visitor centre and gave us the opportunity to stand back, and take in the scale of the grand mountain, 3959-metre-high, its peak partially veiled in cloud. Then on to the Alberta border crossing into Mountain Time and turning our watches forward an hour. Situated on the Rockies, Jasper is a small adventurer's base town. On main street we sat outside a coffee shop and enjoyed some people watching. Our morning tea was serenaded by a couple of musicians who had just started to busk across the street. Unquestionably surrounded by beauty, I had expected the township to have more rustic charm, but we really only saw a portion before heading out to explore. Just out of town, the Maligne Canyon hike gave us an opportunity to witness how mother nature has mixed time and abrasion to carve rock intricately into a showpiece. It was so intriguing that Imogen walked all the way to the fourth bridge and back without a complaint about how far it was. Maligne Lake was a much further drive out of town. We encountered several bear jams as we hugged abrupt limestone cliffs, something we have not seen in person before. Mount Rushmore's famous President sculptures derive their white hue from limestone as well, making me think of how a carving here would have a confronting allure. But I suppose they are spectacularly dramatic just as they are. Although we had prepaid our cruise on the lake it was booked out. I know! How does that work? Judging by the irate line up in front of us, we were not alone in our disappointment. I didn't even bother waiting my turn. Instead we hiked a few trails and checked out the lodge. Fascinating old photos of pioneers and indigenous families from the 1800's hung from the walls. Among the images was an original map roughly scratched on a piece of parchment. Drawn by Samson Beaver, it was used by the first white people, the Schaffer family, to find the area.

After two nights in the cabin at Tete Jaune we treated ourselves to a night at the up-market Jasper House Bungalows with views of the Alabasta River from our living room couch. We hung around the resort for the afternoon, played a bit of bocce and horseshoes. Just generally relaxing, which was a nice change. At about six in the evening I went for a walk upstream on the Alabasta. The sandy flats alongside the river were covered in elk tracks. I assume they come out early in the mornings. Several whitewater rafts glided past full of happy waving adventurers. I was on the lookout for bear. They had frequented the lodge of late, prompting the receptionist to advise us to look out the window before we opened the cabin door just to make sure we didn't have an unwelcome house guest. Our stay coincided with the opening ceremony of the Rio Olympics, so we watched and explained the concept of the event to Imogen. In four years I am sure we will remember where we were. A large thunderstorm hit during the night and put on a great display. The front door rattled so hard that I thought the wildlife wanted to come in and shelter. Maybe they did but I just pulled up the blankets and went back to sleep.

Full of anticipation, the next morning we set off along the Icefields Parkway on route to Lake Louise. The highway followed wild river systems for most of the way affording close up views of untamed beauty. Both Athabasca and Sunwapta falls were outstanding examples of nature's force and the mountains between the two were eye catching. These massive plates of rock had simply given way to tectonic forces and distinctively crumpled up at an acute angle. Surreal! The edges were so sharp that it looked as if it had been a recent event, not millions of years ago. We stopped at a small roadside camping area for lunch. While Anna was cleaning up, Imogen and I went for a discovery mission down to the creek. We hopped over a few streams and bounced our way across the spongy muskeg to the water's edge, crouched under branches and spider webs down to where the creek reached the highway. Imogen loved our little adventure so much that she had to go back and guide her Mum through the course with commentary equal to a wildlife documentary. Great to see her immersed in nature and enjoying it.

Thus far the day had been sunny and cold but as we rolled into the car park at Athabasca Glacier things took a turn for the worst. Having prepaid our transport up onto the ice and knowing we wouldn't be coming back that way anytime soon, we decided we had to give it a go and boarded the huge, red, purpose built bus which would have looked more at home in an open cut mining operation or on Mars. Massive tyres and over-engineered cabin, I reckon that beast could have driven headlong into a cataclysm and came out the other side. On our ascent to the middle of the Glacier our Kiwi driver kept us entertained. His humour was certainly familiar but lost in translation on many of the North Americans. He didn't seem to mind. The ice was very slippery from the rain, but we tentatively wandered around taking some great photos while doing our best to shield our cameras from the rain and sleet. Imogen was very excited about it all which made it all the more special. After half an hour on the ice we were driven to the skywalk and had the disconcerting feeling of walking out over the cliff face on a semi-circular, glass platform. By the time we disembarked we were all tired and excited about our day but there was still an hour drive to Lake Louise.

Rolling into our hostel about seven pm, we were greeted by friendly faces. The car was parked a hundred meters away from the front door and our private dorm, up three flights of stairs. No lift! Unpacking was an endurance training bootcamp but a warm shower and some hastily prepared dinner down in the communal mess made it all ok. Everyone in the hostel seemed to be over thirty or under ten, making an unexpected family feel about the place. Understandable, I suppose, due to the surrounding accommodation being astronomically priced. The room was simple, with a toilet inside and a communal shower in the hall. I could stay in a four-star hotel back home for the same price but we didn't come to sit in a hotel. Nature was the star of the show in these parts. Five minutes' drive to Lake Louise, twenty to Moraine Lake and under an hour to Banff. I am happy with the investment for four nights.

My toes were cold. The covers must have fallen off, or so I thought through my early morning daze. A shaft of soft light crept through the solitary portal in the wall. Through squinted eyes, I began to make out the dormitory style double decker bed I was lying on and spartan surroundings. The question "Was I back in boarding school?" flashed across my mind until slapping me back to the present. A good night's sleep and the anticipation of the day ahead had me in an upbeat frame of mind. Lake Louise's five kilometre shore trail was a fine place to begin. At breakfast we sat in the mess hall surrounded by Australians. We arrived at the lake around nine thinking we would beat the rush. Think again. We were very fortunate to get one the last few car parks in the main area. Later in the day there were cars parked on both sides of the road for several kilometres. At the entrance, main viewing platform and the promenade in front of the hotel, there were hundreds of people. All shapes, sizes and many in ethnic dress. I stood there pondering how many nationalities were represented on that one morning. A testament of how unique the place is. On our previous visit, the icy tongue of the Victoria Glacier lapped at water's edge. But on this day a small creek ran in its place. It was a strange feeling to walk on the beach where several feet of ice and snow had recently sat. On route to the trailhead, we stepped around another episode of dueling tripods and selfie portrait posers in the middle of the path. Heavy fog enveloped the lake until around eleven o'clock, which made the escapade even more special and the photo opportunities diverse. After the hike, we wandered through the Fairmont Hotel taking the time to enjoy its grandeur. Old world furnishings, photos of Indians Chiefs in full headdress and khaki clad pioneers, some with scout style felt hats, high leather boots and puffy trousers. The view through the full length, arched windows of the restaurant down the lake was breathtaking. Like an Escher artwork, a view that demanded a daydream. We sat out front in the garden and unpacked our little picnic in front of the best view in the house. I didn't even want to know how much it cost to stay at that place. We were experiencing the best of what it had to offer.

The Bow River ambled its way through the Lake Louise township in the typical Rocky Mountain style of effortless beauty. We had planned an afternoon walk but noticed bear warning signs erected at the trailhead so made a visit to the Park Ranger at the Samson Mall. He reported that bears were running a muck along the creek, chasing hikers and bikers. Apparently, they usually move higher up the mountain as the snow melts and berries become available. But not this year! The wolf pack were also on the ran-tan, raiding a nearby campground for food. We stayed on the town side of the fence, still able to explore the feeder creek behind the mall. Imogen enjoyed throwing rocks and climbing boulders, so much so that she made us come back in the evening for a picnic dinner. We sat on top of the flattest rock, which wasn't that flat at all, and tucked into a cooked chook, hoisin noodles and a bottle of Australia's finest sav blanc. Nice! Opulence on a budget. The sound of vibrant blue waters gushing over the rocks interjected at regular intervals by trains clickety clacking over the nearby bridge. After dinner we worked on Imogen's throwing technique. She was letting them go too early and the rocks were going straight up and straight down, sometimes hitting her head and shoulders. The poor child had resorted to putting one hand over her head for protection. Time for some urgent parent intervention. Back to the hostel and an early night. I heard a few bumps during the night. Poor Anna bumped her head so many times on the bunks that Imogen and I were concerned that if she left to access the restrooms in her semi-concussed state, she may not be able to find her way back. Insensitively I pointed out that each time she bumped it made a different sound.

With predicted cloud and rain, we decided to drive the Bow River Parkway in search of wildlife. It was unexpectedly quiet, except for one bear who had created an impassable jam. With the distinctive Castle Mountain observing the antics, people readily tempting fate by jumping out of their cars with little kids on their shoulders. By the time our car passed the action, we only caught a glimpse of black fur through the undergrowth. We were not quite sure what to expect of Banff, but we loved it. Sure, the main street was touristy, but it is a tourist town. Where Banff Avenue hits the Bow River there was a large park. The sun had made an unpredicted appearance. During our picnic lunch a scruffy band of backpackers entertained with their slackline and frisbee acrobatics. The things you can master with plenty of free time! We followed the path along the river and across the bridge spotting a caribou, our first. Imogen played hide and seek with a squirrel around the trunk of a tree. Every time she moved, it repositioned just out of her sight. They both seemed to enjoy the encounter. Not expecting to go far, we were dragged along by the beauty and before long had arrived at Bow Falls. I never knew it existed, what a find. Rafters were heading off downstream and tour buses regurgitated their weary load for a quick look then back down the hatch.

Never was the saying "You snooze you lose" more apt than when visiting the major attractions of this region. Even the less know Moraine Lake had a roadblock erected by nine am and only let people drive in if someone came out. We beat the herd by leaving before eight and had our breakfast in the brisk morning air. It was only six degrees but the sense of achievement at getting there made the cereal and freshly brewed tea, taste all the better. We entertained the other adventurers with our make-shift breakfast table and portable gas burner in the gutter in front of our car. Moraine Lake is a different shade of blue to Lake Louise, I suspect it must be the minerals the water runs through. It is more of a cerulean blue green and changes throughout the day with the light intensity. A pleasant slap to your senses like the emerald greens in a damp, dark, rainforest jungle. The shore hike was invigourating, but very cold. The mountains blocked out the morning sun. When we got back, the canoe hire shop was just opening up. Despite the price tag, this was one of those things we just had to do. For over an hour, we explored the entire shoreline. After lunch Imogen and I tiptoed over the floating log jam at the end of the lake and climbed the rocky outcrop. She just loved it, but safety is not yet a consideration. Several times I had to clamber up and catch her as she attempted to climb some rock that her little legs would not allow. Anna took the path and we met up the top for unparalleled views of the lake and surrounds. We took several photos that could easily have been used in a travel brochure. The trail to Consolation Lake was at the base of the lookout so decided to have a look. Not far along, we came across a chirping sound then Anna spotted the elusive Pika, a cute little mammal with large mouse like ears. They live in burrows within the rocky piles which provide plenty of protected living space. Further up the trail we could hear gushing water beneath our feet but could not see the creek beneath the boulders. An unusual experience. Then came a sign which read "Groups of four people minimum, must carry bear spray". We reluctantly turned back, not keen for face time with a bear. That night, utterly exhausted, we hit the bunks by seven and fell straight to sleep.

The following day we moved onto the Banff hostel in a detached family room. Although we didn't spend that much time inside, it was nice to have some extra room to move, a couch and a tv. The communal kitchen again proved handy. First stop on the cold wet morning was Lake Minnewanka. This twenty-one-kilometre-long, one hundred and forty-two-metre-deep, glacier fed lake was given its name by the native Nakoda. It translates as Water of the Spirits. We boarded a cruise boat to check out the scenery, but the windows were all fogged and the rain was coming in almost horizontal assisted by a strong breeze down the valley. The lake was actually a massive manmade dam and prone to bad weather. Waves have been recorded up to six foot tall, which was hard to imagine. A guide explained the wildlife and history of the area. A township lies at the bottom of the lake and is popular with divers. Especially in winter when boats are not stirring up the water. Why anyone would want to jump in, is beyond me. The water temp is a constant three degrees all year round, just the top metre or so freezes in winter. Imagine having to bore a hole through the ice to get in. It must be a bit scary knowing that you have to find a single hole to escape the depths without the aid of sunlight. Maybe they use a GPS. As we disembarked, there were a family of long horn sheep crossing the causeway at the top of the dam wall. The guide said that because they blocked the access road, this is called a Dam Ram Jam. If there is a collision with a car, it is called a Dam Ram Jam Slam. Very Dr Seuss indeed! On the drive back to town we thought about this a bit more and all decided that if a car stopped for a Marmot to cross the road it should be called a Marmotlaide Jam.

In the afternoon we had one of our most memorable adventures. A horse ride around the hills surrounding the Fairmont hotel, along the banks of the Spray river and an exciting river crossing. We had read that children rode ponies, but Imogen was given a full-size horse named Zoro. Anna had Dunny who had a penchant for peeing, anytime, anyplace. My faithful steed was Jangles. All three were very well trained and responded to the slightest pressure on their reins. Imogen was asked if she wanted to be tethered to the guide or ride alone. No surprise, she opted to be independent and took to riding like she had been doing it all her life. She seemed to form an instant trust in the large beast. I was fortunate to be just behind her on the trail and was in awe of her ability to follow the guides instructions, steering and gently kicking with her heels when Zoro was going too slow or wanted to stop and eat grass. I must admit I was worried a few times as we climbed steep sections and when the horses were unsteady at the river crossing. It was such a long fall for a little girl. I kept quiet though and she handled it with aplomb. The trail was verdant, topographically diverse and sufficiently challenging. They could have led us around in a circle in the paddock and taken our money. Another great experience. We have already planned to go riding on Magnetic Island for Imogen's eighth birthday, where they gallop down to the beach, take off the saddles and let you ride the horses bareback into the ocean.

From every perspective Banff affords a rugged untamed Rocky Mountain vista. Riding the gondola up to the top of the observation deck spectacularly highlighted how perfectly the town integrates with its surroundings. The rivers, lakes, wetlands and bluffs seem larger than life. In the evening the girls treated me to a night at the cinema to watch a compilation of the best films from the previous year's Banff Film Festival. What better place to indulge than in Banff itself? We sat amongst a legion of nationalities. The films didn't disappoint with rafting trips down the Grand Canyon woven into historical stories, rock climbing, mountain biking and skiing. All very professionally filmed and an inspiration.

Calgary, we had been told by many not to bother but were glad we stayed a night and wished we had scheduled longer. This clean, modern city had some great architecture, especially the futuristic Peace Bridge. It reminded me of the wonderful DNA inspired Helix Bridge in Singapore. Of course, the Calgary Zoo was the main reason for our visit. We spent about four hours wandering around the exhibits, ogling at the many and variety inhabitants. Our highlight would have to be the hippos. These huge, tubby, water loving beasts put on an agile and acrobatic underwater performance that any Olympic synchronised swimmer would be proud of. We sat in awe just a few steps away from the thick glass walled pool enclosure. I'm sure she was enjoying the attention and did watery somersaults, pirouettes, jete and plie with precision and finesse. I closed my eyes and imagined her in a tutu, it wasn't difficult.

Up early, we escaped the Calgary traffic and were soon on the quiet, straight, Alberta highways. The flatlands were unseasonably green with pastures and crops reaching to the horizon in all directions infrequently punctuated by clusters of farm buildings, wheat silos and lonely oil rigs. Our destination, Drumheller, the home of the world-renowned Royal Tyrrell Museum of Paleontology. Opened in 1985 smack in the middle of a fossil bearing prehistoric jungle and shallow seabed, which is now the Alberta Badlands. The landscape changed dramatically, just before reaching the township we drove down into a canyon bordered by heavily eroded, steep hills. Dry and void of vegetation except for the sagebrush and a few unknown, hardy specimens. This geographical feature was independently given similar names by different groups for different reasons. The Lakota Indian called it "Mao Sica" or "Land Bad", because of the dry harshness of the environment to sustain hunter gatherers. Then the French came along and called it "Les Mauvais Terres Pour Traverse" which translates to "Bad Lands to Travel Through". The French had travelled from the East, all the way across the prairies to colonise the untamed West Coast when they encountered the long canyons. Having come so far with their wagons, progress was stalled significantly. It took a lot of earth moving, by hand, to construct makeshift roads for the carts. Visiting the area is also exciting on another front. As the crow flies, we are not very far from the US Badlands. Towns like Deadwood and the legends of Annie Oakley, Wild Bill Hickok, the Sioux Indian Chief - Sitting Bull, General Custer and Buffalo Bill Cody start to crowd my memories and my imagination. I would have loved to visit this cowboy country with my Dad. To wander around ghost towns in North and South Dakota, imagining the comings and goings of the past.

Red Deer River rambled through town allowing unexpected sanctuaries of irrigated green. When the dinosaurs roamed it was tropical coastline. A return to that would certainly lift the real estate prices. Drumheller struck me as a neat, little town. The locals we had contact with were very friendly. In the bottle shop I said hello to the bloke at the counter who responded by telling me "The Australian wine is in that section down the back". This man not only picked my accent he understood what I was saying, wow. I grabbed a couple of bottles and as I paid, he told me that he married an Aussie and lived in several places around the continent for over a decade, he had permanent residency but when the marriage failed, he came back home. He said moving back was his worst regret in life.

Over forty dinosaur species have been identified in the Drumheller surrounds, including the well know Tyrannosaurus Rex and Stegosaurus. Many adaptations of the Ceratops family evolving through the Jurassic and Cretaceous periods including the fascinating Triceratops and one of the region's most common, the Hadrosaurid or duck billed dinosaur previously wandered this land. In the morning we went for a short walk through the Badlands to a site where a simulated dig was set up. After a talk about how to recover bones without damage, we put on our safety glasses and set about gently chiseling, scraping and sweeping away at the bones in our patch of dirt. Imogen loved it and was all business. What an experience for a kid and well done by the young Paleontology students supervising the activity. We also learnt about the peculiar rock formations called Hoodoos which are dotted around the place. Created by the soft rock underneath a boulder, eroding away to leave a natural pedestal for the cap rock. By the time we got back to the Museum it was literally crawling with people. The line to get in was at least fifty metres long. We were able to jump the queue with our pre-purchased tickets but inside was just as crazy. The displays were world class, life size prehistoric reptiles looking at you from every vantage point. Well preserved skeletons and dioramas provided an insight to how these creatures lived and died. We saw a prehistoric Buffalo skeleton and what stood out for me was the vertical bones protruding for each vertebrae. They seemed to be similar, but shorter, to the Dimetrodon. The one with the sail on its back. A little research revealed that I was not alone in this observation. Even more interesting is the mystery around this Dimetrodon's anatomy. Scientists now seem to believe that the previous hypothesis around the function of the sail were totally wrong but cannot yet explain its purpose. The more we humans learn, the more mysteries we expose. What a fascinating area of research! Later in the afternoon Imogen did a fossil casting workshop with some other kids and came out full of stories and excitement.

Since humans have had spare time, outside of hunting, gathering and hiding from nasty beasts, we have endeavoured to climb the highest mountains. So, as we rounded the bend in town and fixed our eyes on the enormous and kitschy, world's tallest dinosaur sculpture, we knew we had to take it on. We have shamelessly conquered the big Gumboot and the big Pineapple so why not. Of course, it is not to scale or painted authentically or even anatomically correct. I am sure the paleontologists cringe every time they drive past on their way to work. But it looked like fun, so we did it and were rewarded by some decent elevated views of the town. After our expedition the girls did the laundry in the hotel, which was now full of Australian farmers on an agricultural tour. Anna had a nice talk to them while I set about replacing a headlight bulb in the carpark. The part only cost a few dollars but then I had to buy a socket set. Thank goodness for the internet how-to-guides, as I would never have thought it logical to remove the whole front grill of the car and several other brackets to gain access to the headlight. The actual replacement took less than a minute, the other took considerably longer. Surely car design could focus around maintenance and not just aesthetics. With a sense of achievement and the knowledge that a mechanic would have charged me twice the price for labour alone, it was an afternoon well spent. Groceries were much cheaper in Alberta, especially the beef. We made sure to buy a few big, fat steaks for the BBQ.

Off again in the morning, heading south toward the US border. The flat land stretched out ahead. Wind turbines, combine harvesters, fields dotted with cylindrical bales of yellow hay. Many of the small communities looked like they were transitioning through the last stages of becoming ghost towns. Imogen, clearly affected by what she was seeing out her window, asked "Who lives here? Is this what a ghost town looks like?" The facades on the buildings had that weathered wild west patina. All that was missing was tumbleweed rolling down Main street. We stopped in one place for refreshments and the few people around looked surprised to see us. The small museum across the road read, "access by appointment only" and the petrol station bowsers were frozen at a time when fuel was much cheaper. It was midsummer. If ever there were going to be people about, it would have been then. It was a one-horse town and he was lame. Further south, on our way to the beautifully nostalgic named Old Man River Crossing, the green deserted while the brown waters languorously rolled on. The desolate countryside panorama was as dry as a wooden god. In some ways it reminded me of parts of outback Queensland, long bus trips with sports teams, bad renditions of Kenny Roger's songs and a window view. Vast, dry and unchanging. The makeshift bar in the back seat helped break the monotony. Back in Alberta, First Nation's land bordered the strip of tar which narrowed to a single lane. Like cubes of sugar cast recklessly across a bland tablecloth, we passed many spartan dwellings, almost all were a significant distance from the others. It left me with a forlorn feeling for the inhabitants. How isolated each pod must feel in depths of winter?

Now I am a huge Star Wars fan, but Star Trek has just been a passing interest over the years. I watched a few episodes on TV as a kid and seen one or two of the movies, but a Treky I am not. However, what is that saying, "When in Vulcan do as Vulcan's do". We approached the small town of Vulcan, Alberta midmorning. I could feel the steering wheel pulling to the right like we were under the influence of a magnetic field. It funneled our car into the park beside a large replica of the franchises Starship which sat alongside a visitors centre with alien chic architectural design. Pure white, interconnecting geometric shapes, portholes and a plethora of antenna like appendages. We had to investigate. A teenage girl with dyed, several facial piercings and matching scowl blurted out the scripted "Howdy, welcome to Vulcan. What do you want to do" "Well what can we do?" "Some people dress up in costumes and pose beside Star Trek cardboard cutouts. If that's your thing?" she said with raised eyebrows, a slightly curled lip and a large dose of contempt which made the idea sound even sillier than it really was. I thought to myself "teenagers never do silly things, do they?". When she realised we were from another civilisation far, far away, her demeanor instantly shifted. Her eyes sparkled and she even smiled when she said, "One day I'm gonna save up enough money and come and see Australia". I hope she does. We declined the dress up opportunity but checked out the memorabilia and posed for some photos outside, doing the Vulcan salute of course. Mission accomplished.

After some wrong turns and rough dirt roads, an unexpected herd of Bison appeared just beyond the fence line. We were traveling towards, the descriptively named and rather long winded, Head Smashed in Buffalo Jump. A UNESCO world heritage site at the foot of the Rocky Mountains just outside of the town of Fort Macleod. Blackfoot Indian people live in this part of the Province and are part of a confederacy which includes the Montana Blackfoot Indian whose tribal reservation land is one of the largest in the United States. This site is significant to Blackfoot culture, a story of tradition and ingenuity. The Museum was built into the side of a bluff and although it blends extraordinarily well with its prairie surrounds, a closer inspection revealed bold architecture. For centuries the Blackfoot had returned to the sight to harvest buffalo in preparation for the harsh winter. These people knew their prey very well and devised a system where strong young men were disguised as wolves and young bison. They knew that if a young bison became detached from the herd the group would move across to protect it. So, they steered the herd to where they wanted them. Then the ones dressed as wolves would scare the herd into a frenzy which was funneled over the edge of a cliff. The funnel was made up of rock cairns and members of the tribe waving blankets and branches. The women were ready at the bottom to process the meat, bones and fat. It seemed to be sustainable and they would not return every year. Back to the name. The legend has it that a member of the tribe wanted a closer look at the buffalo as they plunged to their death. He positioned himself under the ledge but was unfortunately crushed by the beasts as they piled up. A sad story.

Around five in the afternoon, we arrived at our destination of Waterton National Park. Within minutes several Bambi impersonators and their mothers wandered over to the front of our motel and grazed on the grass. We took some great photos. These deer had become very adept at dodging cars and people. They strutted around as if they owned the place and I suppose they did. After settling in and cooking up some prime Alberta steak on the communal BBQ, we took a twilight stroll around the village. Set beside a vast lake which straddled the US border and surrounded by numerous craggy peaks, this low-key destination was every bit as beautiful as up on top of the Rockies, minus the crowds. The lights were starting to reflect off the water, little curio shops catered for the families returning from their day's adventure. Live music gently drifted from the pub where knots of patrons sat recounting their escapades. Serene. All this perpetually watched over by the historic Prince of Wales Hotel, a sentinel on the hill high above the lake. We spotted a crowd around an icecream shop and decided we needed to get in on the action. Seventeen dollars for three cones, but gee they were good.

Early the next morning I went down to the bay and discovered a grand old timber motor cruiser readying itself for a day of transferring hikers. Its lacquered timber trim glinting in the rising sun. Flags gently applauding a clear start to the new day. Black, brown through orange, red and white, the distinctive palate of pebbles lined the shore. Smoothed by time. A few early morning joggers passed by and deer continued to strut around choosing the sweetest shoots of grass. I think this herd may have been photographed more than a Hollywood starlet such is their ease around humans and propensity for posing. My girls enjoyed a well-earned sleep in before heading out to Red Rock Canyon. As the name suggests, the rocks are red, the same red as the pebbles in the lake. Not a coincidence I am sure. There were not just seams of red rock, the whole high walled creek bed was this monochromatic freak of nature. We hopped up stream some distance and stood in the freezing stream until we could stand it no longer. Imogen had a ball and didn't want to leave.

I vividly recall disembarking an overnight train from Chiang Mai, at Bangkok Station. Sleep deprivation was instantly erased by the smells, colours and sounds of humanity, but not as we knew it. We were profoundly grateful that we experienced a scene that had hardly changed in over a hundred years. Arriving at Washington DC's neoclassical, Beaux Arts designed Union Station from New York had a similar effect, with its incredible arches and ornate ceiling. I stood there imagining the historical figures who had tread those tiles. Monroe, Kennedy, Roosevelt. Thirty-six million passengers pass through each year. I was not, however, prepared to be moved by a step back in time on this particular adventure. We hadn't arrived by train, but we could in the past. The Prince of Wales Hotel is a national historic site, built in 1927 for the burgeoning rail tourism market. It retained an imposing rustic, swiss chalet styled architecture. Turrets, green roof and white trim. The moment one enters the foyer, a massive picture window leads your view beyond to the ever-diminishing headlands, each a subtly different shade of blue. Ethereal. It demanded I stop and let the moment seep into my psyche. The waiters made me smile in their heavily starched white shirts, tartan tie, kilt and long socks. How wonderful to find a place like this in the twenty first century. I could imagine some famous writer sitting in the corner sipping scotch and penning a masterpiece. Maybe a movie starlet, to the other side, being chatted up by several suit clad gentlemen. We moved past the dining section into the bar with equally magnificent views. The walls were lined in fox and hound wallpaper, original I suspect. Although it was only mid-afternoon, we would have stopped for a beverage if there were a free table. Outside there was lawn but no gardens to speak of, probably due to the harsh environment. Another family pointed out three bears swimming and playing at the water's edge, way down on the opposite side of the lake. They looked just like a human mother and children having a day at the beach but alas we could not see any golden locked girl with them. Maybe she was hiding in the shadows.

The next morning, on our way out, we took a detour to the Bison Loop where these massive creatures are protected in a fenced in part of the park. Anna especially enjoyed this up close and personal with these enormous creatures. We took some great photos of them lounging about in the dust. Onward crossing into Montana at the low key, Chief Mountain US border crossing. A thin strip of asphalt guided us through cattle country and small communities until we reached St Mary, the entrance to Glacier National Park's renowned Going to the Sun trail. This serpentine strip cuts across the continental divide, past lofty mountains, deep green valleys and lakes. Waterfalls of snowmelt fell to the road intermittently under the keen eye of long horn sheep only visible in dirty patches amongst the mid-summer ice and snow. The slow going due to traffic congestion suited us fine allowing time to take in the wildflowers and ogle at the procession of bright red tourist buses. Leather roof, concertinaed back, full of smiling faces. This was no jalopy, but a polished throwback from yesteryear. Some of the driver's even wore safari hats. We stopped briefly at the historic Lake McDonald Lodge with its well-preserved guesthouse, before continuing our journey.

Hungry Horse, Flathead County. Population 826. You can find it where the Flathead River splits into South Fork and Middle Fork. We pulled over at the spur of the moment to grab a coffee but soon realised we had arrived smack bang in the middle of Huckleberry season. Roadside stalls sold them fresh, but we opted to visit the Huckleberry Patch Cafe, not to be mistaken with Huckleberry Land just down the road. They sold huckleberry pie, huckleberry jam, huckleberry fudge, huckleberry milkshakes, huckleberry .... What an inventory, these people have caught on to the value adding caper. We browsed the wares, laughed at the clever t-shirt slogans and picked up some goodies. A god-fearing young man served us while giving a bit of a sermon to the people in line. The town oozed character. I am sure more time spent there would have revealed many a tale worth telling, but alas we needed to get to Columbia Falls, our camp for the next few nights. The name hungry horse reminded me of a joke my Dad used to tell us when we were kids. It goes like this. How do you spell hungry horse with four letters? Answer - MTGG. You have just got to love Dad jokes.

In the morning we checked the map and decided that the town of Whitefish sounded interesting. A short drive brought us to a delightful little town centre with old buildings, trendy shops and a playground down near the river. Bears are front and centre in this area. I overheard two people in a store talking about a recent fatal Grizzly attack and looking up at me from the front page of the local rag was a photo of a large black bear sitting in the branches of a cherry tree having a wonderful time of it all. They are not as shy as we had been made to believe, certainly when there is food involved.

We had planned to drive north on route 93 to Rexford in hope of a glimpse of the Amish, then down along the scenic Koocanusa Lake. But local advice suggested we go the shorter route via Kalispell. Sure, glad we did. Serendipitously we stopped at a café in downtown Kalispell. Before long, people gathered, and a parade rolled along the road with floats, horses, marching bands, vintage cars and clowns handing out lollies. I asked the young waitress what was going on and she excitedly told me that the Flathead County Fair started that day. It was reminiscent of our youth and the Maraka Harvest Festival in Ingham. We enjoyed the parade and decided the opportunity to take a look at a County Fair was too great. Being a working day, we avoided the crowds and visited all the animal pavilions before having a few shots at the rifle target range. Yes, a real rifle, only in the US of A. Trying to explain to Imogen how to line up the sights was a pleasant amusement that only a Dad can appreciate. Sideshow alley was small but a perfect introduction to show rides to our little one who had never been before. She was quite brave, took on a roller coaster and several other spinning, twirly things. Anna didn't fare as well and looked a bit green for the ensuing hours. We stopped to watch the inaugural drone obstacle race, amazed by the agility. Our stay was longer than planned but we thoroughly enjoyed our day. The afternoon drive took us past lakes and deep jade forests. The small towns of Libby and Troy were quaint even though we didn't spot any Amish. Apparently, the traditionalist collective who live in this neck of the woods prefer mountain bikes over horse and sulky but still adhere to the customary dress and minimal use of most modern technology. I wonder what the criteria are.

    We rolled into our campground just outside one of the small towns that clung to the Kootenay River. The whole region is drop dead gorgeous, dotted with forestry along with silver and copper mines. The rustic cabins were neat and tidy with shared bathrooms in the centre of the park. At sixty-five greenback a night, it was perfect. I ventured into the office to check in and on entry I heard "Hello old chap! I'm in the same boat as you! Don't know where she has gone" I looked to the side to find a man with thin wispy facial hair, John Lennon spectacles, a tie dye shirt and heavily pleated khaki kilt. His accent confirmed he was a Scotchman a long way from home. When the proprietor eventually appeared, he bought his KitKat and wandered off singing some indistinguishable song to himself. Now I would love to hear that fellow's story. Mad maybe, quirky at best. Then it was my turn. I said, "My surname is Scott and I have a night booked in a cabin" she gave me a puzzled look, lent over the counter toward me and said, "I didn't understand a word you said." I took a deep breath and thought to myself "So you understand that bloody mad Scotchman and I can understand your twangy Montana version of English, but you can't decipher a word I say, really?" Then I simply smiled and repeated my statement really slowly, but hopefully not slow enough to offend. We eventually sorted it out, she understood the bit about me wanting to pay upfront, then told me she encounters a lot of Australians coming through. Amazing in such an out of the mainstream little outpost. We cooked outside on our portable stove, entertained by squirrels, and all slept well until early morning when the cold woke me. I stumbled around in the dark searching for extra clothes and more blankets to throw over the girls. I wasn't sure what temperature it was then, but when I woke just after six it was one degree inside, and this was the middle of summer. We had just slept in an icebox. I mentioned this at checkout and was confronted with a sort of nose chuckle and a flippant "No that is normal".

We crossed the border, high up in the Idaho panhandle, where the car number plates proudly proclaimed, we were indeed in the "Famous Potato State." Bonners Ferry, on the banks of the Kootenay River, is a sleepy little frontier town built to service the gold rush miners need of supplies and a ferry to cross the river. By the mid 1800's the railway brought new opportunities before forestry became the mainstay. The town is now protected by a dyke, but all the historic buildings along Main Street were two story to allow for all the gear to be moved upstairs during the regular floods. Hard to imagine the languid late summer flow rising to rush through town. Strangely most businesses were closed but we did find a great place run by three sisters which sold food and old-world curios that just begged to be investigated. As we left the store, once again locals appeared from the woodwork with fold out chairs they set up on the footpath. We had stumbled across the annual fair. The Boundary County Fair to be exact. After extracting directions to the fairground on the outskirts of town, we roamed the parade marshalling area, stepping around tractors, a fire truck and the usual mish mash of floats. This Fair was free to enter and what it lacked in rides and fast food vendors, it gained in homestyle hospitality. We wandered through the halls where sample bags from the various community groups and several churches were thrust into our hands. We gratefully accepted bottles of water, school stationery supplies and various other goodies. A nice touch. It must have been Sheriff election year. Several stalls were run by candidates. As we passed by, one well-dressed fellow gave us a nod of his large white Stetson adorned head, then flashed us a smile. I am sure his gold tooth sparkled in the sunlight. Again, we checked out the fruit, photography, baking and all the animals. Out of the blue Imogen popped up and said, "Dad I want you to buy us a farm." "Oh yes dear and who is going to look after all the animals?" Great to see her take such an interest in animals in this increasingly digitised world. A stall advertised Elephant Ears, a large flat disc the size of a dinner plates made of doughnut mixture and smothered in brown sugar. Thanks, but no thanks. We left around two pm, not having traveled very far at all for the day, leaving a long drive ahead through Sandpoint, across the Colville Forest to Kettle Falls in Washington State. The week in northern USA was heartwarming. Nature, great little towns and real hospitality that we will never forget.

Much of the area we travelled through during the week was traditionally Kootenai Indian territory which extends to both sides of the international border. The Kootenai are a very interesting race. In the 1850's they refused to sign a treaty with the US authorities and in the 1970's declared war on the government. It was a peaceful demonstration which resulted in Congress allocating them twelve and half acres of land in Idaho for a reservation. Curiously they speak an isolate language called Ktunaxa. What makes it unique is that it formed independently to surrounding cultures, using totally different oral sounds. It is endangered. Other good examples of this are Tiwi in Australia and Basque in Spain.

Kelowna has a small modern airport, easy to get in and out of, a rarity these days. My sister, Louise, arrived after a very long flight from Australia. We were all glad to have her with us for the following month. Having crossed the border the previous day, we overnighted in town, keen to get an early start to show Louise some of our favourite places. We briefly detoured through Barnard Street and along the Kelowna foreshore before heading to quaint little Peachland for a picnic, its casual beauty achieved without trying too hard. Then onto to Summerland for some wine tasting. Nothing like a drink to remedy the jet lag. First cab off the rank was Haywire Crush Pad winery. They used concrete vats instead of oak barrels to ferment their wines. Something I had never heard of. It certainly gave the wine a distinct taste. Up the hill, Dirty Laundry Winery offered views over the valley, our visit punctuated by the toot toot of the Kettle Valley tourist train passing through the cutting below. The tasting hosts were dressed in typical early 1900's, lady of the night couture. Fishnet stockings and flowing dresses, all in deep red. Black laced bodice and a flamboyant feather in their hair. They colourfully retold the story behind the wineries name, which broadly involved a laundry owner making a little extra cash utilising the upstairs rooms of his establishment during the evening. Clever businessman catering for the needs of the community. Clean clothes and happy men, surely the indication of a flourishing town. We stayed in Penticton that night and walked the esplanade after dinner. Kids were swimming but looked a light shade of blue as they emerged from the cool lake waters.

   A new day found us weaving through the vineyards and orchards of Oliver and Osoyoos, we even spotting a skunk on the edge of the road. Unfortunately, it had been hit by a car and had gone to the forest in the sky. This didn't stop the three girls making me stop to allow them to investigate the poor thing. Just before the US border we took a dog leg turn east along the sparsely populated Highway 3, pleasantly surprised by the unpretentious cowboy charm of Greenwood. I reckon Hollywood types would only have to cover the bitumen with dirt and put a few horse rails out front of the businesses to make it ready to film a western movie. It turned out that the township had been used as a set for the movie "Snow Falling on Cedars", a period piece set up to resemble 1950's Washington State and the fictional island of San Piedro in Puget Sound. Further along the road, Grand Forks looked like a tidy village. I suspect a great town for a kid to grow up in or a place to retire. Sitting a stone's throw north of the US border, it grew around the copper mines in the late 1800's and several distinctive old buildings still graced downtown. One of which housed the Borscht Bowl run by Doukhobors. Like the name suggested, the star of the menu was the deep purple, traditional Ukrainian beetroot soup. This part of BC has a fair size Doukhobor community, who have a long history in the region. In the early 1900's, several thousand members of this religious sect fled persecution by the Russian Orthodox Church and ruling Czar. They were communal living pacifists who rejected the opulence of the church and the need for priests to be an intermediary between them and their faith.

Our stop for the night was Castlegar. In the absence of outdoor furniture, I crouched in the gutter and cooked up a storm on our little gas stove. Later in the evening we walked across a suspension bridge out to Zuckerberg Island in the Columbia River where we were fortunate to spot a Muskrat foraging in the weed. About the size of a large water rat, it creates a lodge similar to that of a beaver. On the outer edge of the island a few men were fly fishing. Good to watch but there are easier ways to catch a fish. I suppose when the scenery is that good it really doesn't matter. It is more like meditation while holding a fishing rod and I can't argue with that. I must admit these days when I go out, catching a fish is only a bonus. A day cruising the islands and a dip on the reef, it doesn't get much better than that.

    Nature again smiled upon us the next morning happy to reveal one of its wonders. On only the third day my sister had been in the country we spotted a young black bear on the side of the road near New Denver. A real treat. We stopped for lunch in Kaslo, another picturesque lake side village brimming with history. A large dry docked, paddle steamer built in 1898, took pride of place on the front street serving as a museum. A relic of Victorian grandeur. It delivered its last passenger almost sixty years ago but had been lovingly restored. It must have been a very civilised mode of transport back in its day. Across the road a two story, red brick shop sat comfortably and content with its prime position. Views of the lake's comings and goings. These days it housed a vintage bookstore, a perfect use I thought. Between the slender windows with accented arched brick treatments protruded large bold numerals proudly showing its age "1886". I stepped inside and around piles of books, magazines and comics, funneled deeper by floor to ceiling bookshelves into the dimly lit reaches. I half expected to be offered a phoenix egg, pirates treasure map or a leather bound "Conspiracy Theories of the 20th Century" hardcover signed by the author. Seemingly out of nowhere a tall man with greying hair, and a gentle face, materialised from behind a shelf, jolting me out of my musings. Gathering my composure, I asked him about a copy of "Snow Falling on Cedars", he smiled and walked straight to a tall pile of paperbacks and pulled it out from near the bottom. He then proceeded to tell me all about the author and his other books. I bought the book for Anna and then found a copy of "Uncle Tom's Cabin", a classic published in 1852, even before Mark Twain got started on Huck Finn. Louise bought it for her son. I hope he cherishes it. This bloke sold stamps and comics, magazines from some forgotten time and of course books. Lots of them, but the most enduring quality was himself. The friendly proprietor suggested we should take a look at the Museum up the road which focused on the Japanese internment during WW2. As we left the store, I had a sense that I had just experienced something rare and special. The museum contained some interesting material. Anna continued to morph into a history buff, taking twice as long as the rest of us as she read every plaque and story board.

As I like to do when I travel, I picked up a copy of the local paper at the front street market and checked out what made news in these parts. The local constabulary were kept busy over the previous weekend following up reports of bears roaming the town. This was confirmed by a man ahead of me in the queue. He was telling a friend behind me that three bears had set up camp in his backyard for the last week and nothing seemed to deter then. The poor chap wanted to get out and do some gardening. A few stores along I spotted a sign which read "Hutterite dressed chickens for sale". No not a fancy French cooking term but evidence of that religious group we first heard about in Nakusp Hot Springs. Not sure if they are free range, chemical free or blessed. A walk around the foreshore revealed poo, lots of poo. Unbeknown to me, the girls photographed several specimens, as you do? Later that evening, with the assistance of internet images, they identified it as bear poo. Now I am talking about two educated women getting very excited about bear scat. There must be something in the water. A good topic for a cocktail party back home.

Just up the road we stayed at a cheap and cheerful motel next door to Ainsworth Hot Springs. As the cool afternoon breeze rolled across the lake we ventured across for a dip. This facility was unusual in that there was a tunnel off the pool where you could walk straight into the mountain, waist deep in hot water. The steam and sulphur were a bit much and burnt our nostrils. Definitely a unique experience. In the change room I noticed men lining up to put their togs through a machine which squeezed the water out. Never seen that before. It might be ok for a cheap pair of budgie smugglers, but I doubt too many Aussie girls would want to put their hundred dollar plus bikinis through that thing.

A makeshift sign peaked out from the dense forest verge announcing, "Salmon Spawning". It dragged us off the road and down a dirt track to Kokanee Creek Provincial Park. According to the Ranger, we were in luck; they were having a good run of the smaller landlocked Kokanee Salmon. Nature never ceases to amaze; here I was thinking that the whole salmon cycle involved the fish returning from the ocean to spawn. These fellows had evolved through necessity. Instead the lake was their ocean and they moved up the tributaries to spawn. The extensive trails beside the car park followed the creek, where hundreds of reddish pink fish worked against the current to climb the natural stone steps up stream. An absolute delight to witness, vibrant darts of pure determination. We were warned that plenty of black bear had been seen feeding along the creek that morning but not to worry as they were too full and preoccupied to pay humans any attention. We didn't see bears, they probably saw us, but we did see areas where the grass had been flattened by their big backsides.

Nelson, the bohemian village with an extra dash of the eccentric, perched on a lake amongst the Selkirk mountains begged to be explored. Amongst the Victorian architecture and rich history, both native and pioneer, lies a reputation for fostering Hippies, locally referred to as the Granola set. During the Vietnam War many US draft dodgers developed a penchant for the place and never left. The relaxed, anything goes feel, was certainly different from many of the other sleepy Canadian towns we had encountered. The cafe culture was strong, which brought people out onto the streets to enjoy buskers and the many interesting stores along Baker Street. It was a chilly August day when we arrived. Across the street from our carpark I noticed a very aptly named surf clothing store with a sense of humour. It was simply called "Never Summer". Further along in a used bookstore, which also sold gemstones and hippy fashion, I spotted a book in the glass display cabinet titled "How to hypnotise yourself and other people". I have sat through more than a few pointless meetings over the years and now know where the speakers have found their inspiration and unique ability. We rented a fifth-floor unit right on the main street with a coffee shop gracing the corner below. Location, location. It was in an old building from the 1930's, now housing several legal firms and meeting rooms rented by the likes of the Nature Society. Ours was one of several residences with industrial lino floors, heavy cedar doors and long hallways. Many rooms came off each wing, giving the distinct feel of an institutional building of some sort. A bit of questioning at the museum next door revealed it to be the old Medical Arts building. Our room was smaller than it looked in the online ad, but adequate. It had a rather curious mix of furnishings that included a full size bust of Beethoven, Philippe Starck Ghost chairs around the dining table and framed needlework on every wall. To our surprise, it had no elevator and no parking. After several trips up and back with luggage, I set off to find somewhere to park which allowed me to stay overnight without acquiring a fine. The game of carpark tag became a regular sport over the next four days. Unfortunately, the first night I parked under an acorn tree only to find the car covered in sap the next morning and in urgent need of a wash before it baked in the sun. While the girls got organised for the day, I went for a stroll and spotted a poster advertising a street party on the Baker Street that evening. One event was the Drag Races where bikes were tied to timber pallets, then raced along the road. A cool interpretation. Sounded great. We arrived around six to a street blocked off to traffic and a large crowd taking in the market stalls, food trucks and bands playing at stages on either end of the festivities. The revelers closest to us were being held captive by a long, curly haired, ginger bearded singer belting out some heavy rock. A cross between Braveheart and Jimmy Barnes. He wore a wide mesh shirt that looked as if it would catch fish, tartan kilt and bobby socks with large hibiscus flower patterns. His enthusiasm was appreciated by the crowd. Imogen took a long look and I wondered what she was thinking about it all. We had a taste of a few offerings, browsed the stalls and just enjoyed the energy of the place.

In the morning it was sunny, so we hired kayaks and a paddleboard down on the bay. A backdrop of mountains and a distinctive orange, utilitarian bridge. Very nice to be out on the water and not needing to wear a jumper. After seeing US department store candid camera snapshots on the internet for years, Louise demanded we show her through the local chain store, which thankfully was uneventful. However, to the innocent bystander it would appear that the regional green leaf economy was strong. The smell of wacky weed drifted heavily on the breeze. A friend said he thought Nelson was one of the most liberal thinking places on earth and told a story of when he went into a bar for a drink. His fellow patrons consisted of bikies in full leathers, men in suits having a long lunch, hippies with their dog sitting under the table and two cross dressing chaps. All having a whale of a time. Shades of Lewis Carroll's Alice who said, "But I don't want to go among mad people" and the Cheshire Cat replied "Oh you can't help that. We're all mad here!" But in a nice way of course.

On the day we were leaving, everyone rose early to get a head start on the road to Radium Hot Springs. The drive was mostly uneventful, and we arrived at Radium mid-afternoon with time to check in and have a stroll around town. No surprise, Imogen spotted a playground. Not far up the street we ran into a man riding a scooter. He wore a pointed red, felt, conical hat and long, draped, red robes. I never found out his story, but my sister managed to get him to stop for a selfie. He never said much but his long wispy beard split into a wide smile and the tuft of hair under his bottom lip twitched. We went down a side street and were amazed at how big the town was. Full of accommodation. I decided to go and reserve a table for dinner at the Pub or risk missing out. When I asked the barmaid for a table for four and said I would be back at six, she gave me that now familiar look as if she didn't understand me but then said, "it is six thirty already". I realised then that although in British Columbia the town must run on Alberta Mountain time. "No worries we will be back at seven". The Horse Thief Creek Hotel served up good tucker and entertainment via a few locals who were watching the Gridiron up on the big screen. I excused myself for a toilet break and was amused to see a blackboard hanging above the trough. The scratchings were mainly rants about Donald Trump, both positive and negative. One bloke, who must have had way too much grog, suggested that Trump should replace the Canadian Prime Minister. All the while I am thinking, who stands here long enough to write this stuff and who wants to touch that stick of chalk? Our Motel was old, but the manager was very friendly. It had all that we needed for one night but couldn't help having a laugh at the solution to protecting the floor. All the chairs had a tennis ball shoved over each leg. More than a bit bizarre but at least they were all the same colour, a fluorescent yellow. The manager had previously spent three years in Sicamous but explained he couldn't stand the lack of sunshine. We certainly knew what he meant.

Monday 29th August.

As we packed the car in the crisp morning air, Imogen yelled, "Look! Look!" We turned in unison to see a bighorn sheep grazing only a couple of metres away. This iconic leader of the zodiac sure looked impressive and it was easy to see how Aries became synonymous with courage, honesty, passion, confidence and aggression. It clearly had other plans for the morning and bounded up the steep incline and across the highway with no consideration for the traffic. We were all excited but didn't manage to get a good photo of him. The road through the Rockies from Radium to Banff did not disappoint. We stopped along the way for a short hike into a place called the Paint Pots. An ochre clay deposit historically used by the Indians, who mixed the clay with animal fat and applied it as a dye to clothes, teepees and for war paint.

Having visited Banff before, we were able to quickly find a park and take Louise through the town to buy some souvenirs. We then hiked the Bow River Falls where Anna and Imogen had driven the car and set up a picnic. Our trusty steeds came past with new riders and Imogen was most excited to see Zoro again. A short walk up the hill from the Falls took us to the back of the impressive Fairmont Hotel standing on a ridge like a European castle. Built in 1888, it was by far the most opulent member of the Fairmont chain we had seen. We investigated each floor and got lost once or twice. Stone, marble, spiral staircases, rich carpets and window treatments throughout. In the foyer a woman dressed in long flowing medieval dress played a large golden harp. We loitered around long enough to take it all in. The music meandered through the building and before long the audience became a crowd. The Pied Piper effect. Very surreal.

By the time, we approached Lake Louise Village it was starting to get late but I thought it might be our best chance to get into Moraine Lake. Sure enough, as we arrived the road barriers were being removed, allowing late afternoon entry. Imogen took on the role of tour guide to this ridiculously beautiful landmark and led the way across the floating logs and up the rocky outcrop to the lookout. Louise was suitably impressed, and I was glad we made the effort to come back this way with her. On the way down, we even saw Chipmunks and Pika, which made it all the more special.

Field, British Columbia, population 169 on a good day. Nestled in the confines of the magnificent Yoho National Park. Only twenty minutes from Lake Louise and much shorter to Emerald Lake. It had impressed us so much on our previous visit that we made it our base for a few nights. As a treat, we booked into the offbeat Truffle Pig Lodge and Bistro. Super friendly staff and comfortable rooms. Once again, we cooked dinner outside on our gas stove perched atop of an upturned esky. Our makeshift kitchen creating a curiosity for passers-by. From the communal outdoor lounge on the lawn, the views were spectacular. Sheer mountains and vast river flats. We dined alfresco on Asparagus and Ravioli with Alfredo sauce, enjoying the dancing magpies and rapidly retreating sunlight shift across the many peaks.

After a good night's rest, we were off early once again to secure a park at Lake Louise. The shore trail beckoned as we optimistically strode off wearing only shorts and sandals, telling ourselves the day would warm up rapidly. It was barely five degrees and the sunlight only joined us for the first ten minutes of the trail before being masked out by the mountains. We came across an explosive bowel movement spread out on the trail like a thin pizza with a berry and leaf topping. It appeared to be only slightly digested. The path through the bear's digestive system must have been rapid. Anna and Louise were way too interested and concurred that mammal must have had a case of Bali belly. I think this pair are working towards their own cable reality television show. The Poo Detectives or maybe Excrement Examiners. Would it feature on the Food or Nature channel? The views were impressive as ever, as we forged on to the end where the girls wanted to play around writing names in the sand and taking photos. I spun on my heels and marched back like a moth to the flame and did a bit of sun worshiping while I waited. Once I had feeling back in my fingers I leant against a tree and observed the diversity of humanity around me. People walked their dogs; others clasped a morning coffee while decked out in the latest fitness garb. Some were loaded up with ropes, helmets and carabiners ready for a day of rock climbing. Kids ran ahead splashing in puddles and giggling, others appeared to be pushing themselves hard, one foot after another. Just to the side a woman, crouched amongst the grass seeds, in deep meditation. So many ways to enjoy and be nourished by this rare slice of nature. A few days after this visit it began to snow and the temperature dropped below zero, so in context our day was warm. Later on, we showed Louise the view from the picture windows inside the Fairmont and milled around the gardens. The consensus was an easy afternoon back at the Truffle Pig and a night at the adjoining bistro.

The evening meal was fun, a bit of a late birthday party for me. The rowdy bunch of British at the table next door kept us entertained. They were interrogating the young waiter about his marital status. He said he had a dog and that was more than enough trouble. Then they asked what he did in his spare time in Field. The reply was interesting. He cross country skis up as high as he can get in the backcountry then clips his special skis together to form a snowboard, enjoying the wild, pristine, white stuff all the way down. No wonder he looked fit! On the morning we were leaving a thick fog hung over the stationary trains in the siding below and fanned out across the Kicking Horse River flats. The first rays of morning light glistened off the geometric limestone cliffs and washed down, illuminated the top layer of the low-lying cloud. It screamed photo opportunity and every man knows it is a good idea to get out of the girl's way when they are packing. As I reached the side road, a fit, but aged man emerged and gave me a knowing smile. He too had come to enjoy the morning. Clearly glad to see another soul, he came towards me and asked what brought me to Yoho. Without prompting he said he was there for his 50th wedding anniversary. His children had traveled from all over the world to celebrate with him and his wife. "This place is special" he said. As soon as his kids were old enough to travel, he had bundled them all up in the car each summer and drove all the way across from Ontario to camp and hike. Since his retirement, over a decade ago, he had lived half the year in Israel. Intrigued by this I asked about life in Israel and how it compared to the nightly news coverage of the conflict. He lived only thirty kilometers from the Lebanese border in the Galilee Basin, which is seven hundred meters below sea level. Sometimes they heard shells being fired but for the most part his little town was safe. He was a ham radio enthusiast who said he had spoken with a person in Australia who lived a crazy life. When asked to elaborate, he explained his radio friend lived and taught in the Torres Strait Islands and visited surrounding Islands by small boat on a weekly basis. Having taught with people who had done this, I never really thought of it as unusual, just reality in our sparsely populated country. Although I could understand it probably sounded very exotic to be moving between tropical islands to work and that, I suppose, it is. By this time the fog had evaporated, but that was ok, I had been privileged to hear someone's story. One that is so removed from my own.

    Back at Blind Bay we set about showing Louise around the district before Imogen and Anna started the last term of school. In Canada it was the start of term one with a new class. The weather had not been kind since we had left for our second leg of Summer. It had rained most days and that continued. Louise was desperate to have the "Canadian experience" so we made her cherry pie and set a fire in the backyard to try out s'mores. She bought a beer and bottle of the clam and tomato mixer for us to try but Anna and I politely declined. We did enjoy watching her face when she had her first sip. An acquired taste she said before tipping it down the sink.

The Armstrong Fair, also known as The Interior Provincial Exposition and Stampede, was on and with a name like that who wouldn't be curious. Armstrong does not look much from the highway but a closer inspection across the rail tracks, reveals a thriving little community. This was clearly the event of the year and a large crowd gathered for the fifth and final day. Cowboy hats, large garish belt buckles and heavily embossed high boots were de rigueur. A large central stage pumped out live music, plenty of old tunes which brought back memories. Before I was old enough to go to school or stand up at the kitchen bench without a stool my Grandmother would put on one of her vinyl records and we would cook. This happened every day, a hot lunch for Grandad and some type of sweet. The music and the cooking have left an indelible mark on me. The old farmhouse was a happy place at a happy time in my life. We forged our way past the menagerie of fast food stalls, most of which required a cast iron gut and the constitution of a donkey to digest. We arrived at the Grandstand just in time to catch the end of the Clydesdale team's precision carriage display. These monoliths of the equine world are strong but appear to be so gentle. Preened to perfection with shaved mains and various adornments. Next on the dusty arena, we went from one extreme to another. The miniature chuck wagon crews galloped in. The announcer summed it up when he said, "these little horses don't think they are little" and man did they have attitude. The quick-fire heats between two wagons powered by a team of four horses ran over a figure of eight course. They had no self-preservation and put every sinew into their work, clearly enjoying it as much as the crowd. We learnt that they even have their own world championships. The best in the world were racing on the day. Next stop was the big tent where a surprisingly professional Iron Chef style cooking competition was being held. Chefs from the region were invited to compete and today was the final. They had a screen where they showed live video close ups of what was going on. Curly bells were full to the brim with a respectful silence and a compare kept us entertained. The chefs had access to a whole range of local produce. They were also tasked with incorporating a mystery ingredient. Today it was sumac. I have used it at home for middle eastern meals. A reddish spice with a lemony flavour. I was surprised to find that this Sumac was foraged from the local forest. There are two types that grow in BC. The white berry is poisonous, and the red is the edible one. They created a three-course meal and explained each. Very entertaining.

The Lumberjack show was next. Corny jokes mixed with skillful axe, crosscut saw and chainsaw exhibitions. A lot of fun and something totally different. They even had pole climbing races and floating log rolling where both competitors got wet, just some more than others to the delight of the crowd. But the best part of my day was accompanying Imogen through sideshow alley. Her little hand in mine. We started off with the carousel and then onto the Hungry Caterpillar roller coaster. I was too big for that one, but she tentatively jumped on by herself. Well she wasn't really alone there were plenty of others with missing teeth and barely three foot tall. To my surprise, it travelled quite fast. Very adventurous. We fished rubber ducks from a swirling pool and shot cans with a cork gun to win an assortment of plush toys. I had forgotten long ago the excitement that the show brings to the little ones. Her sparkling eyes and wide smile jolted my memory. I just loved every minute of it and am acutely aware that these special moments need to be cherished as they grow so quickly. I hope she remembers this as I remember the show as a kid. A huge event in a little country town, especially in the 60's and 70's. My Grandfather would take me around to the one arm bandits to push money in the slots. Sometimes winning little bits of shiny junk that became part of my stash of priceless childhood trinkets. Of course, in those days, spruikers would channel you into canvas tents with promises of such delights as the half man half women, the headless woman and a plethora of other freak shows both human and animal which would now be deemed politically incorrect. Ram Chandra "The Taipan Man" was a favourite. I also watched with wide eyes as the boxing tent organiser banged his drum and taunted young fellows in the crowd to try their skills up against the seasoned pros. The tent was always strategically positioned next to the bar, so Dutch courage played a big part.

Louise continued her culinary quest to try out the "unique". A sign on one booth read, "Buy your Horse Blankets here" so she enquired, "Ah, they are like Beavertails" we were told. As clear as mud! This oily, sugary batter concoction were the same large disks of deep-fried doughnut dough that we had seen in the States, only they called them Elephant Ears.

Labor Day holiday in British Columbia and the rain continued to fall. We took Louise on a wine tasting tour at a couple of the local wineries, then a cool walk up to Margaret Falls, now a tranquil stream compared with the snow melt gush earlier in the year. The Shuswap region is around 50 degrees north, home to the highest latitude wineries in North America. Berlin natives grow grapes at 52 degrees but the world's most northern growers are in Norway at 59 degrees above the equator. Where there is a will there's a way. I recalled a local historian describe how one of Townsville's earliest pioneer families successfully grew a significant amount of vines at Kissing Point right on the ocean. Somehow, they conquered the sea spray, the heat and humidity at a latitude of only 19 degrees south. Alas, a cyclone put an abrupt end to the venture, but they shook off the disappointment and replanted just a little further inland at Belgian Gardens. That kind of determination when faced with adversity is what lay the building blocks for our wonderful country. In the afternoon, the neighborhood kids congregated inside our house to play as bears had again been in the street pinching peaches from gardens. Several bear bangers went off during the afternoon, plotting our furry friend's progress through the village. The kids made the most of their forced internment by trying on every costume in the dress up bin and putting on an impromptu performance.

With the girls back at school and despite the cold wet weather persisting, Louise and I decided to pack up the kayaks and head out. We drove to the beautiful Gardom Lake and although chilly, the rain stopped. Not surprisingly we were the only people on the water and glided past the islands with their weeping willows gently caressing the surface. Although I would not dream of chopping one down I sat there estimating how many cricket bats could be made from just one of the massive branches. I tried to photograph a diving Loon and nearly tipped the boat. Louise was more successful and took some great panoramic shots. She really enjoyed the morning and commented how much our mother would have liked it.

We declared the next Saturday was prime time for a do it yourself Produce Tour of the district. Starting our jaunt down at the Sorrento markets where Anna and Louise tasted the offerings of the local organic brewery. It was not even 8 am. They had Gael's Blood potato stout and the curiously named Back Hand of God which, despite its name, was smooth and apparently prescribed to new mothers to get their milk flowing. A First Nations couple cooking Bannock under an awning. To my surprise, they were deep-frying the batter. Surely, a vat of bubbling oil was not a traditional cooking technique. I later found out that they used to wrap the dough around a stick and cook over an open fire. Not too far removed from our Australian damper. The lady explained that the recipe and the cooking method had changed over the years. In the early colonisation period, the indigenous used to trade yams for baking powder to make the brew more palatable. Like most of these types of things, including scones, they are best eaten fresh. Next stop was the cheese maker and dairy on the outskirts of town. We were able to pat some beautiful, light fawn calves that were only three days old. We purchased some cheese and cured sausage for lunch. Just around the bend was another farm selling direct to the public. Louise bought a large orange pumpkin to do a premature Halloween carving and we chose another oversized, flat, deep red variety called a Rouge de Fleur. Translating to Red Flower, an apt name. It must have a high water content because when roasted it seemed to collapse into a mush. It made some great soup. Further along we foraged for wild apples on the side of the road. They appeared to be growing like weeds in the gully maybe the remnants of a hedgerow. Small but surprisingly no worms and they tasted really good. Lunch was had in the picnic area beside a barn which sold local produce to the public. We visited their menagerie of animals. Just past the enclosure, a sign urging us on to the corn maze. We managed to get briefly lost, which is the point of a maze I suppose. Our attention diverted to the family of wild rabbits darting in and out of the foliage. Last stop was the new winery to the region. It was run by a young woman who studied viticulture in England. A couple from Texas joined us. You couldn't fill a room with three more distinct accents. The British winemaker smiled and said she always gets told she is Australian; one person was so adamant that she would not believe otherwise. From our vantage point overlooking the young vines we all had a laugh and enjoyed some nice dry wines.

The Ice Hockey season had begun and another attempt at understanding the rules beaconed. Of course, it was really about the spectacle of something different. The wonderful gorilla mascot, the cold arena, the physicality of the challenges. A sign that read "Pucks regularly leave the ice. Pay attention to the Play" helped maintain our focus. Another good game with several brawls. Louise got a ticket to sit right on halfway underneath the scorer's box. She sat beside a couple of old timers who were able to explain the subtleties of the contest.

Lou's final week was upon us, so we crammed in as much as possible. Monday a paddle across to Copper Island and the walk. After school drinks at the Marina Grill and dinner beside the fire pit. Tuesday, we paddled Skmana Lake and viewed the Beaver lodges. It doesn't get much prettier. Wednesday, we visited a local Beekeeper. An interesting old fellow who explained how he had bred his bees over many years to have a less aggressive trait. Who knew that was even possible? We learnt how the world's bee populations had started to fight back against the parasitic mites that threatened their existence. Apparently in some bee communities the drone workers are assigned the task of picking off the mite and dumping them away from the hive. Amazing. He had an electric fence to stop the bears from trashing his hives and metal plates across the front to stop the woodpeckers. We ogled at the pen of cute rabbits before he told us that they cleaned up all the scraps from the vegetable garden before spending the winter in the deep freeze. I will not tell Imogen about that.

On the Thursday, Louise went on a fly-fishing guided trip up north of Revelstoke. She had a great time, hooked a few fish and walked through rivers laden with migrating salmon. Complete with waders and several layers of warm clothing she looked the part. Finally, a trip to Kamloops to watch the Gridiron and see the zoo. The weather was atrocious which made the walk around the animal enclosures uncomfortable. Trudging through the mud and cold gusting rain ripped away our normal thirst for wildlife. Even the Spirit bear decided to stay in her den, out of the rain. We did get to see the grizzlies up close again and on reflection over a hot drink, that alone was worth the elemental exposure. In the afternoon, there was a clearing of the clouds, so we dressed for the game only to be thwarted by a late thunderstorm. Louise flew out early the following week, excited to be homeward bound.

PART FIVE

Autumn

We were making our final lists and checking them twice, ensuring we took all the opportunities that presented themselves on the homebound stretch. The 22nd of September and the first day of the Autumnal equinox. Salmon Arm held a low-key Apple Fest in a blocked off downtown street. There were a few stalls and some wonderfully weird characters wondering around on stilts, but the main attraction was a mobile apple juicer where locals were enthusiastically depositing their freshly picked produce onto a conveyor belt. The fruit was mechanically washed, pulped, squeezed and pumped into clear plastic wine flasks. Not something we have seen before and judging by the interest, a novelty in these parts as well.

I had been confronted with confusion or corrected every time I uttered the word "Gridiron". Others quizzed "You mean Football?" I wondered why this anomaly. Outside of North America, the well-known sport is referred to as Gridiron, yet they claim to not even recognise the term. I know that many of codes around the world refer to their chosen sport as football, including Rugby League, Rugby Union, Aussie Rules and Soccer. But you wouldn't find an Australian who couldn't rattle off the real name of their preferred code. Surely North Americans know a bit of the history of their game. The word gridiron evolved way back in the fourteenth century where a crisscrossed metal grid over a fire was referred to as a "Gridiron". In the early stages of the popular game's development, from the eighteen hundreds through to the early 1920's, the playing field was heavily marked out into a grid. The name was coined sometime in the early twentieth century and stuck, despite the removal of much of the grid pattern. Regardless of all the confusion and with some defiance, I was very keen to watch a match. We had missed out twice in Kamloops due to the weather. So, on a very cool and overcast Sunday morning I convinced my little tribe to drive into Salmon Arm to watch a junior league match. The boys looked to be around ten or eleven. Although it was hard to be certain through the copious amounts of body protecting padding. It all looks cumbersome like an inflatable sumo wrestling suit. Salmon Arm were playing Vernon, the local derby! Excited Mums, Dads, Aunts and neighbours enthusiastically bellowed one-eyed support from the curly bells. A Symphony of Rivalry "No Love Lost" in E sharp minor. In fact, one boy's mother had a very sharp tongue. The referees, or whatever they are called, were very good and helped the teams get into correct position with an ample dose of patience. There was a distinct lack of action. The constant prolonged stoppages of play and the revolving door of players for offensive and defensive plays made for a disjointed affair. I bet if the kids had their way it would be continuous like they do in the schoolyard. I doubt any of the players raised a sweat or increased their heart rate much.

Anna's birthday fell during the first week of October. An evening of revelry took place at the local restaurant. Tori and Aiden joined in the celebrations. Tori gave her a gift of home-made elderberry tea to help get us through the colder weather. A nice thought and it tasted great too. I was not aware the berries grew wild locally until the bush was pointed out to me on a hike. Another special event followed shortly after. European celebrations of Thanksgiving in North America can be traced back to the fifteen hundreds, but of course Native Americans had been celebrating the abundant harvest for much longer. The actual first celebration is disputed however there are accounts of Spanish, French and British all formally setting aside a time to give thanks in various parts of the continent. Each year the States and Canada celebrate abundance and kindred spirits at different times due mostly to geography. The harvest finishes earlier above the 49th parallel and therefore Canada celebrates in October. We had planned to get into the spirit of things as much as possible. I had researched traditions but didn't anticipate the opportunity of spending the whole weekend celebrating with a family. When Tori and Aiden generously invited us to join their family, at her parent's house right on Christina Lake, we jumped at the chance and are eternally grateful. This significant gesture of hospitality, in what is a special family time, was not lost on us. Very special. Loaded up with homemade chocolate mud cake and plenty of good wine we headed off straight after school on the Friday. It was a five-hour drive south east, to a long thin stretch of water very close to the US border. We joined Tori's Mum from Spokane in Washington State and her brother's family from Seattle. The large, modern house hugged the rocky shore on the east edge of the lake with living room views straight down the waterway. A private jetty and beach completed the scene. It is no wonder they all make the long pilgrimage as often as possible.

Saturday morning was cold and wet as we got acquainted with the rest of the family and took the opportunity to learn how to play some new board games. While both Tori and her brother were born in the US and have dual citizenship, it would appear that she calls herself Canadian and her brother is a proud American. Isn't it funny how things work out. Her brother and his wife worked in IT and aeronautics respectively. Nice to mix with people outside of our field of expertise, get a different point of view and quietly reflect about different workplace pros and cons. Despite their ages spanning from three to fourteen, the five kids played so well together all weekend. Their happy faces running here and there, truly made for a memorable time. Imogen had a ball. In the afternoon, the rain abated, allowing us to rug up for a hike. It wound its way up the nearby mountain, rewarding with a vantage point above the lake. Great to get outside even though it was on the chilly side.

Although Thanksgiving falls on a Monday, most families seem to celebrate on the Sunday evening so travellers can get back home the next day. Tori's Mum, Elise, had two large turkeys, an assortment of vegetables and crochets in the oven when we woke. Pilgrims to the New World utilised the ingredients they found around them developing the tradition of roast turkey and pumpkin pie. After the war of independence, many British sympathisers moved north over the border into Canada bringing with them these new food traditions. The sun came out and a game of golf was on offer while the birds roasted. Tori and her sister in law, took all the kids for a hike along the river for a picnic. That left Elise, Aiden, Anna and I, to bundle into the car and head down to the Cascade golf course on the banks of Kettle River. A wayward golf stroke from the US border. You could potentially need a passport to retrieve your ball from Washington State. I was not expecting such a beautifully manicured facility in this small community. It included an 18-hole course with a par three alongside. We had the place to ourselves and before long were out in the sunshine chasing a little white ball. I hadn't played golf for years and expected a round of slicing and miss hits but was surprised how well they were coming off the stick. I must have been relaxed. When I was younger, I tried to hit the coating off the ball, but with some restraint, I found I could actually hit it further and in somewhat the right direction. Nice feeling. We sat down to dinner at around four in the afternoon. The spread abundant, the atmosphere exuded love and warmth amongst family banter. How incredibly special to be a part of. Around the table, we all had an opportunity to share what we were thankful for and for me it wasn't very difficult. I was experiencing the world with my little family and sitting amongst new friends. After the main course, everyone exited for a stroll along the bay to help digestion before the dessert came out. Pumpkin Pie, Apple and Raspberry tart, fresh whipped cream and ice cream.

    Feeling content and a bit lethargic, the kids watched Mary Poppins while the adults gathered around to see the second US Presidential nominees' debate. As a bystander, I was intrigued and a bit worried in the context of both United States and World affairs. At times reality resembled an over the top political satire. Allegations of foreign government interference, the rise of targeted social media influencers based on user profiles and misinformation spread like wildfire. Questionable logic and sketchy pasts revealed. Choreographed political party rallies complete with entertainment, celebrity appearances, catchy slogans, merchandise and fever pitched chanting of the cause. Suggested pressure from the Tea Party and the gun lobby. Fast news. Fake news. Real news. When did fact checking become optional in the news cycle? I had followed some of the unsuccessful candidates from each party and heard their platforms. It made me appreciate my homeland's political system for the first time in my life. We were able to discuss the situation throughout the afternoon. The US members of the family happy to explain what it meant to them. I appreciated their frankness and patience. Most people steer clear of politics.

We slept in the next morning. Something we had not done for months. Elise put it down to the tryptamine in the turkey, but I know it was because we were made so welcome. We were relaxed. By the time it came to leave, we felt a little bit like part of the family, which is a testament to their generosity and hospitality. Imogen made a new friend in Tori's niece and they gave each other big hugs when it was time to leave. A fantastic experience making indelible memories. Big family gatherings were a part of my childhood, my Grandmother was one of nine children and some of the extended family would come to our beach hut over Christmas and Easter. We would make fresh ravioli, play cards, catch pipis on the beach, play bocce and just generally have a good time. Our Spanish and Italian neighbours added extra flavour to the mix. All these things were taken for granted as just a normal existence. Of course, until they were no more. Many have passed on and the rest have moved away.

On the way back over the mountains we drove through snowfall as the car thermometer dropped down to zero. By morning, frost had settled on the ground, rooftops and anything it could find. Cars left outside had a thin sheet of ice on their windscreens and the surrounding mountains had a beautiful dusting. Winter was beckoning and it was only October. We arrived back to Blind Bay at about 5pm the previous evening, loaded up with leftover turkey and a carcass. The following morning, I made soup, lots of soup. We had roast veg and turkey for tea that night and turkey pie later in the week. Thanksgiving had indeed been abundant.

"Ice possible. Drive with care" flashed on the dash as I drove the girls to school. The morning's weather report read – "Frozen fog, minus 5, feels like minus 9". An ominous prediction. Besides, what is frozen fog? A quick bit of research revealed it to be fine ice crystals suspended in the air when it gets really, really cold. As I stood at the petrol bowser, on the way back to the house, I reflected that they got the "feels like minus 9" part right. On the following day's commute, Imogen said she didn't want to play outside anymore because it was so cold the previous day that the sand pit had frozen solid. Now that is a new one. Lucky her Mum was the teacher and let her stay in the room with a friend during lunch.

I started to notice the Canadian Geese, which had been in the hundreds on the lake mudflats, begin to head south. Many of the human residents of Blind Bay had also left for their winter homes. In addition, we had not seen gopher, squirrel, chipmunk or raccoon for weeks. Not sure where they were hiding. Therefore, it was pleasing to come face to face with a coyote as it sauntered across the highway on our way back from school. It had obviously had a good summer and now had grown a very healthy, heavy coat ready for the snow. The local paper reported a wolf encounter by a couple in Salmon Arm who saw their cat run into the barn and followed to see what was wrong. As they turned to walk out a wolf poked its head inside. They froze with fear. The woman described it as the size of a small bear and believed it could have killed the three of them if it wanted. It showed most interest in the feline, so once they picked it up, the wolf disappeared into nearby forest. Around the same time, our neighbour told us about her encounter with nature at the Sorrento community garden. A moose wandered out of the forest and eyed balled her before disappearing. Everyone told us that moose are scarier than bear. Just goes to show how careful you have to be, especially with young children. My recent experiences had been far less frightening. That morning a flash of black caught my eye just outside the dining window. A large red capped, Pileated Woodpecker landed on the cedar just outside the window. I sat very still and watched it look for grubs. A bit of magic that lasted the whole day.

Outside the humidity was low. Inside the house it was as dry as a wooden god. The central heating sucked out every drop. My skin was parched and itchy. Static electricity ruled. Everything I touched gave me a wicked kick. Power points were the worst. In the dark I could actually see the sparks kick out like a donkey. I previously had never put much thought into this phenomenon but now could appreciate how nature's display of force brought down the Hindenburg. The daytime temperatures hovered around eight degrees for the month. It could have been worse. I heard on the radio that a spot up in the Northwest Territories recorded -35.

Curling. The art of sliding along a slab of ice holding a rock, releasing it at just the right moment and force, to slide and stop where you want. That is a mouthful and a skill. I have played plenty of Bocce and had a lot of fun at barefoot lawn bowling events but playing on a man-made ice cube is a whole new world. We attended a beginner session on the Saturday just for curiosity. I mean you do not get opportunities to have a go at this type of pastime every day. Having said that, I was not too surprised to learn that back home in Brisbane, Sydney and Melbourne there are curling leagues. We even have a national team, which narrowly missed qualifying for the 2010 Winter Olympics. However, I digress. There is a lot to concentrate on, all at once. You have to push off a foot peg while holding the 20 kg polished, squashed, spherical lump of granite in one hand and a broom in the other. Then glide several meters to a line and release the rock with a flick of the wrist to get it to curve in or out. They use the broom to hold you up during the slide. What could go wrong? They use special shoes to supposedly stop you slipping over. Just before takeoff you step your non dominant foot into a sliding shoe. Sound complicated? Well it was. They let Imogen join in and she loved it, despite the rock being nearly as heavy as she was. Anna had a heavy fall on the ice and quickly developed a lump on her knee the size of a golf ball. But not before she was photographed in full flight by the local newspaper. Intent on the young journo noting that she was from Australia, just visiting. Later in the week, she appeared on the front page of two local papers to the delight of her family and several of her students. We grabbed a few copies of that edition and someone posted it up on the school notice board. She was a bit sore and sorry for a few days. We were rugged up for our lesson. Not surprising considering for all intent and purpose we were standing in an esky. We all snuck out into the foyer to thaw periodically. Curling was not always such an exact sport with custom made paraphernalia. Created by the Scottish in the 1500's, it was played on frozen lakes using any rock you could find that looked like it would glide. That sounds like a strange concept but remember theses folk also invented golf. In these frozen countries, people needed an excuse to get outside and socialise. Curling has a tradition of heavy drinking which the governing bodies now try to stamp out. However, several locals told us they didn't play because they didn't drink enough. Even the trophy is called a Tankard; you know the vessel designed to drink copious amounts of beer.

We needed to start making a dent in our supply of frozen pumpkin soup, compliments of the massive Rouge de Fleur we acquired in the summer. I decided to have a crack at making fresh bread to accompany it. Since we enjoyed a loaf of Ciabatta the previous week, that sounded like a good place to start. But maybe a simple loaf may have been a better idea for a novice. Contrary to popular belief, Ciabatta is a very young bread recipe invented in Verona, Italy in 1982 as a substitute to the wildly popular French baguette. I know that kids think anything invented last century is already ancient, but we know otherwise. Mainly because we came into the world in the wonderful twentieth century and we are not old let alone ancient. The story goes that a baker named it so because it reminded him of the shape of his wife's slipper or ciabatta in Italian. It quickly spread across the world to become a staple in many bakeries. The recipe I chose required the batter to ferment overnight. It is essentially a mild sourdough and despite its twenty-four-hour process, it seemed a lot easier than the other real sourdough recipes I found. Once baked it sure looked like bread and had the required holes in it. It even smelt like bread, only problem it was tough. I put it down to some unidentified novice mistake and just had to dip it in the soup a bit longer before eating.

Card games had become a daily pastime. It was good for Imogen to learn new games and it had helped with her Maths. As a kid I used to play a lot of cards with my parents and Grandparents but lost interest in my early twenties. It was about the time the Grandfather whom I played with the most, passed away. The thought of cards made me a little sad for a long time. But having Imogen has made it fun again. The other night we were playing Old Maid. It came down to the last two cards. I had the Old Maid and she was picking from my hand. She picked the other card and I was stuck with the hag. I congratulated her on a good choice. She replied, "Oh it wasn't that hard Daddy, I could see the reflection of your hand in your glasses". Well she is honest and shows initiative. Good girl.

With Halloween just around the corner, one of the local fruit barns held a fundraiser. For a coin donation we gained entry to the field at the back of the barn. The festivities included food stalls, a live musician and two bright orange, custom made cannons shooting large pumpkins at a couple of wrecked cars some one hundred meters away. I know, bizarre! Nevertheless, when in Rome. It was an outing and certainly something new. The cannons consisted of large compressed air tanks with three-meter-long, thirty-centimeter diameter pipe barrels. Fed diligently a constant supply of orange ammo in true muzzleloader cannon style. An old-world pirate would have been proud. First went a handful of hay wadding, pushed down by a ramrod. Then the pumpkin projectile was checked for size and trimmed with a steel blade contraption before ramming it down the barrel. The hydraulic trajectory control was adjusted. With a flick of a lever, there was a loud boom which gave Imogen a terrible fright. The orange missile hurtled forward just clipping the back of one of the cars. The crowd cheered and it was loaded again. You couldn't dream this stuff up. We moved on to the pumpkin carving competition and brought to life a happy faced protagonist. He put on a large, gappy tooth smile for the judges. The prize was all you could carry pumpkin.

On the Sunday we joined a group at a winery to learn how to make Mozzarella cheese by a young artisan cheese maker from Enderby. She owned a herd of sheep along with Jersey and Nubian cows. Over the years, we have dabbled with simple Labna and watched an Italian friend make Ricotta, but this experience was much anticipated. The obvious benefits of doing it at a winery cannot be understated. The arrival wine tasting included the privilege of trying a few vintages that were not yet on sale. Our favourite was the gewürztraminer. The merlot was also excellent and at about seven degrees, it was certainly the weather for red wine. Imogen did not miss out with a tray of antipasto seemingly to herself. The bubbly young instructor told tales of her animals and large family. She started making cheese at fifteen and now worked as a full-time cheese maker in the valley while continuing her business on weekends. Cheese called Mozzarella originates from southern Italy and used water buffalo milk. Byzantine monk's text references to the cheese go back to the twelfth century; however, the monks had been living in the region since the 800 BC. Although water buffalo were not introduced until sometime in the thirteenth century, I suspect variations of the cheese have been made for a very long time as a way of using up excess milk. It remained a local delicacy for many years due to its short shelf life. Refrigeration latter allowed it to spread across the country and the world. This mild, delicate cheese is great in salads, but it really shines on pizza, another southern Italian staple. I had not seen any water buffalo grazing down on the Shuswap, so on that day we substituted with cow's milk. Technically speaking were making Fior di Latte. After bringing the milk and rennet up to the correct temperature, we all donned gloves then stretched and formed the cheese before dropping it into ice water. All in a rustic tasting room with views across the young vineyard devoid of foliage for winter. Everyone was friendly and interested, which made for a great time.

All Hallows Eve or Halloween. As the name suggests, is the night before All Hallows Day. In Australia we call it All Saints' Day followed by All Souls' Day. Evolved in a melting pot influenced by traditional harvest festivals, pagan worship of the spirits, Christianity and last but not least, consumerism. It is the Day of the Dead in Latin America, Japan has the Obon Lantern Festival, Cambodia has Pak Ben and it goes on. It appears retail outlets in North America know when they are on to a good thing. Available in a multitude of places are costumes, pre-packed boxes of treats for the convenience of the homeowner and every ghoulish decoration or accompaniment imaginable. Dismembered limbs hanging from chains, family photographs that change to skeletons as you walk past and even a decapitated head cum sweets-dispenser. Just lovely?

We carved our Jack o Lantern with a sweet smile and heart shapes cuts for eyes. A happy vibe, however walking the neighbourhood it was obvious that executioner chic was in vogue. Wicked ghostly props, skeletons, witches suspended by hangman's noose adorned many an eave, tree and balcony. There were broomsticks and black cats, spiders and their webs, skeletal arms reaching out of the front lawn. One house even had an electric chair. Oh yes it was all very cheerful. My childhood awareness of Halloween was via Disney's Donald Duck Halloween special and The Headless Horseman cartoons. Scary enough for me. Some local farmers had set up corn maze where people paid to be sacred out of their wits each night by chainsaw wielding zombies. The craziness has no bounds. People phoned the radio station to tell the world they were dressing their dogs and cats as sharks, puffer fish, minions etcetera. We baked, Boo Biscuits. Well that's what we decided to call them. Having purchased a ghost cookie cutter and some black, licorice flavoured icing some weeks back, it was time to put our plan in action. We found a recipe on the net for a biscuit dough that held its shape, they tasted great as well. Not that kids seem to mind what stuff tastes like as long as it is sweet or is covered in tomato sauce. We covered the ghosts in white icing then drew in various features with the black. Lots of fun. We made a batch of thirty-six to take to school and none came home.

Arachnophobic Nation, the locals seem to hold their breath at the mention of any creepy crawly. If it is a spider, fear, loathing and hysteria prevail. Many have told me that they will never visit Australia because we have big spiders. At first, I tried to explain that they are easy to avoid. However, when met with disbelief I decided to play the game and ask if they had heard about our bird eating spiders. Such is the collective trepidation to our hairy eight-legged friends that the obvious choice of costume for Imogen was Spider Girl. No not anything to do with the comic hero. Fluorescent spiders strategically sewn onto her black outfit with an extra-large hairy specimen wrapped over her shoulder and around her neck. A spider web drawn across her face and a veiled hat dripping with more spiders. She could not contain her excitement at the prospect of scaring the teachers and students. On Halloween morn, I dropped off Spider girl and my wife dressed in black with a cape, pointed hat and scraggy black wig. I did not call her a witch or blurt out any broomstick jokes because everyone knows not to incur the wrath of an enchantress. The school day consisted of macabre games, a costume parade and a bit of a disco with tunes like Monster Mash and Time Warp pumping out of the auditorium. These teachers sure know how to give the kids a good time.

The fog sat thick and heavy across the highway for the whole day. It hung low enveloping the surrounding mountains allowing only glimpses of the treetops. A monochromatic scene, everything a shade of grey. Cold drizzly rain and an unusually quiet road provided the perfect eerie start to the day. I saw no horseman carrying their head nor black cats, however there were some scary sights at the shopping mall, but that is another story. None of us eat candy so I managed to grab a box of fifty mini chocolate bars. Just in case we did get a visit from some door knocking ankle biters on a sugar high that leave you wondering whether they are the result of bad breeding or have a good costume. At least any spare chocolate would not go astray. My sister emailed and said she had a couple of teenagers come to her place. All she had to give them was a banana, maybe that will catch on or maybe her car will be egged. Only time will tell.

Although the kids had a great day, every little trick or treater had really been waiting for night to fall on that very auspicious day. Five-thirty, almost Autumn sunset, we rendezvoused with Moira and her family over near the golf course for our Trick or Treat adventure. The locals took it seriously. They knew their stuff and apparently "this part of Blind Bay was historically well festooned and handed out the most booty" they said while tapping their finger to their nose. The girls had been planning this for some time and organised their parents well. Despite the rain there were several families with younger kids doing the early rounds. The etiquette was as follows, lights on and a simple Halloween decoration meant "the house is open for business", lights out meant, "we are not at home or we want you to think we are not home because we don't like children". The girls and Moira's little brother excitedly ran up to each house and politely yelled "trick or treat". Moira's Mum was really into the Halloween scene and dressed resplendent in a Pumpkin costume; she advised of the best houses for the kids to visit and took Anna to one that handed out hot apple cider for the parents. Moira's dad joined us a little later, he parked his patrol car out of sight and caught up to us dressed in full uniform. It was hilarious watching people's brain tick over thinking, "is that a costume or is he a real cop?" We walked on for an hour and a half until our children's little legs could go no further. They were ready for bed but unsurprisingly disagreed with our assessment. What a great night for all. The Pumpkin and the Mountie were good people. Later in the evening, we did get a group of three kids from across the road come knocking at our house. Imogen got just as much excitement handing out the treats as she did gathering them.

Monday 7th November.

The days continued to shorten and the roll back of daylight saving only compounded the feeling. It was pitch black by 4.30 pm. The sun, or should I say the dim glow through grey clouds that gave just a hint of something big and bright out there, didn't make an appearance until 7.30 in the morning. Cabin fever rose to new heights. The ensuing weekends and after school were filled with jigsaw puzzling, card games, scrabble, chess, and monopoly. We tried hard to keep ourselves sane. Movies, cooking, painting, playing guitar all got a guernsey. My girls even tried their hand at dying a T-shirt with natural dyes from the garden. They gathered maple leaves, rolled up a white shirt and boiled it for an hour. The result was eh, interesting. I even sat and wrote a few poems, which made the girls laugh. We did venture out for a kid's birthday party held, of all places, at the pool in Salmon Arm. Surreal feeling to be going swimming when it was 6 degrees and raining out, even though it was a heated pool. On reflection, I suppose if Canadians waited for good weather to do activities, they would never do anything. Piles of coats, sweaters, hats, boots and gloves, littered the extremities of the building where people disrobed down to their togs. It was packed and noisy, with a warm chlorine haze that burnt our eyes and nostrils. A day at the beach it was not, but it was the closest thing they had and there were plenty of smiling faces.

Sensing it was time, we placed our car for sale. With crossed fingers and toes we posted it on no less than six online sites, adverts on community pin boards and a sign taped to the window. A couple took it for a test drive the second day and there were a few sniffs via email. Then it went quiet for a week and we started to worry. Thankfully, on the Sunday a retired couple from Kamloops came and had a look. Seemed like really nice people. They had spent their lives living up in Whitehorse, way up in the Yukon, wedged between Alaska, the Northwest Territories and the Arctic Ocean. I instantly thought why, before they explained they were gold miners. How exciting in a harsh, but beautiful part of the world. Alas, they did not buy the car, but we were thankful for the chat.

In 1984 I was just out of high school and bought my first car. A XD Ford Falcon. Back then every good car had a cassette player. In my opinion, there was a lot of quality bands about, but one particular cassette was played until it almost wore out. It was Bryan Adams Reckless album, including hit songs like "Summer of 69". His music is associated with many good times in my life. On Friday night, we took our little girl along to her first rock concert. Bryan Adams played Kamloops, some thirty-eight years on. Man, has he aged well and proceeded to put on two and a half hours of both new and classic hits. Several times, I closed my eyes and was transported back to the fabulous 80's and my eighteen-year-old self. Like old Plato said "Music is a moral law. It gives the universe soul." Imogen was a bit apprehensive at first but was soon clapping her hands, swaying with the music and singing along with the packed stadium. It was a good thing she got moving because it had dropped to below zero by the time we exited the stadium. The fireplace at the entrance to our downtown hotel, was a most popular spot when we burst through the revolving entrance doors.

Earlier in the evening, we treated ourselves to a night out at one of Kamloops finest restaurants. It was warm, stylish but unpretentious. The wait staff were pleasant and the food was memorable. As I sat there with my happy little family, I glanced out the window and briefly locked eyes with a homeless man who was shuffling along the street checking parking meters for coins. He must have been around my age or a little younger. At one point, he stopped and gave me a look that did not divulge its intent. It was not mean or spiteful or even sad. I couldn't help but ponder his existence and felt so grateful for my own life. I sincerely hope his situation improved and he found food and a place to sleep on that very cold night. It put one's first world problems into perspective.

The 24th of November, Thanksgiving in the States. It brought fond memories of our rather wet visit to New York, a few years back that coincided with the holiday. We took Imogen in a stroller to the Macy's parade marshalling area to watch the balloons inflate figuring the parade crush might be too much with a little one in the wet rainy metropolis. Despite the weather, it was exciting to be part of. New York was fun but I cannot help wishing we had visited in summer when Central Park would be at its best and those arctic winds that swirled in from the Atlantic and up the Hudson a distant memory. In fact, I am strongly considering that all our adventures from now on will be during the country's summer. Chase the sun.

We had only two goals for the following week. Find the fish a new home and sell the car. The fish were now acquainting themselves with a new upmarket "real" fish tank environment, they were truly over the ice-cream container they had been circling for months since Imogen won them at a birthday party with strict instructions not to return to said Birthday girl under any circumstance. I kid you not. You would think if they were giving out fish as prizes, they could have been a nice fillet of salmon or trout. The car was in the carport, unfortunately the one attached to our house. I discounted it on the Wednesday to an even better bargain compared to similar on the market, but still no offers. Finally, on Sunday night I received a random text that read, "I want the car. I can wire money into your account now and arrange a semi-trailer to pick it up in the next few days." No name was given; they required no information from me and didn't want to check the vehicle. I smelt a rat but replied that I needed payment by bank draft. The back and forth went on for some time, he even gave me a web address to contact about the legitimacy of his preferred money transfer. A quick web search revealed this was a common, sophisticated fraud where they send out links to dummy banking websites. As soon as I mentioned scams and ringing the institution, the texts stopped. Disappointed was I. We need to trust but know in whom we trust. The Dodo bird was not silly like the aspersions suggest, they were just over trusting souls. I even parked it down near the store with a big fat for sale sign in hope of some attention. Not everyone searches online, especially in the community I was living in.

December 2nd. Imogen had butterflies the morning of the Christmas concert. I assume that since it was "Aussie Jingle Bells" her class chose to perform; she felt a bit of pressure being the token Aussie. With some reassurance, she was fine, but excited. On cue, the first snow fell as we drove to school. It started as frozen rain on the windscreen but by the time we were around the corner it morphed into large dry flakes that swayed from side to side as gravity gradually took hold. The roadside trees were lightly dusted as the white powder swirled around in the back draught of the traffic. It came down heavily until lunch. They expected a high of only minus 8 dropping to minus 13 overnight, so it was going to be interesting. The sunset at 4pm, but that was irrelevant as not a glimpse of sunshine could penetrate the perpetually cloudy valley.

The new music instructor did a tremendous job teaching and choreographing seven performances, which were far from traditional. Sporting a goatee beard, bald on top with long hair trailing down the back he conjured up a believable version of Ebenezer Scrooge, who as usual, was missing the Christmas spirit. A voice told him that he would be visited by seven Choirs. If he didn't get into spirit by the last performance, the rest of his hair would fall out. I sat amongst an excited mix of parents, Grandparents and friends, all waiting to watch their little loved one up on the stage. Plenty of smiles and chatter mixed with the smell of coffee and smoke infused coats. Scarves, beanies, high leather boots, lumber jackets and baseball caps aplenty. Even the locals were feeling the cold. The performance began with the teacher sitting on a couch getting ready to watch some cartoons when the doorbell rang, and a procession of class groups interrupted him with their performances. There was a jazz Christmas song, another written and performed by a year 2 group and then Mrs. Scott's class sang the Aussie version of the classic. The pride that hits you when your own little one gets up and sings is infinite. I watched her every move as she got into the spirit of things. A didgeridoo solo shocked the audience before the familiar tune kicked in. There were kids in shorts, singlets and thongs. An old rusty ute with an esky in the back and a bloke flipping snags on the barbie. It was well received by the crowd, but I expect much of the lyrics were lost without translation. I saw Imogen after the show, and she was full of excited energy. The final two performances were the year five students who providing the sound effects for two old black and white cartoons of Mickey Mouse circa 1929. The kids were fantastic and to think each animated frame was sketched individually. Wow! It provoked me to remember tales of how two of my two great Aunt's use to play the piano for the old silent movies at the Shire Hall at home. I am not that old to have ever seen them but intrigued nevertheless.

The car selling had gone from frustrating to desperation with the realisation that we were rapidly running out of time and may have to accept half of what we were after. I was unsure what to do. Under duress, I resorted to calling two dealerships, but even they weren't interested. It was either a Hail Mary buyer over the weekend or I would have to plead with a used car salesman, and I knew how that would turn out. Not even the sharks were circling our obvious desperation.

A little Christmas miracle happened next, or was it? I had a phone call from someone in Kamloops very interested in the car and arranged to have a look on Saturday. By 5pm I had given up. They were a no show. I was sick of getting exposure washing the car in subzero temperatures only for it to fall through and the car to get splattered in mud after a drive to the corner store. Later in the evening, I decided to send them a text and discounted it again. They came out on Sunday morning. A father and son. The old fellow thought he was some kind of wheeler and dealer. He made a big deal about not liking the colour of the car and that it was ten years old, before offering one thousand less. They knew they had us cornered and I hated every minute of it. We agreed to the deal through gritted teeth. There was a lack of control over the situation that left me very uneasy, but it was sold.

Another student free day. Imogen and I had a great time, we made pinwheels and decorated paper crowns, sketched a toucan and coloured it in. She is quite the artist at seven and I encourage her as often as I can. We did a science experiment by placing a hot cup of water outside to see how long it would take to freeze. We didn't have to wait long. In two hours, it was solid. On the lookout for something else to amuse ourselves, we found a board game in a cupboard upstairs that we hadn't spotted before. After lunch we sat down and watched the wonderful "Chitty Chitty Bang Bang" movie. How can you not like Dick Van Dyke and the sensibilities of the sixties?

The drive to Chase was as scenic as ever, only different. The seeps of water that trickled from fissures in the sheer cliff faces for much of the year were now frozen stalactite claws reaching out at unsuspecting cars. The normally placid lake had whipped up into a deep shade of indigo. White capped waves crashed against the shore. The predicted -15 C combined with 20-knot winds displayed another side of nature. One we had not seen. Our borrowed vehicle shook several times by strong gusts. The oncoming traffic had ice encrusted over their bonnets and a car transporter was almost completely engulfed in fresh snow. In town, everyone was walking fast, head down, eyes squinted, collars up. The cold effortlessly bit my legs through feeble denim trousers. I tried to cash the car payment check so I could transfer the money straight back home but to my dismay I was told that they didn't have that amount of cash. I couldn't help but chuckle in dismay, it was involuntary. Not sure, what the bank manager thought of that. She assured me that my bank, across the road would honor the check immediately, as they all knew each other. I just had to convey the message and it would be all good. Trusting souls. How the internal workings of a small town circumvent the protocols of a national banking institution with a wink and a nod is anyone's guess. True to her word, my bank honoured the check and I wired the money home immediately. One less thing to deal with and a huge weight off my shoulders. The thought of leaving an unsold car in another country was not palatable.

Minus16 and strong winds forecast. I told Anna not to let Imogen go outside at the breaks, if need be, I would come and sit with her in the classroom. It was simply too cold. I could not believe they send those poor little kids outside. That kind of weather can burn your skin and chill you to the bone. On the Vancouver news, the big story was about the arctic weather down on the coast. They were experiencing the heaviest snowfall in years and it was causing havoc. In fact, it was that uncommon the residents were rushing to install snow tyres. The city council had sold off most of its snowplows some years back and had to rely on contractors. They were opening up more shelters and combing the streets for homeless, fearing they would perish in the elements. The weather in Vancouver had only been down to -7. Back in the interior the teachers stayed inside, the school administrators also inside, most of the parents worked inside but the community as a whole obviously thought it was ok to push their children outside. Madness.

In Vancouver the city council was offering to pay for the damage caused by ice bombs that had smashed several vehicles crossing some of the cable stayed bridges. The snow and ice built up until the weight could no longer be held and came crashing down. I saw some of the cars, nasty! They were expecting in excess of 200 millimetres over the weekend and telling travellers to reassess their plans. The airport in Kamloops was intermittently closed by snow. We quietly hoped Kelowna would not be closed when we needed to fly out. Samantha, from next door, rang after school to invite Imogen to come and play with Hannah in the front yard. It was -11 outside and dropping fast. Imogen went over to play with the proviso that it would be inside. Work Safe Canada was on the radio warning about exposure to the cold and the possible burn damage to exposed skin. It was all happening. What a finale we were having.

It was not my imagination, while loitering once again in the town library I read an article about winter aversion among Canadian citizens. It is practically endemic. In the land of snow and ice there are three types of folk. The previously mentioned snowbirds who escape, the winter sport lovers and the ones that grit their teeth and endure the season because that is where they live and work. The "closed up shop for winter" syndrome is so encompassing to the nation that the health and welfare organisations have developed a winter family challenge which encourages people to get outside at least once a week. Most of the world's population would find this request almost ridiculous. I would have thought going outside each day is like cleaning one's teeth. For goodness sakes, there was a house on the corner only a few doors up that up until the end of April, I had thought was empty. Turned out a family of five had been living there all along. The disconnection with community that winter brings is all encompassing.

7th of December, the day Pearl Harbour was bombed by the Japanese and the turning point in the war. We had been in Hawaii on this day the previous year. We love it there, so much like home, but different. I had pondered many times during the year that our exchange to such an opposite environment might have been too much of a contrast. However, with ten days to go, we realized that we had done so much, adapted and we weathered the storms. It would hold us in good stead for the future.

9th December - It started snowing at around 9am and didn't take long to give everything a crisp white coating. By mid-morning the flakes had become much larger and already the driveway looked like it may need shoveling. Some flakes were almost 15 mm across and resembled torn up tissue paper. In the stillness, each one delicately drifted. Slowly, gently, quietly downwards. Momentarily slowing as their flat sides became horizontal and resisted the inevitable, just for a moment, before the silent touchdown. The brilliant white had brightened the whole landscape from its perpetual overcast gloom and even held off the impending evening darkness just a whisker past 3.30. To think no two of these frozen crystalline structures are the same. Formed around a dust particle and influenced by many forces on their descent through the clouds. The cedars were bracing for their seasonal load and the grass had long become dormant. The decaying maple leaves hidden until spring. If there was any life in the street, it was once again well hidden. Few lights were on at night and the drone of car engines had almost dried up. Pets were confined to the rug in front of the fire. I wonder if they get seasonal adjustment disorder like their masters. The short days and lack of vitamin D were causing havoc on our sleep pattern. There seemed little chance of the mercury getting anywhere near zero before we left. The roads iced up. Our borrowed two-wheel drive pickup relied on a pile of bricks in the back to assist with traction, so we decided it was best not to venture far. We yearned for the moment the plane hatch opened in Australia. Our bodies sucking up the humidity and sunshine like a camel at an oasis. How long would it take to feel our kind of normal again?

It snowed very heavily for three days. A few hours after shoveling the driveway, it was full again. A fresh new snowman materialised in the backyard thanks to the girls. A curious raccoon came to investigate during the night, leaving only his tell-tale footprints. I doubt he would have been impressed that the carrot nose was plastic. We listening to lots of Christmas music online while playing cards. Bing Crosby's White Christmas album getting more than its share of playtime. To our surprise, it was recorded in 1945 and that Bing was the biggest recording artist of the twentieth century. Amazing when you think that last century also gave us Elvis, the Beatles and Michael Jackson. Bing was a trailblazer with postwar recording and the use of technology. The fact that a seven-year-old in 2016 still loved his music is quite an achievement.

We ventured out to Tori's in the late afternoon for a farewell dinner. Anna baked a brie in puff pastry with walnuts and cranberries inside. It was a popular dish. They kept telling us that it was mild weather, but at -10 and dropping, I don't think anyone believed that. I could understand Aiden's point of view. It was better than the -30 conditions he experienced growing up in Alberta. The kids had a short play in the backyard snow but retreated within fifteen minutes with cherry cheeks and red noses. When we arrived our host's driveway was clear and as I feared getting bogged in the snowbound edges of the road, we parked on the concrete. However, when we were ready to leave they said, "Oh you didn't park on the driveway did you? Because it is hard to get up the slope when it's icy". With plenty of able bodies waiting to push I revved up the pickup and after a couple of spins we were out. But not before the Scotts nearly froze. It was about -14 and my muscles at the back of my neck and shoulders seemed to cease up making it hard to function. The girls were shivering and finding it hard to buckle their seat belts. It took a prolonged, steaming hot shower to warm up again.

I chose to drive the girls to school every day of the last week. The roads were a mess and I would have been worried sick about them. The salt-dirt mix was regularly applied, resulting in that slushy muck which later froze into a slippery crackling platform. The roadsides tarnished with an unattractive brown frozen hodgepodge.

13th December

In this part of the world, it was very easy to slip into the ranks of the weather obsessed and now it is well documented that we fell down that rabbit hole very early on in our adventure. We woke to a forecast bleating from the radio "Currently -17 feels like -25". Now that was a new PB. The lake was shrouded in a thick fog that gave the impression of steam rising but it was no hot spa. The skeletal remains of trees reached out with pure white frosted limbs. We even passed a couple cross-country skiers shuffling along the roadside, making the most of the situation. I can now confirm that ducks and snow geese have no feeling what so ever. They huddled on the icy verge of the lake; heads tucked back under their wings. Why had they not joined the rest of their flock down in California? The ice encrusted swimming platforms anchored offshore uncannily resembled icebergs. We thought it was a mirage at first. A small frozen pond, beside a farmer's barn had been set up as an ice hockey pitch, watched over by cattle and horses. We felt sorry for the horses with their thin coats and lack of body fat. Not sure how they cope in such extreme cold. Unfortunately, no reindeer wandered into our backyard let alone one with a red nose. I assume they were busy limbering up this time of year. Raccoons however were still on the prowl. The Husky impersonating Poodles were back out walking the neighbourhood, pulling a sled full of groceries.

At the dinner table we discussed the highlights of our year and chose our favourite places. The consensus was that in British Columbia we really enjoyed Cowichan Bay and Tofino on Vancouver

Island and Field/Emerald Lake in the mountains. In Alberta, we chose Waterton and Lake Louise. Finally, in the US our favourite place was Bainbridge Island with Coupeville and Leavenworth getting a notable mention. There were so many more wonderful places we will never forget and feel privileged to have had the opportunity to travel so far and wide. The hospitality of Aiden, Tori and their family. The friendliness of the people of Idaho, Montana and Washington State. The endless array of wildlife. The lakes, mountains and streams. The version of English, the traditions. The many things that initially confused or frustrated, now make us smile. We are thankful.

Dec 16th

Last day of a fourteen-week term and farewell to Sorrento Elementary. The class were sad to see Anna and Imogen go. They had forged strong bonds with the children through the year. In particular, Imogen was fretting about saying goodbye to Moira. As sometimes happens, the pair had just clicked. Moira's parents invited us around for dinner that night, it allowed the girls a bit more time together. Cooking had been an effective diversion during the year and endured to the end. We decided to make a chocolate tart to take to our host's dinner party. The three of us lined up at the kitchen bench, whizzing, melting and stirring. Of course, we had to taste our wares purely for quality assurance purposes. The evening went well. We had a great chat. It was a shame we hadn't got together more often. The girls dragged out the hugs and goodbyes, we agreed to help keep them in touch and nurture the special friendship. As we walked to the car our bodies instantly seized up once again and a quick check of our phone weather app read it was -20 but felt like -28. Thankfully, that was our last evening out. The following day the girls tried out

Skype. For almost two hours they talked, coloured in, read stories to each other and just enjoyed each other's company. Isn't the internet a grand thing.

The bank accounts closed, mobile phones shut down, excess groceries dropped to the food bank, clothes deposited at the charity store, snow boots to the neighbours and appliances distributed to the first hand up. Rapidly the only trace of our existence in Blind Bay would be in memory and photographs. We had wound it up. Cleaned the huge house, handed out Christmas cards. It was time to go home.

There were no regrets packed in our bags, a good thing, as there was no room. We accomplished what we set out to do. Immersion in another country. Yes, we had at times felt uneasy, confined and misunderstood, but it would be a crime to let the challenges blind us from the beauty and personal growth. We took from it what we could and over time would dismiss the rest. We will not forget the silence of a snowy morn, the redness of our cherry winter lips, the unfamiliar way the light hits the divots in the lake through cloudy skies, tentative strolls on a frozen lake, close encounters with strange animals, a ferry's horn through the fog, trees drooping with juicy cherries and so much more. A way of life so far removed from our tropical home, it was surreal and for many of our friends and family back home, incomprehensible.

We arrived in a snowstorm and as it turned out, we would leave in one. Once again Tori was the one who offered to help out and drive us to the airport, take us to lunch and make our departure run smoothly. We left early to allow for any weather events on our way to Kelowna airport. The road was well ploughed, but heavy snowfall reduced the scenery to shades of white. The road to Kelowna had become very familiar, but this time it was different. The grey skies and empty streets had no impact on my upbeat mood and resolve to complete what we had started years earlier. I had taken my family to live abroad.

I had to climb across Imogen to get out of the car as the left-hand door had frozen shut and would remain that way for much of winter. The wind sliced through our many layers with ease making the journey into the airport a shuffled jog, slowed further by our luggage carts bogging in the deep snow and muddy slush. We have learnt the hard way not to try to move too fast on icy ground. Many flights flashed "Delayed" or "Cancelled" on the departure screen but fortunately our plane was only held up for a half hour to de-ice the wings.

By 5.30pm we were in the Radisson in Vancouver, tired, excited and hungry. That part of town is Asia central, with almost every store run by and catering for expats of the East. A stroll through the mall was like stepping straight into Hong Kong, Singapore and Hanoi rolled into one. A cacophony of produce, live seafood, weird, wonderful and even the bizarre. A mish mash of aromas. Think shiitake mushrooms, brewing miso and fresh durian. I heard no English spoken at all, but that was ok with us.

The big red kangaroo, emblazoned across the tail of our national airline, was a sight for sore eyes and the wonderful Aussie accent, mannerisms and laid back nature of our fellow commuters brought huge smiles to our faces. Our big slumber party in the sky left late on Monday and arrived early on a sunny Sydney Wednesday morn. It was the best sleep on a plane I have even had, probably due to exhaustion. It was fairly uneventful, apart from the time I visited the toilet and inadvertently, in my semi consciousness, pushed the "Request Help" button while looking for the escape latch. I forgot to take my glasses. I got back to my seat just as a hostess ran down the aisle and banged on the door of the dunny asking a poor woman, halfway through her constitutional, if she needed assistance.

Warm breeze, a vibrant blue sky, parrots cavorting in the gum trees. We had landed on Australian soil and it was good, it was right. We were now back where we belonged. The feeling palpable. My smile involuntary. I was standing tall and feeling relaxed and enveloped in a familiar welcome hug of my senses.

A few days later we were home, North Queensland, my personal utopia. The intensity of the light allowed each colour its full potential. Palm trees cast their dancing shadows in that delightfully familiar way, hard to quantify. In the ensuing days the lullaby of the birds and insects at dawn and dusk, the feel of the salty afternoon breeze against my face. Ah that wonderful salty smell of the Corel Sea. Summer rain on a tin roof. Swimming in a warm, blue ocean. The delicious accent and colloquialisms we take for granted. Beauty mate!

PART SIX

Conclusion

There is a certain sense of achievement, a triumph of sorts, having completed a year abroad with a young family. Few would have contemplated, let alone gone through with it. I am sure it has added to our individual resilience and brought us closer together. If indeed, Socrates was correct in saying that "Ultimate wisdom comes from knowing one's self" then I have a feeling we have strolled a little bit further down that particular path. Although at times the disconnectedness and loneliness shouted the loudest, looking through the prism of a life well lived thus far, I have been able to quantify the real and important triumphs. We experienced so much. The low points gave us opportunities to grow. The medicine you need doesn't always taste the sweetest. No one could argue that we grabbed every opportunity; we gave it a good crack. Because of this, we can now sit back and recall all the wonderful memories we created. Special things that only the three of us truly know and understand. How good is that?

Although the exterior changes in Imogen were more nuanced, except for her lack of front teeth, longer arms and legs (ok so maybe lots of external change as well); more profound was her growth as a person. I have watched my darling daughter grow into a more confident young lady who is not a follower but intrinsically motivated. This gives her the wonderful freedom of beating to the sound of her own drum, and that she does. The decision to let her consolidate her schooling whilst abroad has been a good one. She has witnessed all sorts of people, traditions and different ways of doing things, which in time I hope, will manifest into her being a more tolerant and empathetic person. She has had the opportunity to learn and progress at her own pace, to adapt and make new friends. She has become more resilient by just living through the upheaval of transplanting to the other side of this great blue marble. For the most part, we have shown her how to view the world through a positive lens, look for the silver lining and of course embrace the opportunity to grow as a person. I am a proud Dad indeed.

Not that she needed to, but Anna proved to herself and the rest of us that she is an inspirational educator despite the country, demographic, system and available resources. She has a real gift with children. They respond to her nature and ability to find great joy in the simple but special things in life. She also conquered the culture and weather shock. She published an amazing blog and dived into new experiences with gusto. However, most of all we got through it together, the three of us.

Myself. The script for this adventure should be "Learning lessons in the most unlikely places". I was dragged kicking and screaming by my new environment to slow down from my normal fast paced existence. The first few months were tough for several reasons and this coincided with learning to deal with a Canadian interior winter. It was productive in the sense that I had time to write and that alone is an isolating experience without being in the middle of rural Canada in the quiet season. It was humbling, confronting and frustrating all mixed into one. But the adventures which spanned from simple things like shopping at the hardware store and driving on icy mountain passes to hiking the Rocky Mountains, kayaking pristine lakes and coming face to face with the wildlife were priceless. Since our return, as I am drifting off to sleep or relaxing out on the deck, the joys and triumphs roll back into my consciousness to be lived and enjoyed once more.

Travellers! Why do we do it? Meeting people from foreign lands, culture, food, music, art, natural wonders. With television documentaries and the internet, all these spectacles are visually available in technicolour with succinct commentary and choreographed soundtracks from the safety and comfort of our homes. Well for me anyway, each time I step foot abroad, somewhere in my mind's eye sees a large sign. Sometimes it is faded and dusty, others surrounded in glitzy lights or bordered by intricate, traditional timber carvings. It may be drenched in sunshine or lashed with cold winds but always it reads the same thing "Welcome to the Great Unknown". We, the traveller, are drawn to the unexpected, the unrehearsed, and the diamonds in the rough. Of course, there are always problems to solve and irritations to endure, but every experience has a story and a lesson. Fate would suggest it is one we needed to learn.

We are no longer just fair-weather travellers, having experienced a place through every season. Warts and all. It may be tough for those not bitten by the adventure bug to understand. Really, they need not try. So where to next? Portugal has been popping up in conversation and print lately, making a strong case. So has Sri Lanka and something tells me it is time to take on Europe. Italy seems like the perfect way to start. The future is bright and there is much more of this blue planet to explore with my girls. The common thread to all our travels is the opportunity to nourish our curiosity. As I complete the final draft of this book tapping away on my phone, I am sitting in the dark in our tent up at O'Reilly's in the Lamington National Park behind the Gold Coast. We drove eighteen hours from home to get here. It is beautiful with a proliferation of wildlife. Wild parrots land on your head and shoulder looking for a morsel of food. But I digress. This is an unplanned but very fitting place to put one unforgettable journey to bed and start to plan another.

Thanks for the ride Canada!

ABOUT THE AUTHOR

Growing up on a sugar cane plantation in tropical northern Australia, Stuart spent hours discovering the world through his Dad's subscription of National Geographic Magazine and the family's World Book Encyclopedia. He soon developed a fascination of the cultures and landscapes of the world. This curiosity has led to extensive travel through South East Asia, North America, the South Pacific and his native Australia. Nothing brings a smile to his face more than planning excursions and roaming the planet with his wife and young daughter. When not off on an adventure, he lives with his family in Townsville where they enjoy kayaking, cycling and bush walking. Stuart always had an idea he would write a book one day. When he found himself out of work and snowbound on the opposite side of the planet, he certainly had the time and was surrounded by the inspiration. This is Stuart's debut novel.